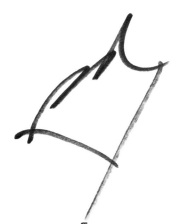

FROM NEW CREATION TO URBAN CRISIS

A History of Action Training Ministries
1962-1975

George D. Younger

C

S

S

R

Center for the Scientific Study of Religion
Chicago, Illinois

Studies in Religion and Society

Center for the Scientific Study of Religion

For a complete list of other publications in the
series, see the back of the book.

Center for the Scientific Study of Religion
5757 University Avenue
Chicago, Illinois 60637

ISBN: 0-913348-25-2

Library of Congress Catalog Card Number: 86-70421

Table of Contents

Preface

Training for Urban Ministry was one important stream in the response of the churches in the U.S.A. to what many, during the 1960's, called a "crisis in the cities." Twenty-seven centers were generated in 22 large U.S. cities, states and regions. All were ecumenical in character and experimental in training methods. This book gives access to that experience, telling the story of that venture of the churches. It details the historical context both in the churches and in the field of training. It tells about curriculum and recruitment of students. It reflects on the accomplishments achieved and the difficulties encountered.

Some widely circulated writing about urban ministry in the 1960's is distressingly shallow. Authors who have neither participated in the events they describe nor consulted the records have indulged in off-target generalizations. Such writing is usually tinged by a negative bias toward Christian activism. This study is an all-too-rare instance of contemporary mission writing by one directly and intimately involved in the story he writes about, and by one who has thoroughly examined the ample documentation.

George D. Younger is a theologian and a historian. For a decade he was pastor of Mariners' Temple Baptist Church, a multiracial Baptist inner-city congregation on the Lower East Side of New York City; at the same time he was a leader in the Two Bridges Neighborhood Council. Later he helped to organize and served as Director for both the Methodist-initiated Metropolitan Urban Service Training program in New York City and for the national Urban Training Center for Christian Mission in Chicago. Since 1976 Younger has been Executive Minister for 237 American Baptist churches in New Jersey, the most densely populated state in the United States. From 1973 to 1986 he participated as a North American representative to the Urban Mission Advisory Group of the World Council of Churches with urban mission leaders from five other regions of the world.

During his career as pastor, preacher, educator and ecumenist, Younger has disciplined himself to do systematic writing. He edited *Foundations*, a quarterly journal of Baptist history and theology, for many years. He has published an often reprinted book of Bible studies, *The Bible Calls for Action* (Judson Press), as well as two books which have become standard works for urban ministry formation: *The Church and Urban Power Structure* (Westminister Press) and *The Church and Urban Renewal* (J.B. Lippincott). In this study, his skill in the methodology of "action and reflection" as a way of education and as a way of doing ministry is applied to the story of training for urban mission.

During the period 1961-1976, some 27 initiatives were undertaken by groups of church persons to establish institutions for training clergy, students and laity in skills for ministry in the city. Fifteen national church agencies, including the Roman Catholics, the major predominantly White Protestant denominations, and the largest Black denominations, as well as smaller and more conservative church bodies, were involved in sponsorship and funding. Although the largest urban training centers were established in Chicago and New York, significant programs were developed in Atlanta, Cleveland, Los Angeles, Cincinnati, St. Louis, Kansas City, Nashville, Philadelphia, Minneapolis, Washington, D.C., Seattle and a number of other metropolitan centers. One center alone records more than 4000 participants during a five-year period in some 100 training programs. Dozens of cadres emerged as training staffs for these centers, and hundreds of clergy, now working in cities all across the country, gained conceptual and practical tools for their ministry in urban areas.

This ecumenical flowering flourished during a period of less than fifteen years. Twenty years after these centers were started, most of them had disappeared. The training centers were vital participants in the ecclesiastical history of their times. Typically they became players in the dynamics of social change in the cities where they were located. Younger traces the suburban flight of Protestant churches in the post-World War II period. Southern Blacks, Puerto Ricans and Mexican Americans were migrating to centers of large cities across the country. Black revolts broke out in major cities. The national push for racial equality was being carried forward in large measure by Black church leaders. The training centers were one way the churches responded to these changes. They were instrumental and effective in developing and teaching new ways for the churches to define and carry out their work in the cities. Younger tells this tale of ferment, creativity and struggle through full accounts of three of the training centers and in briefer stories about each of the others. He also ponders the reasons for the demise of so many of them.

Racial dynamics are always in the forefront of the story. The centers, mostly initiated and funded by Whites, worked to educate White church members to understand and support changes demanded by Blacks. Many of the centers were increasingly staffed with Black instructors and began to develop training designed by and for Black constituencies as well.

Reflection on the urban training phenomenon raises a number of institutional and socio-political issues. Younger analyzes and has advice on such problems as:

- the failure of established forms of theological education to provide formation for effective urban ministry
- controversy about methods of doing theology in urban society
- dysfunctions in the ways national church bodies give support and nurture to local mission action
- difficulties in sustaining funding for innovative ministries, whether from national church bureaucracies, local and regional church sources, or from private foundations and government sources

- confusion and default in the church regarding the getting, keeping and use of power in the city—with particular reference to housing, health care, education and community organization

All of these issues remain critical ones on the church's agenda today.

The Lilly Endowment, which helped to support a number of programs described here, is to be commended for enlisting and sponsoring George Younger to undertake this study. Meager work has been done in the abundant archives documenting involvement of the churches with urban dynamics in the 1960's. Work such as Younger does in this book should be undertaken on such topics as:

- the church's involvement in community organization (including church support for Industrial Areas Foundation organizing and the formation of the Interreligious Foundation for Community Organization)
- church involvement with housing and public education issues
- new church consciousness about obligations to exercise ethical responsibility in investments, leading to the establishment of the Interfaith Center for Corporate Responsibility
- the development of ecumenical institutional structures for metropolitan mission action in some 40 major cities

The author indicates some areas for such further research in Appendix 8.

The World Council of Churches' Office for Urban and Rural Mission, a part of WCC's unit on Mission and Evangelism, was pleased to share in this study. The Urban Rural Mission Office endeavors to give worldwide ecumenical support to the efforts of churches to be faithful to their calling in the countries and localities where they are based. WCC support for this study was given in the hope that North American churches might benefit from this chance to reflect on one important effort to exercise faithfulness during a challenging period in American life. The study certainly has important uses for those who are committed to shaping and carrying out effective training for Christian ministry in cities today.

George E. Todd
New York, New York

(George E. Todd served as Secretary for Urban Mission on the staff of the World Council of Churches from 1973-83. He was a member of the Board of the Urban Training Center for Christian Mission in Chicago during the ten years that he directed the Urban Industrial Mission Office for the United Presbyterian Church USA. He is currently Executive Presbyter for the Presbytery of New York City.)

Introduction

As stated in the title, this work is a study of action-training centers and programs (which originally were organized as "urban training programs") between 1962 and 1975, as well as of the Action Training Coalition, which was organized by those agencies.

The original study was made in 1975, as the Urban Training Center for Christian Mission in Chicago was going through the agonizing process of closing. The major reference materials for the study were already in the collection of the Institute on the Church in Urban-Industrial Society (ICUIS) in Chicago and the files of the Urban Training Center (UTC), which have since been added to the ICUIS collection. A questionnaire was sent to all the agencies that were still operating at that time, as well as to key persons active in the formation of the agencies that had already closed or left ATC. With assistance from the Lilly Endowment, a trip was also made to interview some of the leaders of action-training programs that were operating at the time, and a dozen active leaders and veterans of the formation of the movement met for two days in Chicago on May 12-13, 1975 to review the outline of the study and preliminary results.

The manuscript did not receive major attention again until 1979 when it was placed in rough form, including extensive monographs on many of the action-training agencies. This version of the manuscript, together with a preliminary set of conclusions and findings, was reviewed at a Conference on the Future of Urban Ministry, convened by the New York Theological Seminary, with assistance from the Lilly Endowment, on March 5-7, 1980 at Stony Point, New York. An abstract of the study, together with an expanded set of conclusions and findings, was presented as a paper to the American Society for Christian Ethics on January 16, 1981. During the rest of that year the summaries of the development of the different action-training agencies were brought up to date and checked with persons who had been part of the experience.

The final work to prepare for publication was completed in 1985, including the preparation of the appendices and bringing the summaries up to date for the last time. Thus, what this book represents is a contemporary account, begun in 1975, that has been updated and completed over the subsequent ten years. It seeks to tell the complete story through 1975, while giving word on what has happened with the agencies through 1980.

Because few people will go back to the original sources, this work is a summary of what is to be found there. References are only given for direct quotations, most of which come from unpublished materials that can be found in the ICUIS collection or in the files of the action-training organizations, wherever those may now be kept. Those wishing to do further research are referred to those sources. The appendices have been included in order to fill out the picture with case studies, as well as to provide an overview and suggestions for getting at the sources.

This manuscript is an attempt to go beyond the simple chronicling of organizations, events and people. Therefore, it starts with a summary of the background of training in the church, as well as in industrial society, and of the development of urban mission in the mainline White Protestant denominations as the context. The principal results of the research are found in the summary of different agencies and programs that were at one time members of the Action Training Coalition, and the history of the Action Training Coalition itself. (Other programs and agencies that were also doing training at the same time, but were not members of ATC, are listed in Appendix 1.) The final chapter represents my personal conclusions, as well as learnings, that can be drawn from this study and the experience that it reports.

I wish, first and most prominently, to express my heartfelt appreciation to all the staff members, board members and others associated with the action-training agencies and programs who committed so much of themselves and their lives to the effort to promote change in the churches and in society. They have been colleagues both in the activities reported here, as well as in the subsequent work of research and reporting. I do not pretend to speak for them and their assessment of our common experience, but this record would not have been possible without their full cooperation.

I want also to acknowledge those who in many different ways helped to support and carry out this study, and to bring it to publication: Robert W. Lynn, both through Lilly Endowment and Auburn Theological Seminary; Don Benedict and the Community Renewal Society; George E. Todd, Negail R. Riley and Kenith A. David, and the Urban Rural Mission of the World Council of Churches; Merlyn W. Northfelt and Sadayuki Mouri of Garrett-Evangelical Theological Seminary; Virginia Brereton, James Fraser, Christa Klein and Barbara Wheeler of the Auburn project on the history of theological education; Yoshio Fukuyama and Dorothy Bass of Chicago Theological Seminary; Bobbi Wells Hargleroad, Mary Kirklin and Richard T. Poethig of ICUIS; Keith A. Russell and New York Theological Seminary; and the Center for the Scientific Study of Religion. I am also grateful to three successive generations of typists—Suzanne Bolotin, Connie D'Agostino and Evelyn Yorke; and to Frances Giffin for indexing. Finally, I wish to thank my family for putting up with ten years of clutter and file boxes, along with days and hours of non-communication while this work has been in progress.

George D. Younger
East Orange, New Jersey

December, 1985

CHAPTER I

The Development of Training in the Church

HISTORICAL SURVEY

Training in the churches has traditionally had two foci: (1) the training of catechumens and the faithful in the rudiments of the faith and the disciplines of the Christian life, and (2) the training of clergy and others with specialized vocations. The churches of the Reformation tradition—both state churches and free churches—placed their primary emphasis on education of the faithful, while the Roman Catholic Church after the Council of Trent gave its attention to the training of clergy and those associated with the various orders. Universities and other educational institutions were a by-product of the efforts of Western Christianity to teach theology as basic to the other intellectual disciplines.

In the United States during the Colonial period the training of catechumens and the faithful was principally taken care of in the local parish or congregation and supported by the printing of Scriptures, tracts and books, and by local classes for learning to read the printed word. The earliest colleges and institutions of higher education were designed for the preparation of leadership in church and civil state, following the example of the Continental and British universities. This educational endeavor was supplemented by a variety of tutoring programs for future ministers, usually with a professor of divinity at a college or a local pastor in the parsonage.

As disestablishment of state churches occurred in the post-Colonial period, educational patterns changed. Both in an attempt to recoup their lost power and to meet the needs for ministerial leadership on the frontier, denominations began to establish theological seminaries as centers of piety and learning. This pattern has influenced almost all subsequent developments in theological education down to the present day.

Seminary education in Black churches, as it developed subsequent to the Civil War, was directly related to the establishment of academies, colleges and other institutions of higher learning. A recent increasing awareness of the identity of Black Christianity in the United States has produced efforts by Black churchmen and theological students to introduce special programs in Black theology and other Black church studies, a development which has remained institutionally related to the existing pattern of theological education.

Training of catechumens and the faithful took on its own direction in American Christianity with the widespread adoption of the Sunday school.

Starting in England in the late eighteenth century, the Sunday school was designed to give moral and religious instruction to the children of the very poor, as well as to teach many of the pupils to read. In the United States during the early years of the nineteenth century this lay movement joined tract, Bible and missionary societies in vying for the support and involvement of church members. Of all these movements, the Sunday School had the greatest influence upon the local congregation. While it did not replace worship, preaching and catechetical classes in the formation of Christians, it was one area in which lay women and men assumed key positions of leadership. Although locally controlled, it became part of an interdenominational movement and was organized from the local to the national level. As it grew in strength and influence, the Sunday school movement produced a Bible-centered curriculum in the International Sunday School "uniform" lessons. Little wonder that this sort of lay ecumenical effort was a threat to the power of the clergy and, indeed, to some of the denominations themselves.

TWENTIETH CENTURY CHANGES

The twentieth century has seen a shift in the major White Protestant denominations from the Sunday school form of organization to professionalized Christian education. Taking secular education as its model, the Sunday school was termed the "church school." Divided into separate classes according to age groups, it began to use conventional pedagogical methods and a new class of church professionals, religious educators, who took over both the development of curriculum and the training of teachers. In the local church the work of education was reintegrated with the clergy-led work of worship and catechizing. At the national level, boards of Christian education and publishing houses became the principal powers in the conduct and development of church training. Thus, two shifts of power occurred in the transition from Sunday school to Christian education: from lay control to clergy control, and from local control to national control. It is important to note, however, that Black denominations and many Black churches in White denominations, along with religious conservatives, did not make these shifts.

Although this greater professional expertise and national programming might seem uniquely suited to the task of training in the more complex urban-industrial society of the mid-twentieth century, this has not been the case. Both theological seminaries in the scholarly mode and Christian education in the professional approach have had serious limitations in trying to deal with the multiple issues of modern life and have been unsatisfactory in preparing either clergy or laity for the task of mission and nurture in a world where religious institutions are called upon not only to contribute to change in others, but to change themselves as well.

One reason for the inability of these centralized and professionally oriented education programs to respond to the multiple changes in society is clear. Unlike government, where the Federal income tax has given national bureaucracies strong support for their policies and programs, the control of most of the resources of property, money and personnel in religious institutions has remained with local congregations and parishes, shared in some communions with the area judicatory. Even though national denominational and ecumenical organizations possess a steady source of income from current contributions and funds invested from past contributions—an income which grew in the years of post-war prosperity—the principal control has remained local. In fact, a large proportion of the "benevolence" or "mission" contributions made to national denominational bodies represent basically a bookkeeping transaction in which money contributed from local churches through the judicatories is returned to them in the form of grants and services. If a balance of payments model were used, it would show that urban judicatories usually retain a greater share of these contributions, as well as attracting additional funds in the form of special projects and grants from other sources.

Furthermore, the inability of theological seminaries and other Christian education efforts, as they developed in the first half of the twentieth century, to respond adequately to a more complex society can be attributed to the substantial population shifts in the years during and after World War II. People continued to move from rural areas to urban centers, generally in the direction of the North and the West. The advantage in endowments and ability to secure contributions lay with the oldest theological seminaries and those able to attract support from newly-developed wealth, many of which were in the Northeast and Southwest. Since denominational headquarters tended to be located in metropolitan centers in the Eastern half of the nation, their Christian education staffs were oriented more to the controlling institutions and population groups than to the working class and ethnic minorities, who were heavily represented in the migrating groups.

White denominations after World War II followed this shift of population, organizing churches in new suburban areas and putting a substantial effort into the construction of new buildings for them. The heaviest in-migration into inner-city areas was composed of Blacks and Hispanic Americans (largely Puerto Ricans in the Northeast and Mexican-Americans in the Southwest and Far West). When the White population moved out of those areas, their denominations usually took one of two courses. Either they set up "experimental ministries" with largely White clergy and non-White members in the old buildings that were left behind, or they sold the buildings to Black or Hispanic-American congregations. Roman Catholics, with a smaller supply of non-White clergy and greater centralization of diocesan control, tended to take the first course of action.

Most Black denominations continued to remain under control of their Southern leadership, although the pastors of large churches in the cities gained in influence. The strains of the urban transition caused a schism in the largest Black group, the National Baptist Convention, out of which the Progressive National Baptist Convention was formed and leadership shifted to Northern and big-city clergy. In addition, the failure of existing Black churches fully to incorporate the urban poor contributed to the growth of Pentecostalism and many independent congregations unrelated to denominational groupings. It also resulted in the growth of a new, largely urban denomination, the Church of God in Christ.

In this situation the national mission boards and local judicatories of the largely White, mainline Protestant denominations turned away from the theological seminaries and their own boards of Christian education to perform the tasks they felt to be most vital both for their own survival and for the future of the Christian message in an increasingly secularized society. The decade of the 1960's saw the proliferation of a variety of training efforts developed by national mission boards. The first attempts at meeting what they defined as a need for clergy and staff training were: (1) in-service training programs set up by national staff members using inner-city clergy, national staff, and seminary and urban studies professors; (2) training in community organization, using the resources of Saul Alinsky and the Industrial Areas Foundation (IAF) or other community organization specialists; and (3) management training for mission executives either at university business schools or centers of urban studies, or developed by the faculty of those institutions.

Although national White denominations played a significant role in training students and other White churchmen and women active in the civil rights movement, the principal burden of this task was borne by the civil rights groups and Black churches themselves. Based in the Black church, the Southern Christian Leadership Conference (SCLC) used its local campaigns as the training ground for both indigenous leadership and a continually shifting group of supporters. Rallies using the style of Black church worship and mass demonstrations were the principal modes of training. With pressure and financial incentives from White supporters, a number of Black theological seminaries in the South came together on the campus of Atlanta University in the Interdenominational Theological Center, where, after the death of Martin Luther King, Jr., there was established the Center for the Study of Non-Violent Change and the Institute of the Black World. One further development was the formation of the National Committee of Black Churchmen (originally the National Committee of Negro Churchmen) in July 1966, which brought together significant leaders from Black denominations with clergy from Black caucuses in predominantly White denominations.

Another development in church-related training during the same period was the Institute for Advanced Pastoral Studies in Bloomfield Hills,

Michigan. Organized in May 1957 by Reuel L. Howe, who had been an Episcopal seminary professor, with the support of lay leaders and clergy of Christ Church, Cranbrook, IAPS developed a program of clergy training based heavily upon the insights of group dynamics and a sensitive pastoral theology. When the founder retired as director in 1973 and John E. Biersdorf came from the Commission on the Ministry of the National Council of Churches to be his successor, the program shifted to take greater account of social change along with personal change in the church's ministry. Biersdorf brought Speed Leas from COMMIT in Los Angeles to add some of the insights of action training to the Institute's work.

A parallel development during the 1960's was the rise of the training program of the Ecumenical Institute (EI) in Chicago, Illinois. Using an approach based in the existential theology of post-war American Christianity, this group began training clergy and laity in a form they called "imaginal education." At its inception Joseph Matthews, the founder of EI, was a White Methodist staff member of the Faith and Life Community at the University of Texas. Taking over the corporate structure of an agency formed in Evanston, Illinois, following the General Assembly of the World Council of Churches there in 1954, the program was moved to Chicago in 1962. When it took over the property of a theological seminary on the West Side in 1965, EI developed its own approach to experimental ministry in the "Fifth City" program for Black residents of the surrounding area. Most of the program, however, has been the multiplication of its centrally produced curriculum and research design through urban community experiments and in its own houses across the United States, and in overseas seminars.

Against the background described above, the White mainline Protestant denominations began the development of "urban training," later termed "action training." Although theological seminaries and programs for theological students were included in the activity of action-training centers, they were not a natural development of theological education. And, although lay training was considered an important component of much of the program of action-training centers, they were not a continuation of trends in the field of Christian education. Instead, "action training" represented a new start in the training of both clergy and laity, aimed at the situation of urban ministry and mission, and fostered principally by the national mission agencies of the major White Protestant denominations and denominational and ecumenical units related to them.

CHAPTER II

The Development of Training in Industrial Society

ORIGINS OF TRAINING TECHNIQUES

It is instructive to look at the history of "training" in America and the progress of the movement in which techniques of training arose, for what has been often regarded by its recent proponents as a means to social change takes on a different cast when its sources and early uses are examined.[1]

War and social conflict have played the principal roles in the development of training in the wider society. Increased knowledge in the social sciences, especially in sociology, psychology and social psychology, has been quickly put to use by the military services, industry and business, and government. In fact, these groups often were responsible for financing the original research and experimentation out of which that knowledge has come.

World War I produced a need for screening and effective training of relatively unskilled people both in the armed forces and in war industry. Extensive use was made of psychological testing with draftees and potential workers in Great Britain, the United States, Germany and Austria. In addition, in Great Britain and Germany psychological techniques were used in war industry, both for purposes of morale and for training the unskilled. It was, indeed, the needs of the military services and defense industry in the United States that resulted in the publication of the first general textbook in applied psychology and the first edition of the *Journal of Applied Psychology* in 1917.

Following World War I, those who had been Army psychologists formed psychological consulting firms which quickly made an impact on several areas of American life: the development of manpower programs in industry (Henry C. Link was an outstanding proponent), the creation of the modern business of advertising (an example is the J. Walter Thompson agency), and the application of war-developed forms of intelligence and skills testing to education (an example is the work of John B. Watson). On the Continent a group of German psychologists, including Kurt Lewin, began research on group interaction in a displaced persons' camp in the Tyrol. The rise of Fascism and Nazism in Europe during the early 1930's caused a number of these German psychologists to come to the United States as refugees.

In industry, training principally took the form of foremen's courses in the large companies like Swift, Chrysler and Eastman Kodak. Some psychological testing and screening techniques were used in an effort to weed out potential "malcontents" in the labor force. Once employees were hired, the strategy was to use the influence of foremen and the sanctions of with-holding promotions or firing as ways to keep them in line with management policies and goals. Around 1926 the National Research Council, in coopera-tion with the Massachusetts Institute of Technology and the Harvard Business School, began research on work patterns and efficiency in the Hawthorne works of the Western Electric Co., associated with American Telephone and Telegraph Co. The results of these studies, which showed the influence of "people factors" and informal communication on produc-tion, were incorporated by Elton Mayo of the Harvard Business School into a "human relations" approach for industrial management and supervision. Conflict between labor and management sharpened with the onset of eco-nomic depression in 1929, and the adoption of the National Labor Relations Act in 1935 for the first time placed priority on the ability of management to work with labor in groups and organizations. As a result, personnel depart-ments were increased, and training was directed toward the prevention of unionization and the achievement of management objectives by group sua-sion and personal relations.

As social conflict intensified during the New Deal, labor education arose as a counter-strategy to management's training efforts. Applied psycho-logists turned their attention to industrial conflict. The American Associa-tion of Applied Psychology was formed in 1938, with a special section devoted to business and industry. When the first yearbook of the Society for the Psychological Study of Social Issues was published in 1939, the sub-ject was "Industrial Conflict." This interest of researchers and practitioners in both sides of social conflict was occurring at precisely the time that economic recession was underscoring the intensity of business opposition to the New Deal, while the Roosevelt administration was turning its attention to foreign policy and the growing threat of European and Asian war.

Two other trends that were later to contribute to the development of training began in the areas of social research and psychotherapy. In 1934 Jacob Moreno introduced the technique of sociometry as a tool for the study of social relationships in rural communities. During the latter part of the decade, research in group dynamics and styles of leadership were under-taken with residential communities of youth at the Iowa Child Welfare Research Station. This research gave further knowledge of the way in which people function in group situations. The flight of German and Austrian psychoanalysts and other psychotherapists as refugees to the United States introduced a wide variety of models of human behavior into the previously pragmatic and mechanistic analyses made by American schools of psycho-logy. Although these were not applied at this time to social analysis and group behavior, they provided a broader framework for psychology.

World War II saw much greater use of both psychologists and sociol-ogists in industry and the military services. The armed forces employed psychologists for screening, testing and training draftees, and for studying "morale" among troop units. Training programs were established for essential skills in war industries, and the War Manpower Commission developed a training program for two million supervisors in 16,000 war plants. The inability of individual therapy to deal with the sheer number of service personnel suffering from "combat fatigue" and other psychological ailments led to the use of group psychotherapy in military and veterans' hospitals.

Following the war there was once again widespread dispersion of war developed sociological and psychological techniques into business, industry and government. Motivational research became an accepted tool of advertising, along with more sophisticated propaganda techniques developed for wartime purposes. Industrial psychology expanded its repertoire of skills, and training became an essential part of personnel procedures throughout the business world.

NATIONAL TRAINING LABORATORIES

Further research on small groups, which began in England in 1946 at the Tavistock Institute of Human Relations, was based upon the experience of its founders with the War Office Selection Board and rehabilitation of former prisoners of war. In 1947 the first National Training Laboratory in Group Development in the the United States was held at Bethel, Maine, through the auspices of the Adult Education Division of the National Education Association and the Research Center for Group Dynamics of the Massachusetts Institute of Technology, under the direction of Kurt Lewin. National Training Laboratories (NTL) was established as a separate organization in 1951, with its basic research underwritten by the Office of Naval Research.[2] Much of the present direction in small group leadership and training is a direct result of NTL research and development. Therefore, it is important to note that its origins can be traced to business and military sponsorship. Interestingly enough, although the original effort was co-sponsored by the National Education Association, no attempt was made to apply these learnings to education in elementary and secondary schools until 1959, when NTL held its first occupational training sessions for public school administrators and teachers.

Dissemination of techniques by NTL dates only from 1955 when they held their first sessions for trainers other than researchers like themselves. The first groups included domestic Red Cross workers, and social scientists and educators from seven Western European countries who were brought to Bethel by the Foreign Operations Administration and the European Productivity Agency. In 1956 the occupational training was extended to industrial managers, Puerto Rican government workers and Protestant religious educators. This last group, which included a significant number of Episcopalians, was responsible for introducing group dynamics techniques into the curriculum of some denominational programs of Christian education.

Leaders in community development were not included in NTL training until 1960, and the first contact with community organization was made in 1964 when Mobilization for Youth entered into a contract with NTL for training community workers in New York City. In its earlier years NTL stressed a clinical model of human growth and change, but this has since been modified to include an action research model that permits greater attention to content and organizational structure, and an organizational development model that makes use of the findings of the social science-oriented studies of business administration. It was not until work had been done in Puerto Rico and India that Black Americans were included in NTL training efforts. The first attempt to bring Black trainers together occurred only in the fall of 1971.

Other developments in the training field since World War II have included extensive development of manpower training efforts with Federal grants to educational institutions, local governments and businesses; training for volunteers in both the Peace Corps overseas and Volunteers in Service to America (VISTA), and development of community action training as part of the Office of Economic Opportunity's anti-poverty efforts. Many of these training efforts have been short-lived, and most have made use of existing institutions rather than developing new ones. The requirements of business, industry and government, however, have led to the proliferation of consulting firms and individual practitioners who offer their training and consulting services at a fee to any organization ready to hire them.

IMPLICATIONS FOR ACTION TRAINING

As this survey shows, training in the wider society has had a history in which wars and social conflict have sharpened the desire of military, industrial and governmental agencies to have adequate means of indoctrination for administrators, supervisors and employees, and to produce "managed change" which would remain within their institutions' capacity to control. Both World War I and World War II resulted in quantum leaps in the application of the social sciences to human society, by first using new techniques with the military services and war industry and then at the end of hostilities transferring them to civilian life. When the National Labor Relations Act was adopted in 1935, management was required to deal with employees in groups rather than as isolated individuals. During the 1960's social unrest and rising expectations, especially in the urban ghettos, produced a similar pressure for more sophisticated means of socialization and social control within the large institutions which hold most of the power in industrial society.

This analysis of the history of training and the power relationships of those who have developed its techniques has been necessary because there are those who have been misled by the stress upon individual initiative, self-direction of groups and "change" in much of the literature on group dynamics. Some have been tempted to equate this new methodology with democratic theory, social revolution and even Christian conversion. But such characterizations overlook the auspices under which these techniques have been developed and the purposes to which they have been put. Using the resources of the university, military research and a growing group of related consultants (both firms and individuals), with some support from foundations, the ruling elites of the United States have developed the techniques of group dynamics, planned change, organizational development and applied psychology now being used both by their own personnel departments and by a wider circle of "trainers," therapists and training groups. Because these techniques were developed for the use of elites and on behalf of the dominant large institutions of American society, they carry with them a strong ideological overtone of social control, even though they continually use the language of "change."

In the development of action training by groups related to the churches, many of these techniques and assumptions were uncritically adopted. As the agenda of training moved from service within the institution to the fostering of social change in the wider society, it became clearer that what had been developed by the dominant institutions of society was not suited to the process of resisting or substantially changing those institutions themselves. Moreover, it became obvious that the techniques used by the White majority would not be adequate for developing community consciousness and liberation among Blacks and Hispanic Americans. The dynamic of redemption or liberation for those enslaved or managed by the powers of urban-industrial society could not be achieved on the basis of the assumptions of those who held power and were managers. Therefore, it became necessary to discard or seriously modify a great deal of what had been accepted as viable techniques for producing organizational change and personal growth. In large part, then, the action-training centers, established by the large-scale national religious institutions out of their own organizational need, found themselves placed in an awkward position. Either they had to adopt the subtle means of socialization and social control developed for "managed change" or discard them in search of other means more consonant both with a Christian theology of redemption and with the demands of the poor and oppressed for significant social change. This was the essential problem facing action-training centers after their sponsors had launched them on a more or less independent career, and it underlay most of the discussion about what constituted "action training." Although many of these definitions were clear about their commitment to liberation rather than to social control, the principal activities of action-training centers alternated or were divided between fostering acceptable change within the church and its institutions and supporting or organizing change in the wider society.

CHAPTER III

"Action Training" as Concept and Practice

DEFINING "ACTION TRAINING"

The term "action training" was first applied to action-training agencies at their second consultation on May 24-26, 1968, in Kansas City, Missouri, when they formed the Action Training Coalition (ATC). The participants had been invited to a "National Consultation of Urban Training Centers and Networks," and most of their agencies had been organized as "urban training centers" or "urban encounter" programs. However, by this time the word "urban" in mainline Protestant churches had come to mean "inner city," so they dropped the title "urban training" in favor of "action training."

The agencies which came together to form the Action Training Coalition in almost every case had been organized between 1962 and 1968 by church agencies, largely composed of Protestant bodies, for the purpose of training two constituencies: (1) clergy and full-time church workers, who were to be given preparatory or in-service training for professional responsibilities in urban churches; and (2) lay persons, who were to be given orientation to the urban scene and training for social action.

The context of race, while largely unstated in any formal definition of action training, was basic to the formation and operation of these training agencies. The populations of the cities, toward whom their efforts were directed, had already become increasingly Black and Hispanic. The church bodies which established their programs, the boards and staff responsible for that training, and the lay and clergy trainees were largely White. As a result, action training was inextricably involved in the dynamics of the racial revolution in the wider American society, as well as the churches' own efforts first to speak and act to change the racial situation in the wider society, and later to recognize their own share in the institutional racism that continued to foster discrimination and inequality in both society and church. Even when race was not formally on the agenda of an action-training program, it was part of the context. The staff was interracial, the presentations had been hammered out in the crucible of racial dialogue, and the situations to which the training was addressed had usually been chosen because of their possibility for making a constructive contribution to change in the pattern of race and poverty in urban America.

Also, action training was self-consciously organized in a dialectical relationship with the education offered by theological seminaries, which most of the sponsors and almost all the staff members of the action-training agencies had attended and in which some of them were employed. Action training was intended to be, at the least, a supplement or complement to theological education as practiced by theological seminaries, and, at the most, an institutional alternative to the seminaries. In his first statement on behalf of the newly formed ATC to the American Association of Theological Schools in June, 1968, Robert H. Bonthius underscored three "concerns about the future of theological education" that were the principal areas of perceived difference requiring further dialogue: (1) What kind of "secular involvement" should students have? (2) Should the university or the wider society be the center toward which theological education should gravitate? (3) Can you teach theology in the abstract?[1] The stance which ATC members assumed was held by the seminaries answered these questions as follows: (1) "Secular involvement" can mean any kind of business. (ATC emphasized "engagement at points where people are bent on *changing* things.") (2) The university, with its emphasis on teaching and research, should be the center. (ATC emphasized "the secular world in turmoil.") (3) Theological seminaries already do teach theology in the abstract. (ATC emphasized that it needs to be done "in the context of engagement with society in conflict.")

The formal definition of "action training" offered to AATS described it as "training for social change." When Bonthius a year later edited an issue of *Theological Education* on the theme, "Action Training Centers' Challenge to Theological Education," he gave a fuller definition based on ATC's own definition of membership:

> . . . action training is a process of teaching and learning how to effect institutional changes through supervised experience of engagement in social problems and reflection upon that engagement.[2]

The substitution of "institutional changes" for "social change" in the definition did not mean retraction of the aim of implementing change in the wider society. Bonthius's examples in the article make clear that the principal target is problem areas in the wider society, and that institutional change can include both the churches and other institutions.

However, the concept of action training and its use by those agencies which were associated with the Action Training Coalition was subject to continuing debate and redefinition both inside the training agencies and in ATC. The terms of that debate were set at the second Consultation of ATC in Kansas City on May 24-26, 1968, where the term "action training" was adopted.

George D. Younger, a staff member of the Division of Evangelism, American Baptist Home Mission Societies, who had been engaged to supervise evaluation at Metropolitan Urban Service Training (MUST) in New York City, presented a paper to Consultation II on the subject, "Do Training Centers Know What They Mean by 'Training'?" In that paper he attempted his own definition of "training" based on the experience of MUST and a survey of "training centers" produced for the Association for Christian Training and Service (ACTS) in the Southeast by Meryl Ruoss:

> *Training* is a process of teaching and learning focused on some specified end-results in behavior or perception of the situation. It is directly related to the institutional or social roles and activities in which the person being trained is engaged or is expected to engage.

Younger insisted that ATC members had to answer the following questions:

- What do we mean by "training"?
- What are the objectives and priorities of training?
- Who are the people being trained or sought for training?
- What methods are we using in training?[3]

Training, then, only would become "action training" when it had clear answers about *who* is being trained (constituency) and *for what* (purposes and objectives), as well as *how* (methodology). Although ATC members had differing answers to those questions at the Kansas City consultation and throughout their career as action-training agencies, they were consistent in refusing to consider action training as simply a technique or a methodology that could be applied in any situation by any individual or group for any purpose with any type of individuals or groups.

CONSTITUENCY—WHO IS TO BE TRAINED?

From the very beginning those who established the various training centers and those who served as staff for their programs were clear that this kind of training would need to reach a far wider and more diverse group than the clergy and professional church workers. James P. Morton, associate secretary for urban work of the Protestant Episcopal Church and later director of the Urban Training Center for Christian Mission (UTC) in Chicago, told a Conference on Training for the Urban Ministry, sponsored by the Department of the Urban Church of the National Council of Churches in 1963:

> . . . 99.9% of these instances of urban ministry are secular, are lay, are in the world, and bear no conscious connection with the organized church or its official, set-apart ministry. When any of these persons is a Christian, so much the better, as he may have so much the deeper insight into his life and work and his limitations in this urban world. But this lay character is the *de facto* character of most of God's urban ministry. . . .[4]

The original proposal for the first urban training center in Chicago spoke of training the following groups of people:

1. In-service training for city ministers.
2. Intern program for theological students contemplating inner city work.
3. Training of inner city laity—this task is one which inner city ministers seldom have time to adequately accomplish. Few of the present training programs are directed toward this economic and educational grouping.
4. Ideological training for Peace Corps personnel.
5. Training for college students who need to explore inner city life as a possible vocational choice.
6. Training in the Christian Style of Life for functional groups along lines of Evangelical Academies.[5]

Similar breadth of vision is shown in the categories of trainees listed in the original prospectus for a Methodist Urban Training Facility in New York, drawn up in 1964 by J. Edward Carothers, executive secretary of the National Division of the Board of Mission of the Methodist Church: pastors who are in the active ministry, lay people recommended by their local church, college graduates who wish to engage in volunteer service under the direction of the church, and teachers from colleges and universities who wish to be informed and prepared for Christian involvement in the city.

However, the initial training programs conducted by the Urban Training Center for Christian Mission in Chicago, MUST in New York and most of the other training centers that became part of ATC were principally for three groups of people: clergy and other church professionals from city churches, seminary students and graduates, and lay people from the churches. In only a few cases were the training programs open to—or in even fewer cases, designed for—other lay people who were active in the life of the urban community, or professionals from other disciplines. Because their principal funding and support came from Protestant denominations and churches, and their principal contacts for recruiting were with religious institutions, most of the ATC agencies spent a major part of their training time with constituencies drawn from the churches. The major exception to this pattern was the Center for Human Action, Research and Training (CHART) in Cincinnati, which was purposely set up to train community leaders in conjunction with the University of Cincinnati. Yet because ATC agencies were interested in social change and secular involvement, they were often seen by their religious sponsors, theological seminaries and others in the church as institutions that had gone "outside the church" or had even "left the church."

One example will show the extent to which the religious community has been the principal constituency of action-training agencies. (See Table 1).

Table 1
Statistical Breakdown of MUST Training, 1966-71

	Constituency		
Year	**Religious**	**Academic**	**Other**
1966-67	3,468 t-s 3 pro. En: 100	2,790 t-s 3 pro. En: 55	---
1967-68	3,507 t-s 8 pro. En: 942	3,476 t-s 4 pro. En: 127	---
1968-69	1,399 t-s 14 pro. En: 292	6,001 t-s 6 pro. En: 139	863 t-s 7 pro. En: 146
1969-70	5,906 27 pro. En: 1048	2,577 t-s 6 pro. En: 97	1,561 t-s 9 pro. En: 202
1970-71	2,238 t-s 20 pro. En: 403	411 t-s 3 pro. En: 52	1,604 t-s 16 pro. En: 582
Grand Total	16,518 t-s 72 pro. En: 2,785	15,255 t-s 22 pro. En: 470	4,028 t-s 32 pro. En: 930

Key: t-s = training sessions
pro. = programs
en. = enrollment

By any standard—the number of training programs conducted, enrollment in those programs or the number of trainee-sessions (the only measure which can give comparability to programs of varying length and intensity, because it is based on attendance at individual 2-3-hour sessions)—MUST was principally engaged in programs with a religious constituency, because almost all of the academic programs were conducted with students in theological seminaries and clergy seeking graduate credit.

However, the diversity and decidedly non-ecclesiastical nature of the other kinds of constituencies with which MUST conducted training programs made them more highly visible than the church leaders, both clergy and laity, with whom most of the training occurred. These were the kinds of people included under "Other" :

> *1968-69*: members of a community organization in Albany, New York; school board members, staff, parents and youth in Local School District 9 in the Bronx; adult education students in a class on racism in the schools of Ridgewood, New Jersey; hard-core unemployed workers, and the job trainers and supervisors in the New York office of Equitable Life Assurance Co.; Neighborhood Youth Corps staff in Rochester, New York; poverty program workers in the Watts area of Los Angeles, California.
>
> *1969-70*: faculty and students of the College for Human Services; board and staff of the City-Wide Coordinating Committee of Welfare Rights Groups; adult education students in Ridgewood, New Jersey, and South Orange-Maplewood, New Jersey; White faculty members of Livingston College of Rutgers University.
>
> *1970-71*: staff members of the Food and Nutrition Service, US Department of Agriculture in Albany, New York City and Harrisburg, Pennsylvania; board members of Community Welfare Council, Schenectady, New York; students and staff running a narcotics program at Utica College; Black and Hispanic student leaders in New York City high schools; Southern New York League of Nursing; staff of the outreach program of the adolescent clinic at Harlem Hospital; staff of the National Council of Negro Women's Skills Upgrading Program at Pace College; members of Community Parents, a welfare rights organization in Mt. Vernon, New York; high school students and guidance staff in Ossining, New York.

Other training centers showed a similar pattern of diversity in the non-religious constituency for some of their training programs. However, in most cases the primary constituency was the White churches—their clergy and professional leaders, their lay leaders and seminarians preparing to serve them. The major exceptions were the Ford Fellows program at UTC, which was planned for Black clergy; the attempts to organize centers or program divisions especially for minority constituencies in church or community (like BCETF) in Washington, D.C., and BAT in Cleveland; and the minority-oriented programs at ACTS, COMMIT, CUE-P, CHART, EMM, MTN, MUST, TRUST and UTOA)—and, obviously, PRISA in Puerto Rico.[6] The skills and approaches of the action-training centers were useful to the Black and Hispanic churches and to community groups, but, with the exception of CHART, ATC agencies focused their efforts on a religious constituency.

PURPOSE—FOR WHAT TO TRAIN

Almost all of the action-training centers were set up for the overall purpose of enabling the church to fulfill its mission in an urban society. The initial proposal for UTC said, "The sole purpose of the training center would be to explore and communicate the relationship of the Christian faith to the urban industrial society in order that the church as the carrier of the Gospel may find renewal in our generation." During the planning period for MUST in 1965-66 a Theological Task Force composed of some of the most noteworthy proponents of mission theology, the secular city and the missionary structure of the congregation was responsible for assisting the staff in framing both purpose and program. A similar Curriculum Committee, chaired by Gibson Winter of the Divinity School, University of Chicago, helped to define both purpose and curriculum at UTC. In some form or other, "the mission of the church" was the main way in which action training stated its purpose when the different agencies and programs were started.

As a result, early formulations of the purpose of the Action Training Coalition also carried phrases like "to enable the church to perform its mission in an urbanizing society." (See the more detailed discussion of this development in Chapter V.) However, at Consultation IV in Cincinnati on March 31, 1969, ATC enlarged this purpose to read, "to enable groups and individuals in society to effect institutional and community change for humanization and justice." The church was no longer explicitly mentioned, having been included within "groups and individuals in society"; the mission of the church had been specified as "institutional and community change for humanization and justice"; and the "urbanizing society" (like any other mention of the word "urban") had disappeared.

At Consultation V in St. Louis during October 1969, ATC members solidified this change of purpose by adopting a Social Goal.

> The Social Goal of this coalition is to use and create resources and to employ action training to develop the power of those who are participating in the liberation of society, such as those who are Black, Brown, Red or poor White; alienated youth and women; and disaffected decision-makers within the institutions of society.[7]

At about the same time member agencies of ATC were asked to deposit statements of their basic commitments and methods within the ATC Information Service at the Institute on the Church in Urban-Industrial Society (ICUIS). All of the statements of purpose of the United States agencies that were filed at that time stressed social change in one form or another, but most of them were not so specific concerning "humanization," "justice" and "liberation" as the ATC statements. Only the Canadian training center, Canadian Urban Training (CUT), maintained a mission stance, with references to "the work of the Christian church," "interpret the Christian faith" and "new forms and patterns of Christian service."[8]

Even when operating within a general purpose of "mission" or "social change," the specific objectives of given training programs with specific constituencies were aimed at achieving different results. This kind of difference, which operated in most of the other action-training agencies, was analyzed by George D. Younger in his evaluation of five years of MUST training. Younger distinguished between three different levels of involvement, based on the way in which people participated in the training:

> A. *Orientation*—exposing the training group to information about urban society, racism, Afro-American history or other subject areas in which they had little previous experience.
> B. *Survey and Goal Setting*—assisting the training group (and the organization or institution of which they are a part) in clarifying their self-interest and priorities; beginning to develop workable objectives and future action.
> C. *Analysis and Strategy/Skills for Action*—developing means to move into action, and providing or sharpening the skills by which members of the training group act.[9]

He noted that, while the intention of those who set up MUST was that it would provide "skills for action," much of the training program had been at the level of orientation or survey and goal setting. MUST had a commitment to bring people to the point of strategy and action, but many groups were only asking for the other levels. Also, in many cases the objectives were not achieved in as full a measure as had been desired or planned. As a result, a program that was to result in strategy and action might only get as far as survey and goal setting—or even prove to be little more than orientation.

An even more important qualification on the commitment of ATC agencies to social change was their working distinction between external and internal change, which only showed slightly in the Social Goal of ATC ("disaffected decision-makers within the institutions of society"). Because their primary constituency was among religious groups and their major targets were social issues that affected other institutions in society, much of the language and strategy that characterized the early days of action-training agencies took the form of external change. However, as these agencies had to become more concerned about securing change within the religious institutions to which they and most of their constituency belonged, greater emphasis was placed on methods of internal change and organizational development.

This development is clearly indicated by an analysis of the training and consultation programs and proposals listed in the ATN Project Book, which catalogs some 223 programs proposed or carried out by Action Training

Network of Ohio and its predecessors between 1966 and 1974. The following table gives the results of this analysis:

Table 2

Analysis of Action Training Network Projects from Inception to December 31, 1974

	Pre-ATN Merger (1966-70)	Transitional Period (1970-72)	Post-ATN Merger (1972-74)	Total
Constituency				
Religious	15	53	85	153
Community	1	26	39	66
Religious/ Community	1	3	--	4
Academic	6	3	4	13
	23	85	128	236
Types of Objectives				
Orientation	6	8	3	17
External Change	11	52	60	123
Internal Change	1	17	44	62
External/Internal Change	3	4	13	20
Training of Trainers	--	2	1	3
Other/Cannot Identify	2	2	7	11

METHODOLOGY—HOW TO TRAIN

Edgar W. Mills noted in his consultant's report on ATC's Consultation I that the most obvious theme was "What are you doing that I ought to know about?" Through this kind of sharing at Consultations, through use of each other's written materials, through visits to each other's programs (especially when the visitors were in the planning stage for their own operation), through use of common resource persons, through use of each other as consultants and in training programs, and through taking training from each other, the action-training agencies active in ATC shared much in common in the ways that they did their training. And even if they had not had this amount of continuous contact between 1965, when the first non-UTC program was being planned, and October 1970, when ATC held Consultation

VIII in Atlanta on the subject of methodology, the founders and designers of the ATC agencies shared enough common assumptions and experience to produce remarkably similar programs.

The principal methodology of all action-training programs was "action-reflection." Although ATC's own official definition of membership used other terms like "confrontation, reflection, commitment, skills training and strategy in action" or "engagement/reflection," all members assumed a dialectic between action and reflection in which the training was not on the "reflection" side but involved both action and reflection. (Perhaps it was the "/" although action-training agencies always had difficulty in defining their task so narrowly and their staffs were constantly pressing to be part of the action.) Action was part of reflection, as well as preceding and following it.

On the one hand, action-training methodology assumed that the persons participating in training (whom they sometimes identified as "trainees," but when staff resisted the designation of "trainers" were more likely to be identified by such terms as "members of the UTC community" or "co-workers") were bringing their own experience into the training. This was customarily contrasted with "education," which was seen as "deductive" and "may simply mean the increase of conceptual knowledge" (MUST), or having a practical relevance "predicated on the ability of the student to apply at a later time knowledge accumulated in reflective study" (Center for Urban Encounter, Minneapolis/St. Paul). Action training was in sharp distinction from the clinical model of T-group training, which limited the data to be considered to the experience of persons with each other within the training group (although it had many correspondences with the "action-research model" developed by the National Training Laboratories at a later stage). And action training—even when it used George W. Webber's term, "on-the-job training" —was also considered to be different from the various forms of vocational training that restricted their curriculum to a set of carefully defined skills to be used in a particular setting. Participants in action training brought experience into the training and were encouraged to make that experience part of the training process.

On the other hand, the frame of the training "sessions" or "event" or "program" was too limited to contain all that was involved in action training. The original planning for most of the action-training agencies assumed that they would be involved in a kind of training that could be clearly defined in terms of schedules, dates, number of sessions and number of participants. However, precisely because action training took seriously the experience and context of those who were being trained, the staff members of action-training agencies found that their training work was both spreading into the time preceding the training program and following it.

At MUST the staff in their second year of training came to the startling discovery that the planning, negotiation and recruitment for training programs were part of the training. When a group of Black storefront clergy in

Brooklyn were asked, "How did you hear about this program?" several answered with variations of "I didn't. I planned it." Extra care had to be developed in recording what a group originally asked for and what had happened in the process of negotiation for the training program, because this would continually crop up in the training sessions. The basis on which people were recruited into a program would often limit their expectations of what could be accomplished. Action training, then, did not begin with the opening sessions of a training event but went back into the process by which people were brought from their own action to the training agency.

On the other hand, action training kept spreading into the activity that followed the training program. This was first discovered by UTC when it developed a form of curriculum for its principal group of trainees that provided a "back-home" time between the first and second stages of a three-month-long training process (at first called the "3-3" for the number of weeks spent in each of these stages, and later changed to "4-3-3"). With the employment of Paul E. Kraemer as director of research, UTC tried to engage in two kinds of evaluation—process evaluation, which could be done with feedback and questionnaires upon the completion of a training program, and "back-home evaluation," which tried to take into account what a clergy trainee had been able to do after he returned from Chicago. It was not possible to do very much systematic evaluation of what trainees had done with their training in action-training programs, but the conventional wisdom on this subject was stated by most of the agencies in the following form: We should be evaluated by what trainees do in their own situation, not by what they—and we—do in the training program.

Also, every training agency found that a good share of its consulting work as well as some of the other training activities consisted of follow-up with people who had been participants in a training program. This consisted of requests to go farther with what had been started in the original training program, to share the training with others in their own place of action, or to give assistance with other issues and problems that had not been covered in the original training. Thus, action training was not restricted to what could be rigidly circumscribed as "training events," but spread out both before and after that time and process. Also, there was increasing tendency in every action-training agency or program to go out and hold the training event in the place where people were already working with each other, rather than to bring them in to a training "center."

In describing the work of any of the training agencies associated with ATC, it is impossible to limit that description to what they did in "training," because action training in every case was joined with a variety of other functions and activities. An analysis of the reports, publicity materials, curricula and other products of the ATC agencies shows the following functions to be included in varying combinations and proportions:

Training	Planning
Education	Strategy Development
Consciousness Raising	Coalition and Network
Orientation	Development
Consulting	Brokering Services
Organizing	Documentation
Research	Publication

Action-training agencies, in other words, were multi-purpose agencies in which training not only included the action of those who were trainees but the other functions of that agency as well.

In an attempt to get the ATC member agencies to consider a definition of "action training" that was broad enough to include all the varieties of programs being carried on or considered by the Berkeley Center for Human Interaction (BCHI), Trevor Hoy of BCHI brought to Consultation I in October 1969 a typology which described action training as "a strategy of planned change which appropriately uses one or more of these methods." The methods listed were: therapy (and counselling), personal growth, "Training I" (with heterogeneous groups using T-group methods), "Training II" (with teams having a shared responsibility), teaching and/or supervising, consulting, career development, organizational development, faction training (issue-oriented), socio-political development and community organization. His list was rejected as being too all-embracing to fit the more limited goals and objectives of ATC. As a result, ATC members learned that their own focus was particularly on methods that were concerned for assisting groups and institutions (rather than individuals through personal growth) to work to secure social change.

Many of the methods used by ATC were included in the list presented by Hoy, but others were not. Although the descriptions of methodology made by eight ATC member agencies in 1969 did not include everything that was being used by ATC agencies at that time or some of the work that has been done since that time, they were representative of the variety of methods that characterized action-training agencies.

UTC, as the first of the action-training programs, developed an elaborate curriculum with policy direction from its own Curriculum Committee and consultation by the Institute of Industrial Relations at the University of Chicago and Basic Systems, Inc.[10] The foundation of this curriculum involved a threefold practice of theologizing, sociologizing and strategizing with action. Three skills were stressed in the training process: analytical skill as a basis for concrete reflection, development of skills in strategy-planning and ministry development. Analysis was directed toward each trainee's "situation, the actual field of action—whether it is a geographical area, a movement, an organization, or even a specific system—in which human beings are found to be interacting within a given identifiable whole of relations and conditions." Situations were to be analyzed in terms of four elements—conditions, structures, agents/actors and goals.

In addition to looking at their own "situations," UTC trainees were also encouraged to identify and define the major "issues" in that situation and to select two "problems" for solving in regard to those issues. "Issue" was defined as "situation and circumstances which present themselves as 'hurts,' which are 'at issue,' and with respect to which a variety of (debatable) proposals for dealing with them may exist."[11] Although trainees were always encouraged to bring issues from their own situation to the training program, UTC developed its own process for presenting them through Issue Forums and other programs, with issues that were current in the wider society or in Chicago, where most UTC training took place.

Strategy-planning and ministry development built from the situation analysis by use of the Three Panel Chart.[12] Problems were chosen for further consideration, basic strategies and models for action were suggested and considered, and field visits, consultation with resource persons and written materials were used to develop possible options. When a ministry strategy had been chosen and critiqued by both staff and fellow trainees, a critical path for action was developed. This included both the next steps to be taken in the preparation of strategy after the trainee had returned home and in implementation of that strategy. It was assumed that carrying out the strategy would be accomplished by reflective and evaluative procedures for testing and readjusting the strategy in view of both critical conditions that affected its performance or were called forth by what had already been done.

The UTC model was elaborate, and even the seven weeks which trainees spent in Chicago were scarcely enough time in which to take apart a situation, look at strategy options and develop an adequate course of action for the future. However, this was more concentrated time than most other action-training programs were able to give their training groups. In addition, with few exceptions, UTC trainees came on their own away from their usual work situation. This was in contrast to the development by many other ATC agencies of training programs that involved a group of people who were already working together.

Whenever UTC training is mentioned, the first picture that comes to mind is the exposure to urban poverty in "the rock-bottom plunge." Put out on the streets of Chicago in poor clothing with a limited amount of money for four or five consecutive 24-hour periods, UTC trainees were given a chance to sample the experience of being anonymous and powerless in the same place where others have great wealth, fame and power. Interpretation of the plunge by UTC staff were varied. Richard H. Luecke saw it as having symbolic value, renewing self-acquaintance, and initiating the procedure of "engagement and reflection." Carl Siegenthaler described it as a "preparation for participation by a prophetic fellowship:"

(1) an effort to act on the commitment *to be with people* in other than our own stream of life in metropolis;

(2) to undertake to communicate in *languages new to us,* within sub-communities with which we are inadequately familiar;

(3) *to be open* to sense the chaotic and redemptive, the horrifying and vivifying forces in our society;

(4) *to begin to isolate social problems-for-solving* from the midst of a more general problematic situation;

(5) to increase our *sensitivity to the Word* as it may be coming to expression in particular situations;

and

(6) an indication of our *willingness with the church to be changed* or to participate in directing change, as necessary.[13]

Hometown newspapers and religious journals carried many articles—often with pictures—describing the experience of White middle-class clergy on West Madison Street's skid row. Ithiel Clemmons, a Black clergyman from Brooklyn, New York, developed a program for Black alcoholics, "Highways and Hedges," as a result of his experience in Chicago, and most UTC trainees remembered the meal and fellowship at the end of their time on the streets as a high point of their training.

At Metropolitan Urban Service Training (MUST) in New York, more emphasis was placed on planning, with assistance from the Department of Planning at New York University, and on community organizing, in which several of the staff members had extensive experience. With the use of survey and goal-setting procedures, MUST introduced trainees to a five-step planning process: (1) define the problem, (2) set objectives, (3) choose strategy(ies), (4) act and (5) evaluate. Field visits, readings, and resource people and consultants were used to assist in the development of plans for future action. Then, simple principles of community organizing and group procedures were presented to develop skills in carrying out those plans.

Based on the experience of careful curriculum building for clergy training under a National Institute of Mental Health grant in the Cleveland Internship for Clergymen in Urban Ministry, Community Action Training Services (CATS) placed emphasis on developing four skills, which follow the UTC pattern:

• Theologizing—relating the faith professed by groups in training to the problematic situations of metropolis. . .

• Analyzing—examining the metropolitan scene with a view to understanding its problems and possibilities. Analysis consists of looking at a situation in terms of its material conditions, the structures which affect these conditions, the agents which function or fail to function in them, and the various goals which are operative in them.

• Strategizing—planning, carrying out and evaluating the means of effecting social change.
• Collaborating—developing effective supportive and working relationships with one's own constituency, with one's peers, with community change agents, and with a range of consultants.[14]

In most training programs CATS sought to work with these four skills in the order listed.

Metropolitan Ecumenical Training Center (METC) in Washington, D.C. based much of its curriculum on "action-research." Using Parker J. Palmer of the Washington Center for Metropolitan Studies as consultant, the staff developed, taught and used a three-step process with groups and individual trainees:

Stage I: Identify central issue through community process.
              Define issue as a researchable question.
              Develop research question.
              Develop hypothesis.
Stage II: Construct research instruments.
              Pre-test research instruments.
Stage III: Collect data.
              Analyze data.
              Draw conclusions for action programs.
              Disseminate findings and promote action.
All Stages: Maximize ways of involving people in research process.[15]

Other methods were used by ATC agencies which tried to bring the real world of experience into the training process. UTC trainees took part in civil rights marches in Chicago and Selma, and had field engagements in Chicago agencies, church and community organizations. Black clergy in a MUST program for mission ministers went to Washington, D.C. to join a rally supporting Adam Clayton Powell's right to remain in Congress. Case studies, both those prepared by trainees out of their experience and those presented by staff or other resource people, were used to give a feel for the complexity of real-life action. Models and model-building were an important part of most training programs. And a few training agencies developed experience in creating and conducting simulations. UTC assisted in developing and disseminating the Urban Dynamics simulation. The Interreligious Center for Urban Affairs (ICUA) in St. Louis worked with Washington University in perfecting and developing simulations of city systems and problems.

One characteristic of all these methods and curricula was their stress on the empirical, which was a consequence of their choice of inductive approaches and a process of action-reflection that tried to stay close to the action. A distinctive feature in action-training centers was the file cabinets and bookshelves full of research studies, planning documents, program proposals and reports, and other compilations of data (usually in mimeographed and photocopy form) that were collected to serve the needs of both staff and trainees. Getting the data on social situations and interpreting those data with a cogent social and political analysis was the dominant activity in most action-training programs.

Interpreting the data in theological perspective was more difficult, however. Action-training agencies discovered that their goal of "doing theology" was hard to achieve even though they devoted a great deal of staff time to the effort, and place was taken in most training programs for theological reflection. In the fall of 1967 UTC called a one-day consultation in Chicago of action-training programs that were already in operation, so that the question of the place of theology in their training could be examined more closely. The general outcome of that session was a renewed commitment to working at the problem, but each agency had to admit that this was one area in which they could not yet report a great deal of progress. Yet important theological work was done in the action-training programs. Only one explicitly theological volume has been published out of the action training experience—*Perchings* by Richard H. Luecke. However, much more of the theologizing that was done in action training is now only available in outlines or mimeographed papers or the oral tradition of those who shared in producing it.

One additional characteristic of action training is that the staffs of action training agencies worked together as a team. In its planning year and first program year, MUST employed Billie Alban to serve as "the trainer" on the staff. However, it became clear that every member of the staff (in fact, every person who was asked to serve as resource for a training program or event) was a trainer, because the training was done by the whole team and not by any particular member of it. This perception underlay the many hours of time spent by the staffs of ATC agencies both in planning and preparing for training programs, and in evaluating and redesigning after they were completed. It also resulted in the use of consultants who helped the entire staff master a new discipline, or change the way in which they had been designing or conducting their training programs.

When ATC was approached in 1972 by the Association for Religion and Applied Behaviorial Science (ARABS) to suggest how an accreditation review process might be set up for "action trainers" (along with trainers in the fields of personal growth, organizational development and experimental education), Speed Leas of the Center of Metropolitan Mission in Service Training (COMMIT) in Los Angeles, California, requested assistance from others in framing a reply. The sum of that answer was that ARABS "should not try to accredit Action Trainers or use the term 'Action Trainers' as a part of their accrediting process." Leas identified the most essential difference between ARABS and ATC to be that action trainers "assume that the only place where training can take place effectively is *in* the systems which are going to be affected by the training . . . They are in the action as well as helping others to be in the action." As a result, action training was not seen as an individual skill but a common achievement of the entire action-training agency, whose staff were not only supervised by each other (their peers) but by their "clients," those with whom they shared common commitments and action. Leas underscored the importance of ATC's process of accrediting agencies, not individuals, which was based on these assumptions about the way in which action training was best accomplished.

EVALUATION

One way to define "action training" is to say it is what training agencies associated with the Action Training Coalition between 1968 and 1974 were doing. ATC was responsible both for the term, and for its definition. And the answer given to ARABS on the question of accreditation of action trainers assumed that only an action-training agency could do action training.

Another way to define "action training" would be the approach taken through much of this chapter, in which no definition is adequate unless it can be specific not only about what it means by "training," but about the constituency to be trained and the methodology by which they are trained. Agencies associated with ATC developed very specific answers to these questions during the period between 1962 and 1972, and those which have continued operation still make use of this approach.

Constituency: Action training is concerned either to get people into action or to work with those who are already acting. Although ATC agencies were principally concerned with training people from religious institutions, they found that their approach was also useful to people outside the church bodies which had brought them into being.

Purpose: Action training is directed toward producing social change, either within institutions (including religious bodies) or in the wider society. Although the initial definition of purpose by most ATC agencies was in terms of "the mission of the church," they later narrowed this down to activity that would produce social change and assist people in working for justice, humanization and liberation.

Methodology: One of the most frequently quoted descriptions of action training is the aphorism used at the Taskforce for Research, Urban Strategy and Training (TRUST) in Richmond, Virginia: "People more frequently act their way into a new way of thinking than think their way into a new way of acting." Agencies associated with ATC were not engaged in action for its own sake or denying the need for careful thought. However, they placed their emphasis on methods of training and learning that would focus on the actual situation in which people were involved and the action they were already undertaking or were capable of initiating. The understanding of action training is that little significant action will occur unless both learning and action are joined in the same process.

CHAPTER IV

The Development of Action-Training Programs

URBAN MISSION AFTER WORLD WAR II

The history of urban mission in the period following World War II begins with the formation of the East Harlem Protestant Parish in New York City in 1948. The founders of EHPP were all students at Union Theological Seminary who had spent the war in prison as conscientious objectors (Donald L. Benedict) or in the military as combatants (J. Archie Hargraves and George W. Webber). Although the members of the group ministry found support in New York City from Kenneth D. Miller of the New York City Mission Society and the executives of several of the Protestant denominations, they set an important pattern for the development of urban mission over the next two decades by going to a meeting of the Home Missions Council at Buck Hill Falls, Pennsylvania to secure validation and financial support for their project from the national mission boards of the major Protestant communions. Within a short period of years, the East Harlem Protestant Parish was succeeded by two other ecumenical parishes established by members of the original group—the West Side Christian Parish in Chicago (1952) and the Inner City Protestant Parish in Cleveland (1954). Drawing their inspiration from the Iona Community of Scotland and the French worker-priests, these young clergy were themselves the example for many others who followed them into inner-city mission work, and the gadflies for denominational and ecumenical bureaucracies that were giving primary attention to the suburban expansion of the church.

The concern for urban mission generated by EHPP was responsible for the creation or revivification of urban church departments in the mainline White Protestant denominations and inclusion of a Department of the City Church in the home missions division of the National Council of Churches when it was organized in 1950. An ecumenical Convocation on the City Church was held in Columbus, Ohio, on January 23-24, 1950, to be followed by an emphasis on "The Church Confronts the City" at the NCC's Division of Home Missions assembly in December 1954 and several denominational consultations in the winter of 1957-58. By 1960 almost every major denomination had a staff member or department for urban mission, and it could list a number of churches, parishes and programs that were principally led by White personnel, usually male clergy, in predominantly Black or Hispanic areas of the major metropolitan areas.

The Episcopal Church had the greatest influence on the initiation and development of urban training through its Joint Urban Program and Pilot Dioceses but the contours of its developing interest in urban mission are similar to those of the ecumenical agencies and other communions. In 1948, under the stimulation of White priests serving in inner-city parishes, the Episcopal Fellowship of Urban Workers was formed, and an exploratory conference was held on the church in urban America. For the next two years Seabury-Western Theological Seminary in Evanston, Illinois, held a ten-day Urban Training Institute for clergy and church workers. In 1952 a Division of Urban-Industrial Church Work was created within the Christian Social Relations Department of the national offices, and G. Paul Musselman was named as its first director.

National emphasis on urban mission for the Episcopal Church was initiated by a General Council resolution (Resolution 13) in 1961, which established a Joint Urban Program linking the home mission efforts of Episcopalians in cities with their social action program. First staff members of the program were James P. Morton, who had served in a Black inner-city parish in Jersey City, New Jersey and was related to home missions, and John V.P. Lassoe, a layman who had worked in community organizations in New York City and was connected with Christian social relations. A Strategy Conference was held in Brooklyn in June 1962 involving clergy and lay persons from across the country and using Perry Norton, professor of planning at New York University, as consultant. The strategy developed as a result of this consultation was to operate in several areas: (1) Five Metabagdad conferences were held in New York, Chicago, San Francisco, Atlanta and Omaha. All bishops and key clergy and lay leaders of their dioceses were involved in a simulation exercise to help them see the metropolitan areas in which they were working as areas of mission. (2) Seven dioceses were chosen to serve as "pilot dioceses." (3) 70 Clergy Conferences were held in dioceses throughout the U.S. between 1963 and 1965. (4) Summer training programs were conducted to prepare inner-city clergy working principally in Black and Hispanic areas to conduct summer work camps and training for seminarians. (5) Participation in the Urban Training Center for Christian Mission in Chicago was, in the words of its first director, C. Kilmer Myers, an Episcopal clergyman who had served in Jersey City and New York, "to give content to the terms *mission* and *ministry* in the metropolis." This was being mounted as an ecumenical effort with other Protestant denominations. (6) Plans were made to write and print an inner-city curriculum for use in parishes. (7) A quarterly journal, *Church in Metropolis*, as well as other publications, was planned to disseminate the program and its learnings in the church at large. As can be seen from this list, the Joint Urban Program placed a great deal of its emphasis on training—in the Metabagdad conferences, in the clergy conferences, in the summer training programs, in parish curriculum and at UTC.

Following the initial emphasis throughout the church in 1963-64, the main effort of the program was to fall on the Pilot Dioceses from 1964 through 1966. Then, the learnings from their experience were to be extended to the church at large following 1966. The model used was essentially that of "R and D" (research and development), as it had previously been used in industry, business and the military. The program was to have three main features: (1) Each Pilot Diocese was to receive national church funds for three-year "demonstration projects for developing creative techniques for urban ministry," which would test the priorities for deployment of money and manpower throughout the diocese, and underscore the necessity for long-range planning. (2) This demonstration program was to be sponsored by a commission representative of the whole diocese, rather than being administered as part of the ongoing program. This paralleled the Manhattan Project style of administration at the national level. (3) There was to be continuous reporting and evaluation, both at the local and national levels. Dioceses to be included in the Pilot Diocese program were chosen on the basis of their variety and ability to contribute to a national strategy. The first five included were the Dioceses of Los Angeles, Missouri, Rhode Island, Southern Ohio and Texas. Tennessee and Idaho were added to make up the original group of seven, and the dioceses of Pennsylvania, Olympia (Washington), Chicago-Northern Indiana and Puerto Rico then asked to be included in 1966. As each diocese developed its demonstration projects, training and theological education were included by several (Idaho, Los Angeles, Puerto Rico, Southern Ohio, Tennessee and Texas). Three centers which were related to the Action Training Coalition—ACTS in the Southeast, the Ecumenical Training Council in Idaho, and PRISA in Puerto Rico—had their origins in proposals made for the Joint Urban Program.

At the same time that the Episcopal Church was developing this highly planned and coordinated thrust in urban mission, it was joining with other denominations in rearranging the way in which they conducted mission efforts in the United States. In 1963 the Commission on Religion and Race was formed and placed in the National Council of Churches to take care of concerns for race and civil rights both in the South and in Northern cities. Robert W. Spike, who had been an inner-city pastor in New York City at Judson Memorial Church and an executive of the Board for Homeland Ministries of the United Church of Christ, was appointed to head this effort. Then, the reorganization of the National Council of Churches in 1964 resulted in creation of an enlarged Division of Christian Life and Mission to unite both social action concerns that had been carried over from the Federal Council of Churches, its predecessor, and home mission concerns that had been lodged in the Division of Home Missions of NCC when the Home Missions Council joined the merger in 1950. DCLM had no specific staff for urban mission after December 1964, and the Department of the City Church was terminated. Three denominations—The Episcopal Church, the United Church of Christ and the United Presbyterian Church in the U.S.A.—found themselves having a great number of common interests in cities and metropolitan areas across the country, especially in support of community organization. The UCC and the UPCUSA had a number of special staff persons for metropolitan areas in many parts of the U.S. Based on this common interest, they held a joint meeting of the three denominations' national urban staffs, board committees and metropolitan urban specialists in Chicago on April 19-20, 1966, which was followed by a meeting of urban specialists that fall. Thus was established the Joint Urban Advisory Group, more familiarly known as "the Troika." Although the initiative for this development came from the national urban executives— George H. (Jack) Woodard, Jr., Episcopal; Joseph W. Merchant, UCC; and George E. Todd, UPCUSA—they were backed by the activist leaders of their national home mission boards, Daniel Corrigan, Truman B. Douglass and Kenneth G. Neigh.

Late in 1966 these three denominations moved to separate their common concerns for community organization and urban mission by working to establish two separate entities—Interreligious Foundation for Community Organization, (IFCO), concerned for the support of local organizing and to serve as their joint funding channel in minority communities; and the Joint Urban Executive Committee (JUEC), concerned for joint action in mission. The initial proposal for JUEC talked of pooling mission funds for joint allocation as an earnest of the day when, as a result of conversations in the Consultation on Church Union (COCU), the three communions would become one church. National funding of local efforts had become an increasingly important part of home mission strategy in the period of post-war affluence, as funds contributed by church members increased and as invested funds (many of them in stocks of industries participating in the heated-up defense economy of the Cold War) produced both increased dividends and capital gains. However, the time had not arrived for surrendering control of budget to an interdenominational entity, and the covenant of understanding voted by the three denominations in the spring of 1967 provided for the following functions: joint planning of urban work, joint funding of limited experimental projects, joint screening of ongoing urban work to see that it met ecumenical criteria, brokering of joint funding from other sources, joint communication on urban matters and coordination of strategies for response to issues.

This coordination of effort by Episcopalians, UCC and UPCUSA at the national level both stimulated and was influenced by the development of ecumenical consortia at the metropolitan level in many of the major cities.[1] The denominations involved and the functions for which they were willing to cooperate varied from place to place. In fact, the three denominations which were cooperating nationally were not always included in the groups cooperating locally. However, the consortia at the local level grew out of a similar experience of having worked together on common issues and dissatisfaction with the existing organizations (usually local or metropolitan councils of churches). Among the groups formed in the same period that JUEC was coming together were: Joint Action in Mission (JAM), New York City; Metropolitan Ecumenical Ministry (MEM), Newark, New Jersey; Board for Urban Ministry (BUM), Rochester, New York; Interreligious Council on Urban Affairs (IRCUA), Chicago; Metropolitan Inter-Church Agency (MICA), Kansas City; Joint Action in Mission (JAM, later JAM-SAC), Los Angeles; Church-Community Action Program of the Greater Portland (Oregon) Council of Churches; and Ecumenical Metropolitan Ministry (EMM), Seattle. Many of the action-training programs and agencies were formed as part of the process of bringing together these metropolitan coalitions, and in some cases were lodged in the ecumenical agency (Center for Urban Education—Portland, EMM, and JOUM). Even where such coalitions of denominational urban work were not formed, the action-training centers were usually allied with those who were striving to move the local ecumenical agency in the direction of greater social activism and denominational accountability. Even when the relationships were not formal, most action-training centers had working connections, interlocking directorates and joint strategies with the ecumenical agencies in their area. And, since most of them were ecumenically based, they were also competing for funds, time and other resources with other ecumenical enterprises.

At the national level, cooperation in JUEC was proceeding. *Church in Metropolis* became a joint publication of the three denominations with the Spring 1968 issue (and went out of existence for a simpler publication the following winter). Screening procedures were set up, and a docket of projects was established for common or joint funding. Although the hope had been to move toward an increased amount of joint funding, the process was usually one of joint discussion and separate commitments. Interest in this common effort was great, and other denominations were inquiring whether they could also join. In January 1968, JUEC was reorganized as Joint Strategy and Action Committee (JSAC), and three other denominations— American Baptist Churches, Presbyterian Church in the U.S. and United Methodist Church—joined the original three. By 1974 JSAC included most of the major denominations, although it placed far less emphasis on the screening of projects for funding, and its original emphasis on urban mission had dwindled to a Metropolitan Mission sub-group of a Mission Strategy Development Group. The coalition style of JSAC was influential both for action-training agencies in their own operation and for the formation of the

Action Training Coalition (ATC). Action-training agencies had a close relationship with JSAC's Training Committee (later Strategy/Screening Task Force in Training Ministries) from its formation in October 1968 until it ceased to meet in 1972.

The period of greatest achievement for the work of urban mission in the Episcopal Church was also the very point at which the structures which had accomplished that work were superceded by a new crash effort to meet the threat of urban riots and the challenge of poverty and race, especially in cities. When the 62nd General Convention met in Seattle, Washington, John E. Hines, the Presiding Bishop, made a special call for an effort to raise funds for the needs of the poor and powerless. The General Convention Special Program was established under the leadership of Leon Modeste, a Black community worker. The GCSP raised and distributed $7.5 million to projects that fostered minority self-determination until October 18, 1973, when the staff received sudden notices of termination. Modeste has analysed this development as follows:

> The Episcopal Church at its General Convention in 1967 made a "political" decision to establish the GCSP . . . . The State responded with the anti-poverty program, cooptation and brute force in an effort to calm the masses. The church followed in like manner and began a strong propaganda campaign to project the image of responding to the need of the poor and powerless, especially Blacks. Its rhetoric was that the church had been moved to make its behavior consistent with its Christian doctrine. . . . However, the real reason was that the church and state were responding to the dictates of the ruling class to stabilize the society at whatever cost. The Episcopal Church did it with "pennies" as it gave the GCSP $1 million annually for grants, while spending on all its levels approximately $300 million yearly. Simultaneously, the Church, like the government, maintained investments in corporations that exploited poor and powerless people as in South Africa. . . .
>
> *Black folk must begin to realize that regardless of how liberal the white church, racism, economic exploitation—capitalism is woven into its fabric, and it will always move to protect it own interest.*[2]

Other denominations moved during this same period to set up similar funds for minority empowerment, which distributed grants to church and community organizations. Among the so-called "crisis funds" the following denominations joined the Episcopal Church after 1967: American Baptist Churches and Progressive National Baptist Convention (Fund of Renewal), Church of the Brethren (Fund of the Americas), Disciples of Christ, American Lutheran Church, Lutheran Church in America (Love Compels Action), Lutheran Church-Missouri Synod, Presbyterian Church, U.S., Reformed Church in America, Southern Baptist Convention, United Church of Christ (Commission on Racial Justice), United Methodist Church (Fund for Reconciliation), Unitarian-Universalist Association, United Presbyterian Church in the U.S.A. (Fund for the Self-Development of Peoples) and the United States Catholic Conference (Campaign for Human

Development). At the meeting of the General Board of the National Council of Churches in Atlanta in September 1967, a "Resolution on Urban Concerns" was adopted, which resulted in formation of the "Crisis in the Nation" program. This effort sought to focus churches' attention on the report of the Kerner Commission on Civil Disorders, which described the growth of two societies in the United States, one White and the other Black, and called for a fight against institutional racism.

Another parallel development during this period, which was also fostered by the mainline White Protestant denominations, was formation of a Black churchmen's national organization. The majority of Black Christians in the U.S. were already gathered in large denominational bodies—largely Baptist (National Baptist Convention, Inc., National Baptist Convention, Progressive National Baptist Convention, Lott Carey Missionary Association) and Methodist (African Methodist Episcopal, African Methodist Episcopal Zion, Christian Methodist Episcopal). However, either as a result of past missionary effort in the South or more recent attempts to gather Black congregations in Northern and Western cities, the mainline denominations had some Black congregations and members, and a limited number of Black clergy, many of whom had been educated at White-dominated seminaries.

On July 31, 1966, immediately following the so-called "Meredith March" in Mississippi when the slogan of "Black power" was first raised to national prominence by intense media coverage, an ad hoc group of Black clergy from traditional denominations and the mainline White Protestant bodies published a full-page advertisement in the *New York Times*. Out of response to this public declaration, the National Committee of Negro Churchmen (later changed to National Committee of Black Churchmen) was organized. At its first convocation in Dallas in November 1967, commissions and committees were established, officers elected and a secretariat set up to organize Black churchmen around issues facing the Black church community. J. Metz Rollins, Jr., who had been serving in the United Presbyterian Church national offices, was elected executive director to serve in an office supported both by dues and by contributions from the Black caucuses that were arising in the White denominations. These included the American Baptist Black Churchmen, Black Methodists for Church Renewal, Black Presbyterians United, the Black Affairs Council and the Black Unitarian-Universalist Caucus.

NCBC issued a number of notable policy statements and developed programs for emphasizing Black theology, promoting technical assistance to African nations (Pan-African Skills Project), electing Black leadership in the NCC, and supporting prisoners involved in the Attica revolt and the United Front of Cairo. After the assassination of Martin Luther King, Jr., NCBC addressed a statement to the White churches on urban mission, calling upon them "to take with utmost seriousness the Black church as the only . . .

link with the inner city for the mission of the church." White denominations were asked to be prepared to negotiate with Black churchmen the surrender of resources that were being expended in "irrelevant, nonproductive, and patronizing missions to the Black churches."

However, the greatest impact which NCBC had on urban mission and the White denominations was through its support of the Black Manifesto[3], which came out of the National Black Economic Development Conference on April 25-27, 1969, in Detroit. The Conference had been called by IFCO to bring together Black community activists from around the country with economists and theoreticians to develop an economic development strategy. Workshops were planned on both urban and rural issues of land, labor, capital and entrepreneurship, based on the assumption that the Black condition in the U.S. was neither urban nor rural but a result of the interrelationship of the two. James Forman was responsible for the wording of the Manifesto, which he presented to the Conference, but its support of self-determination and rejection of both "Black capitalism" and "minority entrepeneurship" represented accurately the consensus of those who had discussed the issues in the workshops.

The Black Manifesto and the concept of "reparations" were brought to the nation's attention on Sunday morning, May 4, when Forman read the text from the chancel steps in the Riverside Church. Two days earlier the Manifesto's demand for $500 million in reparations had been presented to the General Board of the NCC, which referred it to a June meeting of its Executive Committee. By the time that group met on June 23, supporters of BEDC, including NCBC, had made demands on many of the NCC's member denominations, staged sit-ins at denominational offices, spoken in churches and held a one-day strike at the Interchurch Center on June 10. During the first year after presentation of the Black Manifesto, BEDC received nearly $300,000 for its own administration and projects, but a great deal more was given to other groups through IFCO, the denominational crisis funds and the denominational Black caucuses. One estimate in June 1970 was that $127 million was already raised or set as goals by denominations that had given token amounts or nothing to BEDC.

Urban mission, which had begun in 1948 with a seminarians' project to evangelize the city, had by 1970 become a swirling field of White denominational churches and projects, Black churches and caucuses' action, and ecumenical coalitions, all surrounded by a national society that had been newly sensitized to racism, poverty and overseas exploitation but that was asking for surcease and a chance to regain its own good opinion of itself. This mood had encouraged the election of Richard M. Nixon in 1968 and has since kept religious bodies from attempting again to take up the task of urban mission and social change. It was in this field of coalition and confrontation that urban training, later to be called "action training," was begun with the establishment of the Urban Training Center for Christian Mission, to be followed by a great many other training programs, centers and networks, 31 of which belonged at one time or another to the Action Training Coalition.

THREE PIONEERS WITH DIFFERENT ORIGINS AND HISTORY

The development of urban training (later to be called "action training") as a resource for urban mission in the United States was a result of the activity of three different pioneer training organizations, each of which had quite different origins and history. The Urban Training Center for Christian Mission, organized in Chicago in 1963, was created by national denominations' urban staff members, with local initiative supplied by the Community Renewal Society and its director, Donald L. Benedict, who had been part of the original group ministry in the East Harlem Protestant Parish. The Cleveland program, Internship for Clergymen in Urban Mental Health (popularly known as "Cleveland Intern Program"—CIP), made use of funds provided by the National Institute for Mental Health to train professionals in mental health, and the spark was given by Dean Allen Pfleger of Cleveland College, Case-Western Reserve University, who prepared the original proposal in 1964 and was academic liaison for the project through four years of training before it spun off as Community Action Training Services. Metropolitan Urban Service Training in New York City was organized in 1965 by J. Edward Carothers, executive secretary of the National Division of the Board of Missions of the Methodist Church, as a pilot program for training clergy and laity. MUST took its form in New York City both from the proposals prepared by a staff led by George W. Webber, who also had been in the East Harlem Protestant Parish, and participation in policy-making by local denominational leaders who were members of Joint Action in Mission (JAM). These three training centers—in Chicago, Cleveland and New York—were the pioneers, and much of what action training became—or did not realize—was the result of their preponderant size, early definitions and later history. Two are no longer in operation, and the third has moved to quite a different mode of operation; but no understanding of action training is adequate without taking their origins and history into account.

Urban Training Center for Christian Mission, Chicago, Illinois—Whenever action training is mentioned, the first example that comes to mind is UTC, which operated in Chicago from July 1963 through December 1974.[4] This is only natural because UTC was the first action-training center (organization began in 1962), the largest in budget (spending over $3.33 million in 12 years, including $880,000 from the Ford Foundation and $415,000 from the Sealantic Foundation), the largest in staff, the largest in number of trainees (977 in its first four program years, 1006 in the next six), the most widely publicized and the first to try to put content into the idea of "urban training." In addition, at least 15 persons who were staff members of other action-training programs received UTC training at some time, and most of the other centers either visited UTC as part of their planning phase or used UTC staff and board members as consultants.

However, there are many aspects of UTC that were not typical of the other centers and programs. Most denominations considered UTC to be the only national center in the United States, while other centers were regional or metropolitan. UTC had the greatest number of different communions cooperating in its sponsorship and was able to receive a large share of the training funds made available by mainline Protestant denominations during this period. Because UTC saw itself as preparing the pilot curriculum for urban training, its staff and Curriculum Committee engaged in a wide-ranging program of research and consultation. The center was modeled on educational institutions, with the corporation being set up in the State of Illinois as an educational corporation, and the staff being given the customary faculty perquisites of long summer vacations and sabbaticals. UTC developed its own style of training that was, at the same time, a precursor of what other centers did as "action training" and yet less capable than most other programs of learning from its heavily stylized experience. Nevertheless, so prominent was UTC in the public consciousness between 1964, its first program year, and 1974, when it closed for lack of continued support from the national denominations, that many have not realized that urban training and action training did not cease with the passing of this Chicago-based program.

Although several national denominations and the National Council of Churches had already been exploring the possibilities of training for urban church work and mission in an urbanized society, the particular proposal that resulted in formation of the Urban Training Center for Christian Mission was not initiated until the spring of 1961. The precipitating factor was the decision of the Church of the Brethren to move Bethany Seminary, then located on the West Side of Chicago, to the suburban community of Oak Brook at the end of the 1961-62 academic year. Donald L. Benedict, director of the Chicago City Missionary Society, an affiliate of the United Church of Christ, had cherished the idea of an urban-based seminary during the years he was associated with inner-city parishes in East Harlem, Chicago's West Side and Cleveland. He developed "A Tentative Proposal for an Urban Training Center," which was presented to the Executive Board of the Division of the Home Missions, National Council of Churches, and referred to the Department of Urban Church. The purpose of the training center, in Benedict's original proposal, was "to explore and communicate the relationship of the Christian faith to the urban industrial society in order that the church as the carrier of the Gospel may find renewal in our generation." This same concern for the church and its role in urban society is found in the purpose stated in a prospectus developed by a Continuing Committee during the winter of 1961-62:

> The Center is to be headquarters for study and demonstration, for reflection and involvement, for implementing the relationship between the gospel and urban culture. It is to be a demonstration school, an urban laboratory, concerned for injecting the Christian way of life into the urban community so that the church may fill its rightful role in this vast segment of contemporary society.[5]

On November 21, 1961 the Department of Urban Church of the NCC held its Consultation on the Urban Training Center at Bethany Seminary. Robert W. Spike and James E. Gustafson presented papers, and Benedict's proposal was discussed. Action was taken to establish a Continuing Committee for an Urban Training Center, including representatives of fourteen national denominations, with Joseph W. Merchant, secretary for urban work of the United Church of Christ, as chairman. The structure and organization of UTC, and much of its future direction, was actually worked out and established over the next year and a half by this committee and its successor, the UTC Planning Committee, before the first staff member came on the scene.

Among many important decisions made during the planning period, the following proved to be the most critical: (1) At the very first meeting the Continuing Committee decided against purchasing the Bethany property, which had provided the inspiration for the training center proposal. The buildings were subsequently bought by the Ecumenical Institute, which used them as both national headquarters and base for their Fifth City project. (2) The wide variety of possible programs suggested by Benedict's fertile imagination in his original proposal were quickly limited to the following:

> a) to train pastors and laymen in the substantive areas regarding the metropolitan complex and
> b) to engage the students in the processes of urban life so that experientially they are involved in the apologetics and dialogues necessary for relevant urban mission.[6]

(3) A conscious decision was made not to locate the center at any of the Chicago area seminaries nor to enter into a direct relationship with any of them, and, at a later time, not to enter into competition with those schools as a degree-granting institution. Two members of this committee were members of Chicago seminary faculties, Gibson Winter of the Divinity School, University of Chicago, and Marshal Scott of McCormick Theological Seminary.

(4)The organizational base was to be a consortium of interested national denominations, and a process was established to secure approval in principle from denominational home mission boards, to have each name an official representative and alternate, to seek suggestions for changes in the proposal, and to develop a timetable for official sponsorship by each of the fourteen interested denominations—American Baptist Convention, Christian Churches (Disciples of Christ), Church of the Brethren, Church of God (Anderson, Indiana), Protestant Episcopal Church[7], Evangelical Covenant Church of America, American Lutheran Church, Augustana Lutheran Church, Lutheran Church-Missouri Synod, United Lutheran Church in America, Methodist Church, Reformed Church in America, United Church of Christ and United Presbyterian Church in the U.S.A. Although these same denominations were also part of the NCC's Department of Urban Church, they only asked that body to "commend" the project and "lend such assistance as they can." Thus, skillful political maneuvering secured both blanket overall approval from denominations whose support was needed—albeit without final confirming action by each body—and some freedom from the structures of the National Council of Churches, which was about to undergo a drastic reorganization in which the Department of Urban Church would eventually disappear. (5) During this process, only two denominations had substantial objections, the United Presbyterians and the Methodists, both of which were to remain minimally related to UTC through most of its life-span. The major role of the United Church of Christ, Protestant Episcopal Church and Lutherans in the future of the project was underlined by the first officers elected—Merchant, president (UCC); James P. Morton, vice-president (Episcopal); and Walter Kloetzli, secretary-treasurer (National Lutheran Council).

(6) The financial pattern for UTC was established in the prospectus developed by the Continuing Committee. The training year was divided into 3,000 "student weeks" (based on an estimated capacity of 75 students per week for 40 weeks). Participating denominations were then assigned percentages of the budget, based on their total number of communicants, and allocated student-weeks on the same ratio. On this basis, United Presbyterians and Methodists were assigned the largest quotas both of budget and student-weeks, a factor that may have contributed to their reluctance to become full partners in UTC as a national effort.

(7) The member denominations, however, were not expecting to carry the full financial load at the beginning.

> Foundation help is necessary in order to launch the project, while the denominations are gradually assuming the major responsibility for its continued financing. A five-year "staged grant" would be necessary . . . The denominations would underwrite the total cost beginning with the sixth year.[8]

By June 1962 contacts had already been made with the Ford Foundation,

Lilly Endowment and Chicago Community Trust, and a list of national and Chicago-based foundations was drawn up for future contact. Also, the participating denominations were being promised a way to get the project started that provided a five-year delay until their full financial support would be required.

1963-64 was taken up with filling out the organization, electing a staff and planning curriculum. C. Kilmer Myers, a White Episcopal priest who had been an inner-city pastor in Jersey City and New York's Trinity Parish, was elected Executive Director in February and began his service in June 1962. By the time UTC opened for its first trainees in the fall of 1964 Myers had resigned to become suffragan bishop of the Diocese of Michigan, and the Board elected its own vice-president, James P. Morton, another White Episcopal priest, as his successor. By the fall of 1963 Myers assembled a staff consisting of J. Archie Hargraves, a Black UCC minister who was a veteran of the East Harlem Protestant Parish and Chicago's West Side; Carl Siegenthaler, a White United Presbyterian with both theological and social work training; Niles Carpenter, a White Episcopal priest with social studies training (who was replaced a year later by Paul E. Kraemer, a Dutch social scientist) as Director of Research; and Richard Luecke, a White Missouri Synod pastor who had been serving as Lutheran chaplain at Princeton University.

While the Board busied itself with securing financial support and developing by-laws, the staff was principally engaged in building the curriculum under the guidance of a Curriculum Committee, chaired by Winter. Although the original proposal was an "orientation month" as the basic unit of training, the staff developed a three-month training sequence that became the basic module. A significant part of the first proposal was "the Plunge," intended as "a period of intense personal exposure to the problem of unemployment" in which a trainee would "examine his own identity and begin to understand the life-situation of so many where there is a lack of personal and social identity," and discover the church "out there in the heart of the metropolis." During the first program year the curriculum was to focus on three problem areas—school drop-outs, organizing the unemployed and the effects of cybernation on middle-level decision-makers in suburbia.

Full denominational support in the first program year (1964-65) came from eleven denominations—American Baptists, American Lutherans, Church of God (Anderson, Ind.), Evangelical United Brethren, Lutheran Church in America, Lutheran Church-Missouri Synod, Mennonites, Protestant Episcopal, Reformed Church in America, United Church of Christ and United Presbyterians. Seven other denominations were represented on the Board of Directors—Brethren, Disciples of Christ, General Conference Mennonites, Methodists, Moravians, Presbyterian Church in the U.S. and Roman Catholics. Although this line-up represented a very wide spread of mainline Protestantism and Roman Catholicism, UTC, before it had finished its career, had also secured additional Protestant participation from a number of other largely White denominations (Anglican Church of Canada, Christian Reformed, Presbyterian Church of Canada, Southern Baptists, United Church of Canada) and the major Black denominations in the U.S. (National Baptists, Progressive National Baptists, African Methodist Episcopal, African Methodist Episcopal Zion, Christian Methodist Episcopal), as well as Orthodox participation through the Standing Conference of Canonical Orthodox Bishops of the Americas. Few national mission or educational projects have had so wide a spread of confessional participation.

Denominational financial support was easier to gain because the Sealantic Fund made a decreasing grant for the first five years of operation. Denominations committed themselves to tripling their share of the budget by 1969. "Interim space" was secured at 40 North Ashland Avenue, a building attached to First Congregational Church on the largely Black West Side and located close to the Duncan Branch of the YMCA of Chicago. Although it was planned that the Chicago City Missionary Society would later build a joint facility for UTC training and its own use, this never came to fulfillment. UTC spent most of its life at 40 North Ashland, moving in 1971 to an office building in the Loop owned by the Paulist Fathers and conducting training sessions primarily at the YMCA Hotel.

During 1964-65, UTC conducted two three-month programs, called "3-4-3" because they included two three-week periods of resident training separated by four weeks of field exposure in Chicago agencies. The focus on unemployment resulted in heavy involvement with West Side community organizers and Black leadership in forming the West Side Organization, to which funds were channeled in exchange for supervision of trainees. Concentration on the issues of "Power and the American Negro" and "The Reconstruction of the Democratic Society" led naturally to trainees' participation in the Selma-Montgomery March of the civil rights movement and a demonstration on Balbo Drive against segregation in Chicago schools, during which many were arrested. As part of the openness after Vatican II, UTC enrolled two Roman Catholic trainees in its initial year; by 1967-68 they became the largest single group enrolled in the center.

When the second program year began in 1965-66, UTC was both in the process of expanding its original mandate to train for existing church vocations and becoming more heavily involved in theological seminary programs. Curriculum had been developed for five major areas of ministry— metropolitan mission, community organization, civil rights, industrial mission and central city ministries, the last being an attempt to respond to denominational criticism that UTC was not concerned for the church-based programs sponsored by most mainline White denominations. In addition, Sealantic Fund prevailed on the staff to give orientation to Rockefeller

Fellows entering seminary through the Fund for Theological Education, and the Divinity School, University of Chicago signed a contract with UTC to conduct two quarters of its new D.Min. program. During the first year of the program 128 trainees were enrolled in three sequences, but staff also gave five months to the Divinity School D.Min. students and two weeks at the end of the summer to the Rockefeller Fellows. Stanley J. Hallett, a theologically trained planner on the faculty of Northwestern University's Center for Urban Affairs, and Milton E. Kotler of the Institute for Policy Studies in Washington, D.C., were both helpful resources.

The major shift during this year, however, came as a result of a successful proposal submitted to the Ford Foundation. Although no Black members sat on the Board of Directors, no Black denomination was represented in sponsorship, and only one staff member was Black, UTC had asked Ford for assistance to bring Black clergy trainees to Chicago. Award of the Ford grant enabled UTC to add C T Vivian, a Black native of Illinois and Baptist clergyman who had been a civil rights activist, to its staff as Director of Fellowships and Internships. Black participation on the Board was provided by adding at-large members, although no Black denomination was received as a member of the corporation. Thirty Ford Fellows were involved in the last two training sequences in 1965-66. Fifty-one took part in 1966-67, 124 in 1967-68 (including 55 in the Chicago-based CAT—Chicago Action Training—program), 96 in 1968-69, 71 in 1969-70 and 51 in the remainder of 1970 before the grant closed. This represented 350 of the 1983 trainees during UTC's ten program years, and almost half of the total of Black trainees. The basic UTC sequence was changed to a 4-3-3 period, so that Ford Fellows could return to their congregations between the training sessions. This placed their training more in the context of their back-home situations than most of the other trainees, who had Chicago placements during the middle three weeks and were not able to take Ford-financed trips back to their local involvements. Ford trainees added an additional burden to UTC's training capacity, but they brought a concrete involvement with the Black church in the midst of the civil rights struggle, and made possible a larger budget for consultants and resource persons, as well as for research and evaluation.

On December 13, 1965, a special Board meeting was called to consider the resignation of Walter Kloetzli, UTC's secretary-treasurer, who had played an important role in drawing up the original proposal. He charged lack of administrative control, irregularities in use of staff time and budget, and an orientation toward "action" rather than training. The first two criticisms were directed principally towards Morton's stewardship as Executive Director. The Board accepted Kloetzli's resignation, but increased the powers of the Executive Committee to reduce staff autonomy between Board meetings. The third criticism stemmed from the close relationship with the West Side Organization and Saul Alinsky's style of community organizing, which Kloetzli had long opposed. However, it was also the first of several internal Board discussions on the extent to which UTC was to focus on action through the church as well as outside it.

The Ford years from 1966 through 1970 were the most exciting and representative time of UTC training. The staff had already developed the training programs and style during the first two years. Each year there was a core of longer-term trainees who stayed six, nine or 12 months, in addition to those in the basic 4-3-3 courses, one-month orientations and any additional programs that were scheduled. Although different issues would be chosen for workshops each time, curriculum focused on the basic disciplines of theologizing (including questions of liturgy and discipline), analyzing (using a single major topic in the Issue Seminar as the example) and strategizing (in a small group of trainees and UTC staff), and in most cases was directed toward the trainee's back-home situation. Those who took the longer-term courses had a field experience in the Chicago area under supervision of the field agency, with a reflection-review group of fellow trainees to assist in interpreting the experience and developing a proposal for ministry as a final major written project.

According to the testimony of trainees in their own articles and newspaper interviews after they had completed UTC training, the major impact came from the experience of urban living (particularly through the Plunge and UTC's location in the West Side ghetto), the ecumenical diversity of UTC's fellowship both in confessional background and previous experience, the stimulating presentations of speakers and resource persons, and the concrete possibilities for future strategy that were worked out in the proposal for ministry. All of this was received under extraordinary pressure, especially by those enrolled in the 4-3-3 course or one-month orientation. Five and a half days of each week were filled with plenary and small-group sessions. The sense of being in Chicago at a critical time in the history of the nation and of the churches was intensified by constant battle reports brought in from both the city's neighborhoods and the nation's trouble spots. Joint Roman Catholic-Protestant worship, including eucharistic fellowship, was made possible by the UTC's having been designated as a place for liturgical experiment.

Among the issues considered in UTC training during the Ford years were: control and ownership of the ghetto, protests and politics, higher schools and the city, the Black Manifesto and the response of the churches, federal programs and urban community development, White laws and Black power, central city community development and economic development, suburban housing and zoning, suburban youth, ecology, youth culture, and health care. Resources and projects were drawn both from the Greater Chicago area and from a wide variety of national organizations. In addition, Ford Fellows gathered in 1970 for three alumni sessions on economic development (in Atlanta and Seattle) and community schools (in Boston).

A wide variety of other training programs were offered during the same period. In collaboration with Urban America, a national housing coalition in which religious groups played a major role, UTC offered a series of eight workshops on low-income housing development and management, most held in Chicago. Spanish participation in UTC training was encouraged by recruitment of a training group from Puerto Rico who had a one-week orientation in Cayey, Puerto Rico, in 1968 and then attended the fall 4-3-3 sequence in Chicago. Another Hispanic program was set up in the fall of 1969 in collaboration with Ivan Illich and CIDOC in Cuernavaca, Mexico. Another regular offering between 1968 and 1970 were the workshops on social planning conducted by a British social theorist, Richard Hauser, director of the Centre for Group Studies in London, England. Other special programs in this period included: a 12-week course on "Arts in the Urban Context," a two-week Intensive Planning Workshop for denominational executives, a week of training each for regional and national mission staff members, and for district presidents and assistants of the American Lutheran Church; and a session with the senior class of the School of Theology, University of the South, Sewanee, Tennessee. In addition, UTC continued to offer two quarters to students in the University of Chicago's D.Min. program through the summer of 1969.

A continuing challenge for the training center from the beginning had been how it would relate to the Chicago metropolitan area in which it was located. Three of the original sponsors out of whose vision the proposal had come—Benedict, Kloetzli and Winter—were all Chicago-based and had hoped for direct benefits to that city in line with their concerns. Hargraves was deeply involved with the Black community, especially on the West Side, where the UTC headquarters was established. UTC staff had established a wide network of relationships with ecumenical and denominational leaders in the city, as well as with all sorts of local projects and leaders both inside and outside the churches. An example of the way UTC interacted with the life of the Chicago metropolitan area is that during the 1966-67 program year the staff supported the entry into Chicago of both the Taize Brothers from Europe, and Martin Luther King, Jr. and the Southern Christian Leadership Conference from the Southeast.

During 1965-66 Hargraves outlined the possibility of a "Freedom Corps" to train ghetto leadership for Chicago in a paper entitled "Finding and Making New Cats for the New Thing." ("New thing" had been used in UTC promotional literature to describe both the new reality it was trying to bring into being in metropolis and UTC itself.) When this proposal did not fly, he then turned to developing a "CAT" (Chicago Action Training) sequence in a regular UTC training program by using Ford funds to bring Chicago Black leaders, both clergy and lay, for a one-month session in January 1968. During their UTC sessions on strategizing these participants worked out a proposal for creation of a Black Strategy Center to serve the Black community in Chicago. In a parallel development, stimulated by work on racism and community organizing being done at the Center for the Scientific Study of Religion by Winter, Alvin Pitcher and others, Pitcher had brought to the UTC Curriculum Committee in November 1967 a proposal to establish the Committee for One Society as a support for efforts by Chicago's Black leadership to overcome the effects of institutional discrimination and achieve self-determination. Thus, from two separate but related sources UTC was being approached to make the struggle against racism and for Black control of the ghetto its point of entry for training in Chicago.

The strong catalyst of the race issue and possibilities of additional funding gave the Black and White proposals for the Black Strategy Center and the Committee for One Society a better chance for adoption than a proposed joint venture with the Church Federation of Greater Chicago in a Metropolitan Chicago Training Center for church leadership that was already being discussed. On June 7-8, 1968, the UTC Board met for a two-day retreat to consider the two-pronged proposal as the basis for long-term training at the Center. Right after its adoption, Hargraves left to join the faculty of Chicago Theological Seminary, and Vivian took over the relationships with the CAT participants, the Black Consortium and the developing Black Strategy Center.

Relationships with both Black and White groups over the next two years were stormy. Blacks contended that funds were going principally to the Committee for One Society, the White support group, rather than the Black-directed effort for community unity and economic development. The White group developed an inventory for racism, which, in addition to being used with a couple of Chicago businesses, was applied to the YMCA of Greater Chicago. During the spring of 1969 this resulted in a student protest by UTC participants both against the Duncan Branch of the YMCA, in which they were housed, and against the UTC itself as "racist institutions." In the following year the Committee for One Society was spun off from UTC; it expired shortly afterwards. The Black Strategy Center had previously asserted its own autonomy and carried on its activities apart from UTC, although with continued heavy involvement of Vivian until he left the staff in the fall of 1969.

The most basic equation in UTC's career after the 1968-69 program year was the attempt to build a firm financial base. By the end of the fifth year of the Sealantic grant, the member denominations had achieved an overall annual total of $159,601, which was beyond their projected goal of $144,700.

However, the effects of inflation and increased operating costs had raised the annual budget to nearly $300,000. In addition, both staff and Board had become used to a Ford Foundation subsidy that totalled $235,000 in 1968-69. Although designated for Black participants who were Ford Fellows, this money also filled out other parts of UTC program and permitted a higher overhead for library, consultants and staff expense. Thus, UTC came to 1969-70 with an annual budget totalling over $500,000. Many member denominations which had been the Center's heaviest supporters were not making full use of the student-weeks to which they were entitled by their annual grant. Continuation of the Ford grant was needed not only to keep the Black clergy program going but to assist general solvency—and additional foundation grants were needed to subsidize the basic operation beyond the ceiling that appeared to have been reached by the supporting denominations. Morton started to warn the Board of this situation in January 1969. A new proposal was taken to Ford Foundation for the "renewal of the Negro ministry in America" that would include a core group of 20 Chicago clergy (and ability to undergird the Black Strategy Center) as part of a total of 500 Black participants. Another proposal circulated to several foundations asked assistance to establish a Central Training Action Resources Unit to develop "training options with new constituent groups for specialized needs," that would take up the slack beyond what denominations could supply. However, the main hope for survival lay with the member denominations.

The financial sword of Damocles hung over the UTC's head for almost two years until February 1971, when an "unmanageable deficit" of $120,000 and a "cash flow crisis" made it plain that even the budget which had been planned for that program year without the renewal of a Ford grant was severely off-target. Emergency monies were raised by the member denominations, staff members were reduced both in number and in time allowed for their service, and one of the two floors at 21 East Van Buren, to which the Center had relocated the previous summer, was vacated. In June 1971, the Board recommended formation of a "strategy unit" or "Black tube" as a means to secure additional support to supplement denominational grants. Discussions were begun with the National Committee of Black Churchmen to set up a Black training unit to parallel that of the national denominations. Morton, who had been replaced as administrator in July 1971 by Sister Marjorie Tuite, one of the two women who had been added to the staff in 1969, resigned in May 1972 to become Dean of New York Cathedral. A decision was made to have only a minimum staff, and the UTC, along with its board, was divided into a Black Training Center, in cooperation with NCBC, and a Denominational Training Center. Carroll M. Felton, who had succeeded Vivian, was named director of the former; George D. Younger, who had been serving at MUST in New York City, was called to head the latter. All the remaining staff members—Siegenthaler, Luecke and Sister Marjorie—were released or placed on part-time service.

Even in the midst of these convulsions and the two years of intensive care that followed, UTC continued to carry on creative programs of training and resource. An emphasis on health, with assistance from Ivan Illich, John McKnight of Northwestern University and Dr. Robert Mendelsohn of Cook County Hospital, produced a wide range of publications in the field of community health care, as well as support for positive changes in Chicago's health systems. A publishing program under the imprint of UTC Press brought several books to the wider public. A large number of conscientious objectors to the Vietnam War were placed in alternate service in Chicago under the UTC umbrella. Although training events were first cut to a month, and then later to two weeks, the issues covered continued to be timely—economic development, models for mission, low-income housing, Vietnam veterans, consumer education and revenue-sharing. After Younger came to the program, he developed a variety of training contracts and short-term programs, as well as continuing the relationship developed in 1970 with the Urban Ministries Program for Seminarians (UMPS), which had been developed by evangelical seminaries under the leadership of Gilbert James, a professor at Asbury Theological Seminary, Wilmore, Kentucky. (This program was a precursor of the present evangelical urban training effort in Chicago, SCUPE—Seminary Consortium for Urban Pastoral Education.)

However, the 1973-74 year saw a desperate end-game played with declining resources. Some foundation grants and denominational financial support continued to flow into the program, but the national denominations were no longer sending participants, and no subsidies were available for Black clergy who still wanted to attend. At the Annual Meeting of the Corporation in May 1974, decisions were made to cut back further on budget and staff, while a study was made of the long-term future of UTC as a national and/or metropolitan center. In July of that year a "fail-safe" decision was made by the Board to continue with the study through December, guaranteeing the two staff members their positions through December. However, the response of national denominations was so minimal that the Board decided in November to close UTC as "a national operation" and to appoint a Chicago-based committee to survey interest for a continuing program among denominations, ecumenical agencies, and seminaries and other educational institutions in the Chicago area.

By March the committee had determined that there was not sufficient support to keep going in Chicago. Younger took over the task of closing up the offices, which had been damaged by fire, and seeing that records were transferred to a safe depository. In December 1975, almost exactly 15 years after Benedict first became excited by the possibility of locating an urban training center in the buildings being abandoned by Bethany Seminary, the last debts were paid and an official mail vote by the remaining Board members dissolved the corporation, which had been launched with such promise, attracted such widespread support, and created such helpful ferment both in Chicago and more widely throughout the United States and other parts of the world.

The following solid accomplishments and contributions can be credited to the Urban Training Center during its career as a national training center:

(1)*Through its national and international contacts, UTC kept the cause of urban mission before the churches.* As the first urban training center established (at times "UTC" was the generic word for action training), the only national center in the United States and the program with the widest coverage in the secular press and outside the United States, UTC was able to give high visibility to urban mission. Almost 3,000 alumni who had taken part in its training were scattered all over the United States and many other countries. Visitors from overseas were routinely scheduled to visit UTC as part of their itinerary to see significant mission work or experimentation in the United States. A wide variety of news reporters wrote stories about the center which, when added to the articles written by staff and alumni, gave constant exposure to its current concerns in urban mission.

(2) *UTC maintained a constant focus on the interrelatedness of metropolitan life and mission, while emphasizing the need to redress inner-city and minority injustices.* The original vision was for a center that would train church workers in all parts of the metropolitan areas. Starting with its first training sequence, which included both inner-city and suburban issues, continuing through the heated days of civil rights activity, when White strategies against institutional racism through the Committee for One Society were supported along with those developed by the "Black cats" of CAT and the Black Strategy Center, and down to its final training session, UTC tried to keep the whole metropolitan area in its program. However, this was always done with a recognition that the major needs and hurts were in the inner-city and among minorities who felt the pressure of societal injustice. And most participants went away with a heightened sense of the ways in which that injustice tainted the life of modern cities.

(3)*Through its Board and relationships with sponsoring denominations, UTC had a major influence on national urban mission strategy.* All major national religious bodies (except those that were Jewish) were represented on the UTC Board. After the dissolution of the Department of Urban Church of the National Council of Churches, its regular meetings provided the major opportunity for national urban mission staff to gather to share shop-talk, gain a sense of trends and developments, and set direction for the future. After 1966 this fellowship (a literal word, for the group was all-male until Roman Catholic sisters entered the sanctum) included Roman Catholic urban activists and representatives of the major Black denominations. As the fortunes of UTC worsened and its efforts for survival became more desperate, the denominational staff took this to mean that urban training—and metropolitan mission itself—was on the decline; and the closing of UTC occurred during the period when JSAC was no longer able to sustain its Metropolitan Task Force (although it had a thriving Non-Metropolitan one).

(4)*Through Ford Fellows, UTC affected the major Black denominations.* C.T. Vivian used the relationships that had developed in the Civil Rights Movement to recruit Ford Fellows from all over the United States, particularly from the Southeast. Many Black pastors took back from Chicago practical plans to increase their congregations' community ministry. A whole class of younger bishops in the African Methodist Episcopal Church devised their election strategies as part of their "back-home" exercise at UTC. This emphasis on strategy and taking account of the empirical facts of social situations provided a helpful supplement to the wisdom learned from centuries of oppression and the rhetorical zeal of Black Church tradition.

(5) *In the mainline White denominations UTC had the effect of strengthening the emphasis on specialized and secular ministries.* Although UTC staff continually pointed to their inclusion of church strategies in training, several factors contributed to tipping the balance away from that direction. UTC's commitment to experimentation meant that it was trying to go beyond what presently existed in local parishes and congregations, as well as to attempt their renewal. Both seminaries and denominational mission boards gave greater attention to specialized ministries in this period. And many of the White participants who were sent to UTC, particularly for the longer-term assignments, were either recent seminary graduates who did not wish to be placed in the conventional church setting or were seeking to clarify their vocation, or veteran urban missioners who had "burnt out" or who were also seeking different ways than those already tried.

(6) *UTC developed a wide variety of useful relationships and interaction with metropolitan Chicago, especially with community organizations.* Although accused at times of "living off" Chicago or using its churches and street workers as "guinea pigs," from the start UTC made a consistent attempt to relate to leaders and organizations in the Black ghetto, and to metropolitan mission organizations like Community Renewal Society (Chicago City Missionary Society) and the Church Federation of Greater Chicago. The story of civil rights activity and Black community organizations in Chicago could not be told without giving credit to the role played by Hargraves, Vivian, A.I. Dunlap and other UTC staff, alumni and co-workers. West Side Organization received both community organizing

know-how and financial undergirding from its relationship with UTC. And UTC staff, participants and supporters were the backbone of ecumenical mission activity in Chicago throughout the period of its greatest activity during the 1960's.

(7) *UTC helped reshape theological seminary goals and curriculum.* Although purposely constructed as an alternate institution (or even an "anti-seminary"), UTC quickly developed programs in cooperation with Chicago-based and other theological seminaries. Many faculty and administrators came as participants or observers, and elements of the UTC curriculum found their way into courses on Christian social ethics, urban ministry and pastoral theology. Even though the UMPS Program, developed by a consortium of evangelical seminaries, for reasons of theological purity maintained a separate administrative structure from UTC, many of its training components and its overall perspective on metropolitan life were adopted from UTC.

(8) *UTC maintained throughout its career a steady commitment to experimentation and the "R and D" (research and development) approach.* Benedict's original vision—and that of the Continuing Committee, which developed the proposal—was for a center that would take what was being learned in urban mission and ministry and make it accessible to others, but that would also be free to experiment and develop new ministries from scratch. Although tempted at times to develop a "UTC ideology," the Center's staff and Board kept pushing into new arenas, while continuing to develop refinements of models and approaches that had already been found useful. This was particularly true of its commitment to community organizing as a useful tool for urban mission, and potentially for the reformation of urban polity.

(9) *UTC maintained a consistent concern for theology and liturgy.* In contrast to the statements of detractors of action training, UTC never lost touch with its theological base. Richard Luecke was continued on the staff as Director of Studies. "Theologizing" was one of the constant components in the curriculum, even in one-month orientations and short-term training. Ecumenical worship was a consistent feature of every training day and program, and a wide variety of liturgical experimentation was done.

(10) *UTC developed a pattern and style for issue analysis and strategizing.* Although the discussion of terms like "situation" and "issue" could sometimes take off into the abstract or seem like a word-game, UTC's Curriculum Committee and staff developed an eclectic form of social analysis that was very useful in locating social problems that could be changed, analyzing the structures that caused them or were available for assisting change, and evaluating the strategies for change that were being considered. Much of the skill in using this method was in the experience and judgment of the staff members who worked with participants in small groups, but the

printed instructions and background papers give sufficient guidance to be used by others without that type of consultation. Other centers developed other styles, in many cases modifications of that developed by UTC or the Cleveland Intern Program.

(11) *UTC through the period of the Ford Foundation grant had a solid program of research and evaluation.* Niles Carpenter and Paul Kraemer were specifically hired with a job description emphasizing research and evaluation. Both as participant-observers and as evaluation researchers, they developed means for the program to have evaluation in depth. UTC resources were also shared with other training centers through the Research on Training for Metropolitan Ministry project.

(12) *UTC made wide use of academic and other resources to learn about urban life and the role of the church.* At all times in its life, UTC was ready to listen to and secure information from the academic community, innovators in government and business, and a wide variety of resources. Many of these people were brought to training sessions as resource persons, and their seminal writings were shared with participants. Every time that a new issue was being explored for inclusion in an Issue Seminar, staff would make a wide-ranging survey of written, institutional and human resources, out of which they would choose the most challenging or basic to share with participants. This constant search for what was meaningful could at times be overly fascinated with novelty, but it made available in one place what could otherwise have taken years of time and great amounts of money to assemble.

(13) *UTC collected and published a wide-ranging variety of documents.* In addition to a good basic library on theology and urban life, UTC files included all strategy documents prepared by participants, case studies on a wide variety of local churches and specialized ministries in Chicago and elsewhere, and documents on the following areas: addiction, community, cybernetics, education, Freedom Movement, health, housing, industry, model ministries, penal institutions, research, sexual deviation, urban church, urban studies, unemployment, worship, youth and "Other." Mimeographed documents were sold in the following categories—organization/urban theory/worship, training center proposals/curricula, church institutional renewal, community organization and development, racism/Freedom Movement, health, reference materials, faculty documents, curriculum materials. This added up to the staggering total of 549 documents, many of them 20-30 pages long, that were freely available for sale, as well as another 42 that were in the reference category for use in training.

Internship for Clergymen in Urban Ministry, Cleveland, Ohio: Initiative for the Cleveland Intern Program (CIP) came not from the churches but from an educational institution—Cleveland College of Western Reserve University; the major funding did not come from religious organizations but from the federal government through the National Institute of Mental Health (NIMH); and participants did not pay fees or need supporting funds from their religious body, but were paid a stipend of $3,000 a year (later raised to $3,600) to study full-time for 32 weeks.[9] The Internship for Clergymen in Urban Ministry was a "pilot program," but the uniqueness of its circumstances meant that it would not be replicated even though it would make important contributions to the development of action training in the churches.

Dean Allen F. Pfleger of Cleveland College thought of the idea of using an urban university as a base for a program to train clergy on an inter-faith basis to develop mental health understandings and skills that would improve their ministry to their congregations, and through their congregations to the community at large. He worked for two years with an advisory committee to prepare a proposal for NIMH that requested $417,000 for a five-year pilot project. When the grant was made in 1965 for a planning year and four training groups of 15 each in the school years of 1966-67 through 1969-70, the college recruited as director of the program Robert H. Bonthius, a White United Presbyterian clergyman who had been a college chaplain and professor of religion at the College of Wooster and Vassar College, and who was serving then as pastor of Westminster Presbyterian Church, Portland, Oregon.

NIMH made a grant to Western Reserve University to design, administer and test a "model curriculum" (or series of models) that could be used in whole or in part by universities in other metropolitan centers for "the postgraduate training of the clergy in urban ministry." The fundamental assumption of the program was that "mental health is grounded in interpersonal relationships which are affected on every side by continuing changes in urban community." Clergy were chosen as the training group because they have "the double opportunity of working with persons who suffer from the stresses of city life and of helping to change the society which causes these difficulties." Although the clergy participants were important to the Internship program, the focus for the University and for the staff was on the curriculum being developed and used.

Bonthius arrived in Cleveland in March 1966 and had six months to tool up for the first training period. He recruited a core staff—Frederick C. Brechler, associate director, who was a White educator with a background in urban community studies, and Martha A. Sterrett, a White religious educator with urban church experience. He was able to draw upon a wide variety of consultants from the University: the staff of the Division of

General Studies, in which the program was lodged, and faculty members from the Departments of Economics, Education, Political Science, Psychiatry, Psychology, School of Applied Social Sciences, Sociology and Anthropology. He also formed an Interfaith Committee of Clergymen of Metropolitan Cleveland to assist in developing goals and recruitment. In addition, contact was made with a wide variety of community specialists throughout the Cleveland area.

Under the rubric of "re-tooling" clergy for more effective ministry to individuals and groups in the urban community, CIP began with the following specific objectives developed during the planning period:

> 1.To expose clergymen in depth to problems of the metropolis and to explore the bearing of these problems upon the mental and physical health of persons.
>
> 2. To provide the clergyman with a discipline of research (that is, responsible study and analysis of problems) so that this discipline can become a part of his professional equipment in the practice of his profession.
>
> 3. To teach clergymen how to find and use the resources of the metropolis to meet human needs and change urban society for the better.
>
> 4. To equip the clergy with new knowledge and new skills for their unique roles as urban leaders of congregations and community.
>
> 5. To help the clergy explore their professional roles and the roles of their religious institutions.
>
> 6.To enable clergymen to combat urgent city problems and to effect desirable social changes.
>
> 7. To enable the clergyman by this training to impart new knowledge and new skills to other clergy of his own and other denominations.

Ten clergy were to be recruited for the first training year in 1966-67 and 15 in each of the succeeding three years.

The original program design called for participants to spend half their time in field involvement and half in study and reflection. The two opening weeks were given to orientation, three weeks in mid-year to independent study and the final two weeks to sharing their independent study monographs on models of ministry with the rest of the group. Each week's study and reflection included three seminars and two hours of sensitivity experience in a "personal learning group." Two of the seminars of two hours each lasted throughout the year—"the Metropolitan Community," to provide an overall theoretical framework for understanding the metropolitan community and means of effecting change, and "Religious Implications of Urban Problems," to give an opportunity "to review and discuss the bearing of the human problems encountered in metropolis upon their own organizational understanding of human nature and destiny, and the implications of these problems for religious institutions and clergy if they are to deal effectively with the urbanization of man." Major attention was given in a four-hour seminar for each five-week period to the problems of youth, poverty, intergroup relations, health and aging, using experts, change agents and victims from both the faculty and the metropolitan community.

Field placements (called in succeeding years "anchor engagements") were made in different community settings, areas of the city, agencies and institutions. These were chosen by CIP staff, in consultation with the intern and a field supervisor related to a community agency or institution. Each participant selected some organization working with a "crucial problem for Cleveland" during the 32 weeks of the program, so that they could join that group and learn by doing. Involvements in the pilot training year included residential housing renewal in a Black ghetto area, counseling emotionally disturbed teen-agers, working with a White ethnic group, training community residents for participation in community organizations, developing a plan for residential desegregation to be used by a metropolitan housing committee, and sharing in a coalition of professional organizations and poverty groups.

Eight White Protestant and two White Roman Catholic clergy took part in the pilot program in 1966-67. Succeeding years' programs were open to 15 clergy per year. CIP always had a majority of White clergy enrolled with a limited number of Black Protestant clergy and even fewer Jewish rabbis, and all interns were male. A total of 56 clergy participants, 15 of them Black, took part in the four years of CIP program, but the final sequence was shortened to 16 weeks.

In addition to the training staff and the field supervisor, each participant was expected to have a pastor supervisor designated by his denomination to assist him in relating the experience of the program to his organizational orientation and ecclesiastical responsibilities. Thus, both the academic model of intensive seminars and the social work/mental health model of field experience under close supervision were used in developing the training curriculum. Although this particular model, which was the purpose of the NIMH grant, was not influential on other action-training programs and has not been adopted by other educational institutions or continued past the grant period by Case-Western Reserve University, two other initiatives by CIP have had more lasting effect—its role in creating the Action Training Network of Ohio and its contribution to getting research started on action training through the Research on Training for Metropolitan Ministry project (RTMM).

The Internship program was scheduled to close in 1970. Therefore, from 1967 on Bonthius was engaged in suggesting ways to continue action training in the Greater Cleveland area under another umbrella than Case-Western Reserve University. In September 1968, William Voelkel, a White United Church of Christ clergyman who had been a member of the group ministry in the Inner City Protestant Parish and then headed the training program of the Commission on Ecumenical Education of the Council of

Churches of Greater Cleveland from 1965 through 1968, joined the staff of CIP. He and Bonthius organized and incorporated Community Action Training Services (CATS), which was to train religious and secular groups in Northern Ohio. While engaged in running the CIP program, they also were able to serve as consultants, designers, trainers and/or evaluators with a wide variety of national, Ohio and metropolitan Cleveland denominational bodies, colleges and seminaries.

CATS was incorporated in June 1970, and Bonthius, Voelkel and Sterrett were able to continue training by moving their offices to a local church and beginning to operate with contracts from religious and secular groups. In addition, Bonthius and Voelkel were involved in the organization in 1969 of Black Action Training, a program sponsored by the United Pastors Association and developed by six Black CIP graduates. Operating with a foundation grant, BAT looked forward to starting training in the fall of 1970 when three seminars were scheduled in nursing technique, Black family development and youth leadership. However, the program closed the following spring when its Board asked for the resignation of the director, Irv Joyner, a local Black clergyman.

More successful was the effort to form an Action Training Network in Ohio that would bring together the training interests of the Cleveland group with those of Columbus Action Training Associates (CATA) in the state capital and Center for Human Action, Research and Training (CHART) in Cincinnati. The three groups began talking about cooperation in 1968. A proposal was drafted for an Action Training Network in the Ohio region, which was defined as being principally the state of Ohio but having the ability to stretch east to Buffalo and Pittsburgh and west to Detroit. With the help of a grant from the Commission on Continuing Education of the National Council of Churches, George D. Younger, a staff member of MUST in New York City, developed a report on the feasibility of an Ohio Action Training Network that recommended staying within the state boundaries and suggested that a wide variety of training possibilities was open to such a group.

The three groups incorporated ATN in September 1969, and it served for three years as an umbrella under which a wide variety of training was done, especially in Toledo, Cleveland and Columbus. Finally, at the end of 1971, it was agreed to merge ATN and CATS, using the tax exemption of CATS but the corporate name of ATN, an action finally completed on June 19, 1972.

The Research on Training for Metropolitan Ministry (RTMM) had its origins in a small study of UTC participants published by Jeffrey K. Hadden and Raymond C. Rymph, which suggested that there were structural constraints in the congregation that inhibited clergy involvement in social change ministries. Hadden and Edgar W. Mills, director of the Ministry Studies Board in Washington, D.C., initiated discussions with the three pioneer training programs, UTC, which had just completed its second program year and was beginning the Ford Fellows program; MUST in New York City, which was ready to begin its first program year; and CIP, which was also ready to start operations. Shared research seemed to be most possible in the area of curriculum evaluation, since each program was using a model with some similarities and some differences, and impact evaluation, because all three were principally training clergy. In a meeting in December 1966, Paul E. Kraemer, director of research at UTC; George D. Younger, who was conducting evaluation at MUST; and Bonthius for CIP agreed to share in planning an impact study that would try to measure changes in attitudes, ministerial activities and skills. The key to making such a project possible was CIP, because both UTC and MUST had funds from their sponsors for evaluation research. However, Dean Pfleger had to find additional funds from NIMH and his own administration to make CIP participation possible.

With Mills serving as both project administrator and research consultant, the RTMM project retained J. Alan Winter, a White social scientist on the faculty of Temple University, as principal researcher and used the facilities of the Ministry Studies Board to process data. Under Winter's direction, a sophisticated attitude measure was developed, based upon the earlier Hadden-Rymph instrument, and methods devised to measure clergy activities and skills. Studies were made of participants in the longer-term (and a few short-term) programs of the three centers during the 1967-68 program year, compared with a "comparison group" of similar persons nominated by the participants. Nine different impact reports were prepared by Winter and Mills, and the entire project report was published by the Ministry Studies Board through IDOC in 1971 as a paperback book, *Clergy in Action Training*.

General findings of the study were that participants in the three centers' programs during 1967-68 were largely well-educated (college and seminary), young (under 40 years old), White, Protestant, with an urban or suburban childhood, and at the time of the training serving a White congregation with a majority of white-collar, professional or managerial members. The assumption that time spent on social problems in the metropolitan area takes away from time spent as pastor, priest or preacher was disproved, while another pattern appeared showing that time spent in administrative work for the congregation has a negative effect on time working on community issues. The impact study found that a large number of the participants were "pre-program successes," who at the start of the training were already at the point that the training was intended to reach. Also, the training programs produced changes in social attitudes without making any significantly different changes in theological views, as compared with the comparison group. Because all three programs made drastic changes in their curriculum or form of training even before all the results of the study were available to them, RTMM did not have a great effect on the programs of the agencies that sponsored it. However, it did provide an important model of cooperation among action-training agencies that assisted in formation of the ATC, and it gave some data on activist clergy that differed from the highly publicized findings of Hadden, published in *The Growing Storm in the Churches*.

The following accomplishments and contributions to action training resulted from the activity of the Cleveland Intern Program:

(1)*The Internship for Clergymen in Urban Ministry was a gift to the churches from Cleveland College of Western Reserve University and the federal government, through NIMH.* At a time when funds for action-training had to be gathered piece-by-piece from denominations and grant-by-grant from foundations, the Cleveland program provided another agency located in a metropolitan area that had a more local model, sponsored by the Council of Churches of Greater Cleveland, but was unable to sustain it in existence.

(2) *CIP made greater use of academic resources than most other programs.* Because it was administratively related to the University, CIP was able to draw upon all its departments for resources both in planning and in training. Interestingly enough, the results in curriculum and style of training did not prove to be drastically different, especially after the first year.

(3) *Through its career CIP developed close relationships with both religious and community organizations in the Cleveland area.* Although the Interfaith Committee of Clergymen was an advisory group, and most field supervisors and other consultants were contacted individually, CIP developed a wide-ranging network of relationships from the inner-city ghettos to the suburban areas, which included both White institutions and the minority community.

(4) *According to its staff, CIP showed the inadequacy of a professional model of urban training for the church.* The major assumption of CIP was that training for clergy would not only change the way in which they worked with their congregations, but would also produce greater church and synagogue commitment to social change by what they were able to do through their congregations. Bonthius has said that the four years of experience showed that clergy were not the people needing to be trained; they should be trained along with lay persons. Also they learned that training should not occur outside the context of the parish or congregation; people should be trained on-site. Although the anchor engagements gave important exposure to CIP participants, they were not the same as the regular situation in which each clergyman was operating. As a result, CATS and

ATN training worked with clergy along with others within the religious institutions in which they normally functioned.

(5) *CIP staff developed a method of action-training that was widely used by other action-training agencies.* Although UTC had a more sophisticated process for developing urban strategy and MUST developed several components of training that were used by other agencies, nothing had as widespread use both among and beyond action-training agencies as the Action Development Form, based on the schema developed to evaluate interns' models of ministry. It was used by CATS staff with National Welfare Rights Organization members, Bread for the World activists working against world hunger and several other national church-related groups, as well as in other training in the Ohio area.

(6) *Although having a much smaller staff than the other two pioneers, CIP produced a large amount of publication of high quality.* This was principally due to the disciplined writing activity of Bonthius, but it has made available a great deal more of the action-training experience in writing than would otherwise have been possible.

(7) *CIP was used as a base for the development of other agencies for action training and for collaboration among action training programs.* Although CIP and its staff shared in the entrepreneurial zeal and competitiveness that characterized almost all action-training agencies, they were willing to give substantial amounts of time and attention to forms of collaboration, both in the development of national projects like RTMM and the Action Training Coalition itself, and in the emergence of the Action Training Network of Ohio as its own successor. When the Federal grant from NIMH and the support of Case-Western Reserve University were finished, the staff had prepared a successor action-training agency that was able to keep the experience going, and to share with others in Ohio and across the country in action training.

Metropolitan Urban Service Training, New York, New York. The record of the institutional life of Metropolitan Urban Service Training, like that of UTC, is the story of a national project that failed to secure sufficient local support in the metropolitan area in which it was placed to guarantee survival.[10] It is also the story of a large amount of funds being spent by a large staff in a short time on a bewildering variety of programs and objectives. However, the period from 1968 on, in which MUST focused on the priority of racial justice, produced a high quality of training and pioneered many techniques of action training. The results of this training are now most obviously built into the philosophy and curriculum of New York Theological Seminary, but they are also still at work in the action and training being done by many

MUST trainees and former staff members. Metropolitan New York may well have been too large for any single agency to have made a significant dent in either its religious life or the wider community. It is certain, however, that through MUST New York City had a significant effect on action training in the churches.

J. Edward Carothers, executive secretary of the National Division of the Board of Missions of the Methodist Church, first conceived the idea of a training project in urban mission in 1964. He had a vision of a Methodist-related center that would use the resources of a single metropolitan area to provide training for a wide variety of clergy and laity. The purpose of this pilot program was stated as follows:

> This project is directed to the training of clergy and laity for improved skills in Christian mission in the various types of urban setting. New skills are required because the urban setting is new and imposes new obligations upon those who would engage in ministry.[11]

In 1965 the National Division pledged not less than $500,000 (most of which had become available from endowed funds because the stock market had gone up) for a pilot "Project for the Training of Clergy and Laity in the Urban Mission of the Church of Jesus Christ Our Lord" to insure a period of two years "during which it may be proved whether it is a desirable project or not." At the time of MUST's organization, the Methodist Church was not a member of the national UTC in Chicago, although the Evangelical United Brethren Church, which later merged with Methodists to form the United Methodist Church, had been a founding member. Carothers helped establish MUST as a clear alternative to UTC.

At the same time as this pilot training project was being organized and placed in New York City, the Board of Missions of the Methodist Church was engaged with other national boards of the Methodist Church, including the Board of Christian Education, in setting up a team to work with local Black churches, known as the Interboard Commission on the Local Church. The training project at MUST was scheduled to come first and provide experience, as well as trained leadership, for the interboard effort. This led the New York training agency to be known in Methodist circles as "MUST-I," while the all-Methodist board program was labelled "MUST-II."

Originally called "*Methodist* Urban Service Training," MUST came into being as "*Metropolitan* Urban Service Training," an ecumenical agency based in metropolitan New York. Local Methodist denominational and mission executives in New York City had been meeting regularly with their counterparts in other denominations and ecumenical agencies as part of "Joint Action in Mission" (JAM). When the national Board of Missions project proposal was introduced by its local Methodist board members to their colleagues in JAM (as provided in the terms of the JAM covenant), representatives of the other groups asked these questions: Could the agency be ecumenical? Could the main emphasis be placed on training clergy and laity in New York City? Negotiations with JAM resulted in a counter-proposal, drawn up by a group of White urban pastors, including Howard Moody of Judson Memorial Church, George W. Webber of East Harlem Protestant Parish, and George D. Younger of Mariners' Temple Baptist Church. The following modifications were made in the original design and were used by Webber with both the MUST board and JAM as the conditions under which he would accept the call to be MUST's director: (1) the Board would include representatives of other denominations, and the agency would train their clergy and laity, as well as Methodists; (2) the basic focus would be upon the mission of the church in a single metropolitan area, the New York region; and (3) program components would include: the congregation in mission, new forms of missionary presence and service, and student training and involvement (only the last involving trainees from outside metropolitan New York).

Staff planning for MUST began in October 1965, when Webber started as executive director. He was joined by Ellen Lurie, a Jewish community organizer who had been active in East Harlem and with city-wide parents' organizations, and Randolph Nugent, a Black Methodist clergyman who had directed city mission work in Albany, New York, along with a staff trainee, Hooker Davis, another Black Methodist clergyman on leave from the New Jersey Conference. During the 1965-66 planning year, the staff took courses at New York area educational institutions, talked with key leaders in church and community (including 101 participants in 10 three-hour dialogue sessions), and visited other training centers and experimental programs. Younger convened a Theological Task Force, whose membership reads like a *Who's Who* of exponents of mission theology in the Northeast, including Harvey Cox of Harvard Divinity School, Hans Hoekendijk and Paul Lehmann of Union Theological Seminary, Richard Shaull of Princeton Theological Seminary, and Thomas Wieser and Colin Williams of the National Council of Churches, along with Black and White pastors from metropolitan New York and two Bible scholars from Drew Theological Seminary, Howard Kee and Lawrence Toombs. This group's theological conversations fed into the staff's program proposal, as well as being used to reflect on that proposal.

After listening to the needs of the city, the staff was ready by March 1966 to present its outline for the first year's program to the Board of Directors. This called for three elements of training—skill training, on-the-job training and encouragement of new forms of ministry. Training was to be built around a focus of "the agenda of metropolis," and three alternative problems—public education, housing and welfare— were proposed as the major program emphases. In addition, the proposal included as "supportive program elements" (also to be paid out of the budget provided by the Methodist Board of Missions) a variety of student programs (Metropolitan

Intern Project, Judson Urban Vocation Project, Student Interracial Ministry's Northern Urban Project), continuation of the Theological Task Force, public relations and interpretation, and Radio Free New York, a Sunday night program to feature urban community issues.

MUST's first training year in 1966-67 was dominated by two year-long programs; the Action-Training Institute (ATI), which enrolled 56 clergy, laity and the MUST office staff for weekly evening sessions around the combined problem, "The Relationship between Education and Real Economic Opportunity;" and the Augmented Clergy Program (ACP), which enrolled 18 clergy in a full day of seminars preceding ATI evening sessions. The foolhardiness of attempting a full-year program in an agency that had not yet conducted any training became obvious after the first five weeks, when the entire curriculum of the evening ATI was reorganized, the staff person who had prepared it was released, and the rest of the year was devoted to three parallel inquiries on economic opportunity, education and the church in mission.

A second major thrust in the initial year was to be training institutes in local communities. After exploration and negotiation, the possibilities were narrowed down to a group of suburban churches in Greenwich, Conn. Difficulties in getting the suburban group to agree on a significant issue on which to focus in their community left the MUST staff with only the Brooklyn Mission Ministers Community Training Program, composed principally of clergy and church workers in Black Baptist and Pentecostal churches with a median size of 50-100 members. Over 22 sessions with this group studied community issues, African and Afro-American history led by John Henrik Clarke, and leadership skills. One result of the program was negotiation of a building loan fund for this group of Black churches from the Methodist Board of Missions.

All the participants in the student programs were White and in the age range between 21 and 27. Forty-five seminary and pre-seminary students were enrolled in four different geographical units on the Metropolitan Intern Program and the Student Interracial Ministry Project. An additional 10 college graduates took part in the Judson Urban Program, designed for young professionals beginning their careers in the city. The role of seminary enrollment in permitting young men to participate in this kind of experience during the Vietnam War was made dramatically clear as the Judson project lost five of its original male participants to the draft in the first six weeks, while the seminary-related programs lost none. Most trainees in the seminary intern program stated that its major value had been personal growth and help in their search for identity (which was very close to Webber's unstated goal of breaking out of the cocoons of family, school and church) rather than in developing skills for urban ministry.

In addition to this ambitious set of programs carried out with a training staff of six, MUST also conducted several short-term programs for national and metropolitan church groups and sponsored a nine-month course in computer programming, and consulted with a wide variety of church and community programs. MUST staff and office resources were shared with two city-wide organizing efforts—the City-Wide Coordinating Committee on Welfare, which brought together welfare rights groups, and the People's Board of Education, which was working for community control of schools. MUST also produced a weekly mailing that shared printed materials and important meetings around the city with trainees and an action mailing list; printed several papers by Preston Wilcox, a consultant with ghetto-based community groups throughout the city, and the full curriculum on African and Afro-American history prepared by John Henrik Clarke; and introduced Paulo Freire and Mrs. Anna Spaulding, author of *The Writing Road to Reading*, to interested groups in the city.

After the feverish activity of the first year, MUST staff planned that 1967-68 would focus on two models of training—Training for Community Mission, developed out of the experience of ATI and the Brooklyn mission ministers program; and a more limited set of academic programs—three units of the Metropolitan Intern Program with 36 students, continuation of the Augmented Clergy Program for six persons as an S.T.M. Program in Urban Ministries at New York Theological Seminary, which rented space to MUST for its offices; and a Joint Seminary Program, developed in cooperation with the faculties of Maryknoll, New York and Union Theological Seminaries as a semester of urban exposure for 90 seminarians to issues of urban education, racial justice and poverty.

During the fall a group of clergy and lay leaders from Protestant and Roman Catholic churches took part in the East Bronx Training for Community Mission (TCM) which met for 13 weekly evening sessions. The group was predominantly White and resisted trainers' attempts to point out the metropolitan dimensions of the issues of education, housing and intergroup relations, which were the stated content of the sessions, preferring to focus on more local issues and their own congregational survival. The TCM model was not tried in any other community, but three other programs called "Clergy Training for Community Mission" were held with United Methodist Clergy in Brooklyn, Nassau-Queens and Bridgeport, Connecticut, giving MUST visibility with clergy of the sponsoring denomination in its New York Annual Conference.

Another project attempted during this second year was the Congregational Renewal Project, an action-research project to test the feasibility of organizing "clusters" of churches, under the direction of Theodore Erickson, a White United Church of Christ clergyman who received grants from that denomination and foundations to support the program. Erickson also tried to develop local units of organization and training, but was only able to get cooperation in two Queens communities—Richmond Hill, an older White residential area, and South Ozone Park, a relatively recent

Black residential area. Other programs during this period were a two-day New Clergy Orientation Program for ministers new to the city, a Spanish Clergy Program in cooperation with the Fraternidad de Ministros, and a Lay School of Mission Theology enrolling a very limited number of lay persons in weekly evening sessions. MUST also produced Action-Training Clearinghouse, a more unified information mailing that had been planned by trainees in the 1966-67 Action Training Institute.

As the result of a combination of circumstances culminating with the assassination of Martin Luther King, Jr. on April 14, 1968, MUST changed both its approach and its executive director before the end of the second program year. Both Training for Community Mission, the main program model, and the Congregational Renewal Project were not finding many takers among metropolitan area churches. Staff relations were complicated by two sets of tensions—between Black and White staff members, and between those with greater experience and younger people with less. In an attempt to resolve both conflicts, Webber arranged for Carl A. Fields, a Black educator at Princeton University, to hold bi-weekly staff sessions to promote staff trust and improve training techniques. In addition, a "troika" of Webber, Nugent and Rae Hendrix, a Black community organizer who had replaced Lurie in 1966, met regularly to handle administrative questions and prepare agenda for staff meetings.

During the summer of 1967 Rae Hendrix attended the Black Power conference in Newark, and she and Nugent were at the organizing meeting of the National Committee of Black Churchmen in Dallas. While preparing for the Dallas meeting, Nugent brought to the staff on October 20 the following proposal which, although a program proposal, was also a challenge to the way in which Webber had been administering the agency:

1. Select the movement toward racial justice as the primary agenda item against which all others are held.. . . We should seek and even welcome direction in staff from all of our black staff members.
2. Re-evaluate all programs for their impact on the development of racial justice. The basis of such evaluation to be the use and leadership of the black community and the leverage which this can make in the white community.
3. It is clear that the present programs need not be cut back if the proper supporting resources are available. . . .
4. Give the delegate from our staff a free hand to support, as the situation calls for support (i.e., this newly developing National Convocation of Negro Clergy). Unless the delegate is able to operate (even in the name of MUST) without clearing every detail beforehand, or having to check for permission afterwards as the time or situation is presented, he will be seen as a puppet without power, and a tool of the white institution.
5. Check the use of consultants and informants, as many are seen as *real* enemies of progress toward racial justice by the black community. Develop a policy for the selection of consultants.
6. Commit MUST to those meetings where decisions relative to race are being undertaken.[12]

In further discussions of this proposal, the staff moved toward setting a priority on racial justice for the next program year.

But events overtook this orderly process. Realizing that his major interest was the academic program with seminarians, Webber suggested at an all-day staff discussion on February 5, 1968, that Nugent assume the post of director. He submitted his letter of resignation to the Executive Committee on March 11 and recommended Nugent as his successor, while declaring himself available for continued service in a training task. Nugent, after being elected, led the staff in preparing a training proposal that would be presented to the Board on April 9 for its opinions in both the areas of policy and organizational structure. This proposal was to focus on racial justice, and the staff was prepared to develop the 1968-69 program on the basis of the Board discussion.

King's assassination encouraged the staff to abandon this plan and substitute a "crash" program for the rest of 1967-68 based on their own estimate of the gravity of the racial situation. Working all day on Saturday, April 6, they produced a new program design, alerted Board members to the importance of attending Tuesday's meeting (which was also the day scheduled for King's funeral), developed a series of "action" suggestions for Communique, MUST's recorded phone messages for church and community groups, and made up a new Board agenda.

In cooperation with Communications Network, a group of Black church-related activists in several metropolitan areas around the country organized by Isaac Igarashi, a field staff member of the National Council of Churches, MUST was already planning to conduct on May 1 in New York City a Strategy and Training Workshop for Civil Disorders. This event became the core of a program of "continuing crisis training" to proceed in five stages: (1) identification of interdenominational, interracial "clusters" of churches and community groups in metropolitan New York, (2) emergency training in those clusters in May and June, (3) cluster action involvement through the summer, (4) congregational education through trained leaders in the fall of 1968, and (5) cluster action task forces working on issues of racial justice from 1969 on.

The MUST Board accepted the plan, and all programs planned or negotiated for 1968-69 were tested by the principal emphasis of racial justice. As a result, the Congregational Renewal Project was released in June 1968 at the end of the first of what were to have been three years, and student programs under Webber were evaluated more rigorously in terms of their focus on racial justice. Although not acknowledged at the time, the Emergency Training Program, conducted in collaboration with the Interfaith Citywide Coordinating Committee Against Poverty, marked the end of the period in which most MUST training was designed and developed by staff, who then went out and tried to recruit a constituency, and the beginning of the period in which training was negotiated with potential training groups. MUST still conducted a few staff-designed programs—Training for Social Action, Institute on Power, Workshop on Researching Power and Training of Trainers. However, most programs from 1968-69 on were developed in a process of planning and negotiation with the groups that wanted training. Almost all these programs were measured against MUST's overall objective of racial justice.

Two other changes in MUST's operations also occurred at this time. The staff prepared for the Emergency Training Program a detailed curriculum on racism that, together with Nugent's material on planning, became the basis for further training curriculum. Also, several experienced people with personal commitment to Christian mission replaced the younger White seminary graduates: Robert L. Washington, a Black community organizer who had been an ATI trainee and was chairman of Harlem Parents Committee; Dr. Anna Fried, a psychologist and social worker who had been on the staff of the New York City Mission Society; and Younger, who had been doing evaluation of MUST programs while a member of the national evangelism staff of American Baptists. By the end of the 1968-69 program year Webber left to become president of New York Theological Seminary, continuing its close relationship with MUST.

The next two program years saw a wide variety of training programs. In 1968-69 MUST conducted 29 different programs, in addition to four academic programs with seminarians. This increased to 34 training contracts in 1969-70, along with two courses for New York Theological Seminary and three other academic programs. For the first time most of the New York denominational executives on MUST's Board had an experience with MUST training in a series conducted for members of JAM. The United Methodist Church used MUST for its basic training program with organizers in the newly-formed Black Community Developers Program, as well as for follow-up training and evaluation. Adult courses on racism were conducted in the suburban school systems of Ridgewood and South Orange-Maplewood, New Jersey. A contract with Equitable Life Insurance Co. to train job trainers and supervisors and to conduct a pilot orientation Workshop for Hard-Core Unemployed represented an attempt to extend MUST training to business and industry.

Probably the most innovative MUST training program, which built on the earlier experience in racism training and the program for Black Community Developers, was the Institute on Power, held over the weekend of December 12-14, 1969. The full staff used this as an opportunity to pull together insights that had developed out of years of experience in church and community, and to attempt use of both audio-visuals and the simulation, Community Land Use Game (CLUG). Following this program, most MUST training included a sequence on power analysis, as well as the previously developed curriculum on racism, planning and community organization.

On May 4, 1969, James Forman presented the demands of the Black Manifesto in the chancel of the Riverside Church, beginning a period of logistical support from the MUST office both for the Black Economic Development Conference (BEDC), which could not use the IFCO offices at the Interchurch Center, and for Black caucuses and White supporters in national denominations who wished to press for "reparations" from the churches. On June 30 MUST staff conducted a training session with Board members in an attempt to surface their reactions to the Manifesto and to develop alternatives for MUST's own action based on the discovery that White-controlled denominations were reluctant to grant real authority and control of resources to minority leadership. Formally, the Board took action on a motion supporting the demands of the Black Manifesto, promising to approach their own denominations for a positive response and authorizing the staff to develop training around the Manifesto. Informally, however, MUST's staff's outspoken support for Forman and BEDC probably laid the groundwork for withdrawal of support by some national denominations, particularly the United Methodists, who had originally founded MUST and were providing the major share of its budget.

Although the quality and depth of MUST training had never been better, the Board of Directors meeting on April 9, 1970, was the occasion for two announcements that produced shocks from which the training agency was never to recover. (1) Carothers, who had written the original MUST proposal and gathered the funds to support the program for four-and-a-half years, announced that "he was recommending that the National Division, Board of Missions, United Methodist Church, terminate funding of MUST, because, while MUST was moving in the way that the directors wanted, it was no longer moving in line with the goals and priorities of the National Division." MUST would receive only $50,000 for the first half of its fiscal year through December 31, 1970, and then would have to prove itself to the Home Fields Department of the National Division for any further funding. Since United Methodists had provided the lion's share of MUST's budget until this time, this action was a crippling blow for an organization operating on an annual budget of $213,800. (2) Nugent, who had been director for two years, announced that he was leaving to become associate general secretary of the National Council of Churches in charge of the Division of Overseas Ministries. He recommended that Younger be named interim director, which was voted by the board.

The 1970-71 program year was filled with efforts to raise additional funds, as budgets were adopted for three-month periods after December 31, 1970. During the years under Nugent's directorship, MUST had built a fine interracial staff team that could work well with religious or secular groups and was able to train both in all-White and all-minority situations, as well as with interracial constituencies. Much of the training in 1970-72 was done in the New York metropolitan area with local churches, religious programs and community groups. Outside the metropolitan area, programs were conducted in Schenectady and Utica, New York, and in Maine, as well as with national organizations. A contract with the Food and Nutrition Service of the Department of Agriculture resulted in civil rights training for all staff in the Northeast. Staff developed grants for a program of Community Organization Training for Minority Youth with New York City high school leaders in Charleston and the Sea Islands, South Carolina. In addition, MUST's experience was used to develop and conduct curriculum for the S.T.M. in Parish Ministry at New York Theological Seminary, to prepare and evaluate faculty in the Core Group Program of Yale Divinity School's Berkeley Institute, and to consult with staff developing Inter-met in Washington, D.C.

In June 1971 all staff were released except Washington, Younger and a clerical worker. Because Younger and the staff felt MUST's unique contribution in the area of racial justice required a minority director, he remained "acting director" until September 1972, when the program closed, and he left to become co-director of the Urban Training Center in Chicago while Washington joined the faculty of New York Theological Seminary. During this same period MUST offices were moved to 125th Street in Harlem, where the Ministerial Interfaith Association, a group of Black clergy, owned an office building.

As analysis of MUST's finances throughout its history will show, this action-training agency was the highly dependent child of one national mission board, with an assortment of national and local aunts and uncles. Between October 1, 1965, and June 30, 1970, national denominations (principally the United Methodist Church, which gave $804,332 out of $839,417) provided 82.4% of MUST's income. In the next program year their share sank to $80,300 out of a total of $152,244, or 52%. Nevertheless, there had been a self-conscious attempt from the start, on the part of both national and metropolitan New York sponsors, to develop independence and separate status for MUST.

MUST's principal sponsor, the National Division of the Board of Missions of the Methodist Church (later United Methodist Church) desired for the project to operate "on its own" and not be tied down with too many strings. The original prospectus had provided for a Board of Directors selected by the National Division and called for control of the project to be "with the National Division until there is official support and commitment from other denominations in a degree sufficient to make reasonable the relinquishing of the control by the National Division." Within the National Division, however, MUST-I was not seen as a project of the Division or any of its departments, but as "Ed Carother's baby." The same was true of the Women's Division, which furnished a large share of the funds for launching MUST.

Setting up a Board of Directors which included most of the major denominational and mission executives in New York City was considered both to be a way of building a base in a particular metropolitan area and of securing commitments to MUST from denominations other than the United Methodists. Nevertheless, this proved during the first three years of operation to be the way in which "Ed Carothers' baby" became "nobody's baby." At the same time the willingness of New York City's church leaders to let the Methodists carry the ball—so long as their largesse continued—kept them from asserting themselves in a Board that was 50% Methodist. Reorganization of the Board of Directors in May 1969 to include a wider variety of leadership from New York City and national organizations, as well as several former MUST trainees, did not change this basic two-way dynamic in the Board until the Methodists pulled out their support, leaving the New York City members holding a largely empty bag.

Within the staff another dynamic also contributed to the lack of a sense of responsibility on the part of both national and metropolitan New York sponsors. MUST staff sought to retain initiative over the program direction and other policies of the action-training agency. This quest for independence antedated the hiring of the agency's first director. George W. Webber only accepted the directorship after the principally Methodist Board of Directors and the members of JAM accepted his proposal for the general outlines along which the program would be developed. In the first planning year the proposal was developed by staff and taken to the Board for action. However, by the time the Board considered the second year's program, the major action of approval took the form of a vote of confidence in the director, rather than a vote on a specific program proposal. Thus, once staff had been hired and began to function, the project moved rather quickly from the board control envisioned in the original proposal to a form in which "staff proposes and board disposes." By the final year those who still made up the Board and attended meetings were more than glad to accept any training that Younger and Washington were able to negotiate that would provide income to keep the agency going. They had little left to offer, either in finances or advice.

The following accomplishments and contributions were made by MUST in the development of action training:

(1) *MUST developed and sustained an emphasis on combatting racism and encouraging minority empowerment.* Although most action-training agencies were concerned with race relations in a period of civil rights ferment, MUST was the only agency to make the struggle against institutional racism and for minority empowerment its major priority. Even before Nugent became director, this was a major component of MUST training. Some trainees and groups negotiating for training felt that this agenda was imposed upon them, but the sense of its importance led MUST in its later

period to turn down training opportunities that did not contribute to improving the situation for minorities. The training agency insisted that what it was trying to accomplish elsewhere in American life also had to happen in the sponsoring denominations and churches that were its principal constituency, as well as in its own institutional life.

(2) *From the very beginning MUST maintained a primary relationship with the metropolitan New York region.* The original listening sessions in the planning period went to local church and community leaders to find out what they saw to be the principal "agenda of metropolis." The lines of communication opened up at that time were continuously used, and were added to as MUST trainees spread out through the metropolitan area. Although principal financing and half the Board came from a national denomination, the strategy of MUST was continuously coordinated with the work of New York City denominations and mission agencies represented in JAM. Almost all staff members throughout MUST's history were persons who already had years of experience with church and community groups in greater New York.

(3) *MUST affected the Black church principally through relationships with caucuses in predominantly White denominations.* While UTC in its Ford Fellows program was related to the historic Black denominations, MUST kept close ties with the strategies developed by caucus groups like Black Methodists for Church Renewal and Black Presbyterians United. As a result, the training agency was often called in to do training with these groups at critical points in their development.

(4) *MUST led the shift in action training toward negotiated training.* Starting with the insight that training began in the planning period as trainees and training groups were contacted, MUST felt free to break out of the pattern of staff-initiated training after the second program year. This brought its resources to a much wider range of Black church and community groups, as well as developing a larger share of income from training.

(5) *Out of its experience MUST moved to the team approach in training and developed several curriculum innovations.* The original MUST staff included Billie Alban as "trainer." However, experience showed that training was not a set of techniques, but the entire process in which the agency was engaged. As a result, attention was given to developing every staff member's skills in training, so that the staff team could be the "trainer." MUST developed a sophisticated combination of group laboratory methods, social analysis and skills training for its programs on racism that proved very useful in other training with different objectives.

(6) *MUST staff had greater diversity than most other action-training agencies.* In contrast to the usual pattern of having White male clergy as the principal staff members and using others as consultants or part-time staff, MUST from the beginning had minority, women and lay staff members. In

later years the agency also used several young persons, and in training on racism with the National YWCA in the summer of 1969 actually used minority clerical and service employees as part of the training team.

(7) *MUST maintained a continuing commitment to evaluation.* In its first two program years, Younger was used as a participant-observer to develop evaluation processes for MUST training, as well as to prepare summary evaluations. Almost every training program provided for trainees' feedback and evaluation, and staff spent significant amounts of time studying evaluations to learn for future training. Although this had also been a requirement of the sponsoring Methodist denomination, MUST made it a part of its continuing operation.

(8) *MUST contributed significant resources to the development of other action-training agencies through the Action Training Coalition.* UTC, as the nationally sponsored training center, had a mandate to assist in development of other training programs, but MUST gave a larger share of its own staff time and budget to this effort. MUST staff were heavily represented at each ATC consultation, and Nugent served as chairman of the Coalition through much of its history.

(9) *Theological seminaries received a significant amount of MUST resources, and much of the MUST experience is embodied in the present program of New York Theological Seminary.* Although almost no fees were received from seminaries for the various seminary programs that were conducted by MUST beginning with its first program year, both urban orientation and some training in urban church leadership were given to seminary students. When Webber went to New York Theological Seminary, he used the experience with the Brooklyn Mission Ministers Community Training Program and training with Spanish evangelical clergy as clues for the way in which the seminary could develop significant theological education for minority clergy. Washington and Younger worked on contract with Melvin E. Schoonover in developing first the S.T.M. in Parish Ministry for urban pastors, and then the D.Min. sequence. Washington continued on the NYTS faculty in its certificate program and relations with minority Black churches.

(10) *Without sacrificing the ability to meet the agency's needs, MUST used its office and other support services to help a wide variety of community and church groups.* Realizing that the same infrastructure needed to support training could assist groups without an office, MUST helped the City-Wide Coordinating Committee on Welfare, the People's Board of Education, Black Economic Development Conference, *Renewal* magazine, Communications Network, and a number of other metropolitan and national groups.

THE SURVIVORS

Of 31 action-training programs and agencies that were members of ATC, 15 continued in existence through the end of 1975.[13] (Eleven remain active at the time of publication. See Appendix 2.) Seven of these were organized before 1966, and the other eight between 1967 and 1969. The following table summarizes the length of time that each had maintained its institutional life, as of the end of 1975:

Table 3
Institutional Life of Action-Training Agencies as of 1975[14]

	5 or less	6-8	9-11	12 or more	Total
Survivors	--	5	8	2	15
Others	9	4	--	--	13
	9	9	8	2	28

None of the survivors was able to continue by maintaining a principal emphasis on training, although most continued to do some action training. This section will describe the 13 programs and agencies that were still operating in the United States through the year 1975. The succeeding section will speak of the two in Canada and Puerto Rico that had taken a different course. The final section of this chapter will present brief sketches of the other ATC members which had ceased activity by 1975 or on which no data were available at that time.[15]

Although most action-training programs and agencies were organized for the sole or principal purpose of training clergy, lay and/or community leadership for urban mission and social change ministry, they moved in three principal directions as they modified their program and institutional life for long-term survival—consulting, community organizing or education. By 1975 consulting had become the main style of ATN of Ohio, ACTS in the Southeast, the Metropolitan Ecumenical Training Center in Washington, D.C., and Training Ecumenically to Advance Mission in Philadelphia. Community organizing was the principal activity of COMMIT in Los Angeles, CUE in the Twin Cities, and the Black Churchmen's Ecumenical Institute in Washington, D.C. Education was the major emphasis from the beginning of the Ministry in Social Change, a graduate program in the Twin Cities, but developed at a later stage in CUE of Portland. The other three agencies—ICUIS in Chicago, EMM in Seattle, and the Strong Center (originally Berkeley Center for Human Interaction)— had other emphases from the beginning.

CONSULTING

*Action Training Network of Ohio, Columbus, Ohio:*This study has already traced the origins of the Action Training Network of Ohio (ATN) in the Cleveland Internship Project, which had been financed by NIMH through the Cleveland College of Case-Western Reserve University, and Columbus Action Training Associates (CATA), which had developed from an inter-racial team of church and community activists in the state capital. Robert H. Bonthius, director of CIP, had already worked on 23 action-training and other consulting projects before ATN was incorporated in 1969. Between the fall of 1969 and June 1972, when the Cleveland and Columbus components of ATN were merged, using the CATA corporation, the associated group (which also included persons connected with CHART in Cincinnati) conducted 72 projects on a consultant basis. After that time, with head-quarters first in Cleveland and then in Cincinnati, the group of trainers and consultants associated in the network conducted a wide variety of training and work in organizational development, much of it with church and other religious organizations.

The format adopted when ATN was reorganized was that of a non-profit organization with a Board of Trustees composed of persons from the follow-ing categories, all of whom shared personal interest in development of the network: trainers, funding sources, client groups and others. This group decided purpose, goals and program. The major work of the network was organized by a Management Team, composed of full and part-time trainers. Thus, ATN became basically a cooperative of trainers, who formed various teams to carry on consultation and training within policies set by the Board.

The bulk of ATN consultation work was with church and community or-ganizations in the state of Ohio. Particularly significant for work with both type of groups was the Intra Systems Change Model developed by the staff out of experience with action for change in society and for eliminating insti-tutional racism in the church. In Toledo, a project was developed in co-operation with Toledo Metropolitan Ministry to improve the Health Delivery System. A Parish Model was developed and used with a number of local churches in different parts of the state.

Between 1970 and 1974 a major ATN contract was with the Episcopal Diocese of Southern Ohio. After two years of research the Institutional Racism Subcommittee of the diocese prepared a report with 17 recommen-dations for increased participation by Blacks and other minority groups in the life of the church body. In 1974 a follow-up study committee prepared a list of 15 objectives to be accomplished by the bishop, his staff and the parishes. In each case the recommendations were adopted, including an an-nual appropriation of $100,000 to fund programs and projects that would directly empower minority groups in Southern Ohio. Other contracts for anti-racism training, social change and intra systems change were entered into with the Episcopal Diocese of Ohio, the East and West Ohio Conferences of the United Methodist Church, and several presbyteries in Ohio connected with the United Presbyterian Church in the U.S.A. In addition, a number of similar training contracts were developed with church bodies and local churches in the Cleveland area, including the Roman Catholic Diocese.

In the community particular attention was paid to issues of welfare (with the Ohio Steering Committee for Adequate Welfare), public education (with the Council for Planning), peace (with Midwest Conference on Organizing for Peace) and criminal justice (through two grants by the Ohio Committee for Public Programs in the Humanities). As an outgrowth of its relations with groups in Ohio, ATN served as consultant to national conferences or programs of the National Welfare Rights Organization and Clergy and Laymen Concerned. Its director, Robert H. Bonthius, produced two manuals for citizens' group action—*Action for Earthcare*, a manual on ecology printed by Friendship Press in 1972 to be used in local church study, and *So—You Want to Change the System*, published by Trends in 1971.

By continuing to take contracts concerned for issues of social change, and by maintaining a team of consultants that included minorities and women, ATN was able to maintain much of the action-training emphasis and keep true to its motto, "Vision and Power for a More Human Society." About two-thirds of its work continued to be with religious bodies, local churches and projects related to them. The remainder of the contracts were principally with health, educational and welfare organizations. In this way ATN kept close to its purpose:

> To provide consultative, training, researching, and evaluative services and technical assistance to religious and secular institutions and community groups interested in a more human society, in order to develop their capacities for more effective social change.[16]

Association for Christian Training and Service, Nashville, Tennessee. The Pilot Diocese Program of the Episcopal Church, through the Episcopal Diocese of Tennessee, was responsible for the organization of Association for Christian Training and Service (ACTS), which originally had its headquarters in Memphis, the seat of the diocese. The diocesan Pilot Steering Committee, meeting between 1964 and 1966, authorized a request for a year of research and planning for establishment of "a Southern Regional Training Center for Christian Mission." General characteristics of the Center were as follows:

> be interdenominational
> use involvement-reflection training methods

speak to all the people of God
be concerned with total society
use various academic disciplines and skills
be directed to Southern Region
be concerned with research and Mission development
be effectively and responsibly related to the churches.[17]

William A. Jones, Jr., a White Episcopal clergyman who had served parishes in the Nashville area, was called to be the Research Director. He subsequently became the Executive Director.

A Consultation on Southern Regional Training for Christian Mission was held in Memphis on Feb. 23-24, 1967. Forty delegates representing 14 denominations, including five community groups, heard working papers by Jones and Earl Brewer of Candler School of Theology in Atlanta, discussed the possibilities of a center, and set up a timetable that projected organization of an interdenominational Board of Directors by the fall of 1967. Principal concerns of the consultation were: the need and value of continuing ecumenical conversation in the region, the need for more specific goals and purposes, a stress on equipping Christians with skills and understanding of their own situations, an "open door" policy for Christian groups to participate, extension of training to lay leaders, ongoing evaluation and ways for "the predominantly Negro Churches" to be "truly and genuinely included." There was agreement on a pattern of a regionally dispersed, interracial staff to carry out a three-year experiment. Meryl Ruoss, former director of the Department of Urban Church in the National Council of Churches, served as consultant, producing a series of working papers that surveyed nine other action-training programs and proposals, as well as giving insights on the questions of the nature of training, the concept of training for mission, and the possibilities for training for mission in the South.

ACTS began its work of researching, communicating, training and consulting in 1968 with a staff of five: Jones as Executive Director with Memphis as headquarters; Ted McEachern, a White United Methodist clergyman based in Nashville; Neil Leach, a White Presbyterian Church U.S. clergyman; Smith Turner, III, a Black AME Zion minister, based in Charlotte, North Carolina; and Clyde Williams, a Black Christian Methodist Episcopal faculty member of the Interdenominational Theological Center in Atlanta. Before the end of the first program year, Williams was replaced by Mance Jackson, a Black clergyman, who was also on the faculty of ITC and serving as national executive secretary of the National Commitee of Black Churchmen. The staff group used Arthur Cohen, professor of psychology at Georgia State College, as its consultant for development and training. The regional effort was aimed at the 11 states of "the Old South" —Alabama, Arkansas, Florida, Georgia, Kentucky, Louisiana, Mississippi, North Carolina, South Carolina, Tennessee and Virginia; and it succeeded in having significant programs in 25 cities in eight of those states, plus one in Texas.

The dynamic of Black-White relations, plus the pressures to develop an ongoing base for funding when the three-year experimental program was to end in 1971, resulted in Jones's resignation in 1971. McEachern took over as Executive Director and moved the headquarters to Nashville. In preparation for the long run, the Board developed an organization goal, "To accomplish mission action for social transformation within the southeastern region of the United States." Related to this was a set of training, consultation, research, mission development, ecumenical action, coalition and research goals. In November 1973 the Board of Directors was reorganized as a self-perpetuating board for an independent agency that would still be related to its sponsoring denominations.

Throughout its history ACTS has majored in providing consultation, planning assistance, research and training to groups of denominational leaders and local clergy in a number of metropolitan areas throughout the Southeast. In some of those places, it assisted in the formation of ecumenical mission agencies or strategy groups like Metropolitan Interfaith Association of Memphis; Religions United for Action in the Community of St. Petersburg, Florida; Coalition for Mission Action of Jacksonville, Florida; Greater Birmingham Ministries in Alabama; an ecumenical steering committee in Chattanooga, Tennessee; and an ecumenical task force in Winston-Salem, North Carolina. In every urban center where it was involved ACTS concentrated on developing the strategy competence and other skills of a cadre of urban clergy. In addition, through the work of Mance Jackson it trained rural Black pastors all over the region.

Denominational bodies called upon ACTS for consultation and training in connection with their mission strategies and local church research. These included the Cumberland Presbyterian Church, whose churches are concentrated in the Southeast; the Episcopal Synod of Province IV, comprising 17 dioceses in the region; the Presbyterian Church in the U.S., another Southeast-based body, which used ACTS as a resource for the reorganization of its synods and presbyteries and for training new judicatory officers; and the National Division and Annual Conferences of the United Methodist Church, for which ACTS worked with the Hinton Rural Life Center to develop a rural strategy, and with local church, District and Annual Conference leaders to form an Urban Workers Coalition. ACTS also conducted important research projects for individual denominations and ecumenical coalitions throughout the region.

Programs for seminarians were planned and conducted for St. Luke's School of Theology at Sewanee University and Vanderbilt Divinity School. In cooperation with Vanderbilt, a project on the churches in transitional communities was conducted to assist White churches facing community change and improve Black-White relations among the churches. Through Jackson, the relationship with the National Committee of Black Churchmen contributed to the strengthening of that community, as well as better understanding of the Black agenda among the churches and denominations of the Southeast. A Coalition for Criminal Justice was developed, and both consultation and training were provided for a variety of community organizations and agencies.

In 1975 ACTS saw itself as capable of offering the following types of training: Internal Skill Development—working effectively in groups, consultation skills, multiple staff research, conflict and power utilization; and External Skill Development—the church in transitional communities, economic recession and the church's mission, research skills for mission research, urban awareness using the Community Land Use Game simulation. This kind of training tailored to each situation was in contrast to earlier training efforts like the region-wide Consultation on the Church and Urban Life, held in Chattanooga in April and June 1969, which brought together larger groups of persons without a common action base for a program that was essentially orientation to urban mission. By staying close to its regional base, by working steadily with clergy and denominational leaders, and by developing a staff and a network of resource people and consultants who were responsive to local needs, ACTS was able to survive the transition from reliance on pilot project grants to fees and contracts for direct services to the churches and their leadership. In addition, it kept a viable Black-White relationship both within its staff and among the churches with which it has been working.[18]

*Metropolitan Ecumenical Training Center, Washington, D.C.:*With a purpose "to train and equip clergy and laymen to engage in mission directed towards the problems of the metropolitan area," Metropolitan Ecumenical Training Center (METC) was organized in April 1967 in Washington, D.C. In pursuit of this goal, METC was committed to three specific objectives: (1) "METROPOLITAN in location of concern," (2) "ECUMENICAL in membership," and (3) "A TRAINER in function, standing between seminary and ecclesiastical structures, between general education and specific mission strategies, as a complementary facility for all religious bodies."

Impetus for the formation of METC, according to Paul Moore, Jr., Episcopal bishop and first chairman of the Board of Directors, "grew out of a two-year concern among denominational representatives in the Washington area with ways of pooling our resources for training laymen and clergy in the problems of the suburbs and inner city."[19] The training project had been preceded by the Washington Urban Training Program to prepare seminarians for inner-city ministries. William A. Wendt, a White rector of an Episcopal parish, negotiated the first program of WUTP in 1963-64 with Virginia Theological Seminary. By the 1966-67 academic year it included five area seminaries. Tilden Edwards, a White priest who had served in Wendt's parish, was director of WUTP in 1966 and was named director of METC.

Sponsors of the new training center were 11 Protestant and Roman Catholic jurisdictions in the Washington area, along with representatives of the Urban Institute of the Council of Churches, the Archbishop's Community Relations Committee and the Chesapeake Foundation for Industrial Mission. Jewish representatives joined a year later. Moore stated the hopes of the founders of METC as follows:

> But what is really *new* about the Training Center idea? First of all, it is completely ecumenical, including the Roman Catholic Church. Secondly, it will attempt to deal with the metropolis as a whole, and not just the problems of the inner city or of the suburbs. Thirdly, it will be oriented to the training not only of the clergy but also of laymen. Fourthly, with a very small staff it will attempt to provide faculty by using the resources of the Washington community, both in the government and in the universities.[20]

Most of the center's program was church-related. During the first year a Clergy Pilot Seminar was developed to test out training needs and methods, followed by seven Community Forums for laity and clergy on urban issues. A New Clergy Orientation was held every year until the winter of 1974-75, when its purposes were taken over by a year-long Continuing Education Institute. Lay leadership training had a more spotty history at METC, but the agency was successful in training and consultation with geographic clusters of churches, either in all-clergy or all-lay groups. In September 1969 a Mission Development Group, composed of denominational and ecumenical mission staff, developed a strategy that resulted in training programs for several group ministries and some denominational groups and local churches, as well as open programs on conflict in congregational life and working with the youth scene in suburban communities.

METC's concern for the spiritual life, both personal and corporate, was a component of training prior to 1971, when both the Executive Committee and the Board and staff held retreats on "religious identity." During 1972-73 Edwards developed a research project on spiritual growth in congregations, in collaboration with Loren Mead of Project Test Pattern. Training sessions were divided between one for clergy on meditation and the devotional life, and a lay-clergy unit on worship in congregational life. During the summer of 1973 Edwards took his sabbatical with a Buddhist lama, Tarthang Tulku Rinpoche, and at a Jesuit center for spiritual growth. He reported that "the summer has veered me personally toward valuing the uniquely religious task of cultivating a dynamic, ever-deepening, liberating, transcendent faith, experience, and awareness, upon which can be based the fullest sense of human purpose, unity, development, justice and happiness."[21] Following a year-long research project to examine the values and experiences of 29 lay persons out of seven religious traditions, Edwards founded Shalem Institute for spiritual formation, drawing heavily on the Western contemplative and mystical traditions and Mahayana Buddhism.

After a survey of training needs in the fall of 1970, METC decided to give fuller attention to continuing education for clergy, using Hans Scherner, a White Lutheran clergyman who had been working with the Race Institute. In 1973 Roy M. Oswald was called as Director of Continuing Education Development and a Continuing Education Institute was established with its own advisory board. This unit took over the orientation program for clergy new to the Washington area, as well as contracts and consultation with various groups for clergy training.

The Youth-Adult Task Force is an example of a useful program sponsored by METC for four years and then closed when its task was completed. In 1969 the Board adopted a proposal for work with suburban youth developed by Tom Murphy, who had been engaged in youth ministry at Church of the Pilgrims in the Dupont Circle area, where he noted that virtually all of them, "runaways, young street kids on drugs, clients at the Free Clinic, hangers-on at the Mustard Seed," which was a drop-in center, were from suburban homes and communities. He proposed to organize local community action groups in the suburbs to work with youth on an ecumenical, inclusive basis. Community task forces for youth were organized in Bethesda, Maryland, and Springfield, McLean and Fairfax City, Virginia. Training and consultation were offered to adult workers with youth, and youth forums were held during 1973-74 in Fairfax County in Virginia. Finally, a Youth Services Resource and Referral Manual was produced for the Washington area. The program was terminated at the end of 1974 when the staff was only being used occasionally by the community groups.

The Race Institute, committed to "training for human relations specialists in the design of group encounters with racism," also began in 1969 with a sequence to train trainers for work in race relations. The program operated through the end of 1972 with its own steering committee. At that time it went out of existence as a self-supporting consulting network with its own director and became a consulting service and informal learning exchange. During its four years of activity the Race Institute worked more with secular institutions and community groups than with religious organizations and churches, although its original intent had been to work on racism with clusters of churches in White communities. The Institute used problem-solving related to situations of institutional racism.

METC was responsible for the creation of two new institutions, the Black

Churchmen's Ecumenical Institute, organized in 1968 (described later in this chapter), and Inter-met, an alternate institution for theological education, as well as assisting in the birth of Alban Institute. During its first four program years, METC continued to provide services to students from six theological seminaries in the Washington area through the Washington Urban Training Program, which offered field experience and reflection seminars for 12 hours each week. Planning sessions in the fall of 1969, sparked by a $10,000 grant from the Danforth Foundation to evaluate and plan continuation of the seminary training programs, resulted in a proposal for "a full-time, inter-faith theological education facility, based on an engagement-reflection methodology, to be located in Washington." A Central Planning Committee was formed, and John Fletcher took leave from the faculty of Virginia Theological Seminary to serve as director of the Theological Education Demonstration Project for a year, beginning in June 1970.

During the planning year Fletcher led the research of what was now being called "Inter-met—Interfaith Associates for Metropolitan Theological Education." Task forces were formed to plan selection and placement, educational process, accreditation and relations with religious jurisdictions, and finance and management structure. Fletcher remained on the METC staff until Inter-met was incorporated in the summer of 1971. Although the original timetable called for the new seminary program to begin in the fall of 1971, the timetable was postponed until the 1972-73 academic year in order to train preceptors and supervisors, plan for long-range funding and accreditation, and give more attention to "the complex interreligious and racial issues" involved. The experimental seminary program opened as an independent institution, but its offices remained in the same building with METC, and the action-training agency provided consultation and other services to the Inter-met staff. Thus, the concern for seminary training that helped to spawn METC had, in turn, resulted in the birth of a new form of seminary, while METC continued with its original mandate.

Out of this rich background and accomplishment, METC in 1975 was emphasizing training, consulting and research in four areas: spiritual research, congregational leadership research, continuing education consultation, and social justice and quality of life. Its principal instruments for carrying out this program were the Shalem Institute, lay-clergy training in conflict and corporate worship, the Continuing Education Institute and staff work for the Interfaith Committee of Greater Washington, for which METC provided consultation with task forces in three priority issue areas—hunger, housing and criminal justice. This program had grown both out of the needs of the Washington area and the previous experience of METC as an ecumenical agency.

The existence of METC in its developed form ended December 31, 1978, two years after the resignation of Tilden Edwards as executive director. It changed names in January 1977 to the Interreligious Association of Greater Washington, but its functions and incorporation remained the same, with Cecilia Braveboy, a Black woman who had been on the staff of METC, as interim executive director. Tilden Edwards remained temporarily as director of the Shalem Institute component, and Roy Oswald with clergy education and social issues. In 1978 the organization was disbanded after much debate and analysis, to be succeeded by two new independent ones: Shalem and the Interfaith Conference of Greater Washington, the latter focused on interfaith executive level collaboration around statements and actions related to social issues, sponsored by Protestant, Roman Catholic, Jewish, and Moslem jurisdictions.

METC planning and program remained rooted in the situation of metropolitan Washington and the needs of the sponsoring religious bodies. The agency continued to be flexible without becoming faddish or shallow. In a report in 1970 Edwards commented on this characteristic:

> We have paid a certain price for our "flexibility," to the degree this has meant creation of constantly new kinds of programs in relatively unchartered directions. . . . Ideally, it is best to build from year to year on the specific kinds of successes and failures of past programs, and so develop over the years a more and more effective model to accomplish a specific purpose. I think we should try to do this as much as possible, but there are two built-in limitations: first, the "situation" of the religious community and the society shift so rapidly today, that last year's program just may not be relevant again this year, no matter how well it's put together. Second, different groups can respond very differently to the same program: one man's meat is another man's poison.[22]

Constant adherence to the discipline of quarterly reports from the director and staff of related components left a continuous, contemporary record of the research, changes, accomplishments and failures during METC's lifespan. Like most other action-training agencies and programs, it was under constant evaluation, but no other agency has left so full a record of its existence for both friends and detractors to read and consider.

Training Ecumenically to Advance Mission, Philadelphia, Pennsylvania: During the winter of 1968-69 four denominations in the Philadelphia area—Episcopal Diocese of Pennsylvania, Philadelphia Group Ministry of the Evangelical United Brethren Church, Presbytery of Philadelphia and Pennsylvania Southeast Conference of the United Church of Christ—planned the organization of a metropolitan training agency, Training Ecumenically to Advance Mission (TEAM). In June 1969 William E. Ramsden, a White United Methodist clergyman with experience as an inner-city pastor in Buffalo and a denominational executive in Indianapolis and training in organizational development and group dynamics, was called to be executive director. His offices were located in the headquarters of the ecumenical agency for metropolitan Philadelphia, although the action-training agency was not made a training activity within that body.

From the beginning TEAM engaged in a broad program of both training and consulting in organizational development and human relations, as well as working with urban issues and mission strategy. The agency's purpose was "to develop training to help people build a more just and humane society," and to help religiously-sponsored efforts become more effective. In addition to its own programs of training on urban issues, church management workshops and human relations training, TEAM's staff worked with Metropolitan Associates of Philadelphia, another member of the Action Training Coalition, to prepare a curriculum to enable lay ministry. Ramsden also taught courses at Eastern Baptist and Drew Seminaries.

When funding from the sponsoring denominations proved unable to carry the full salary of the executive director and the office expenses, it was voted not to disband operation. The Board was expanded to include individuals and congregations, and the director's salary was made dependent on income from contracts for consulting and training. TEAM continued as the corporate structure for Ramsden's work in the Philadelphia area.[23]

COMMUNITY ORGANIZING

Center for Urban Encounter, Minneapolis/St, Paul, Minnesota: The story of the Center for Urban Encounter in the Twin Cities (CUE-M) is that of one agency which has had two quite different action-training programs, both of which have been effective and well received. From 1967 through 1969 the focus was on orientation for lay leaders and church workers, while the emphasis after that time was on community organizing in the Twin Cities and beyond.

CUE-M began as a project for "A regional Urban Training Center in the Twin Cities," sponsored by the Greater Urban Parish of the Twin Cities, an ecumenical inner-city program engaged in direct ministry with ghetto areas and working-class neighborhoods. The seven denominations that sponsored the parish were responsible for developing the action training agency with the purpose, "To equip laity and clergy for mission and ministry in an urbanized society." Charles Lutz, a theologically trained layman of the American Lutheran Church who had been deeply involved with the Ecumenical Institute of Chicago, was employed as director in the fall of 1966, and training began early in 1967, using the models that had already been prepared during the planning period.

The basic sequence of training called for a lay course of six sessions from Friday evening through Saturday afternoon, to be offered three times a year, and a ten-day church workers course, offered twice a year. The main emphasis in the lay course was on orientation to the Twin Cities and urban problems, with preparation for volunteer service in either their own congregation or a social agency or program in the Twin Cities. Volunteer assignments for a 16-week period following the lay course were made available during the training. Over four years through December 1970, 350 persons, of whom the largest group was Roman Catholic, took the lay course. The church workers course was more intensive, and featured an "urban plunge" experience and discussion of papers.

In addition to these training programs which drew from all over the metropolitan area, CUE-M conducted local church courses in urban neighborhoods. The first such program in April 1968 enrolled 40 persons from 14 churches in the Near-Southside of Minneapolis, which had been chosen as a Model Neighborhood area, for two weekends and three week nights of training to help them become more knowledgeable about their community and develop specific strategies for church response. The main learning from this experience was that "the churches historically have responded through the responsible involvement of individual members in many social structures, and through the stance of local churches acting independently." Areas of possible cooperative action were identified, and an ad hoc committee composed of one representative from each congregation met to plan next steps toward some form of cooperative ministry. A similar program was held in April 1969 in the suburban community of St. Louis Park, where anti-Semitism was threatening community relations in a municipality with the largest concentration of Jews in the Twin Cities area. Six Lutheran, Roman Catholic and Presbyterian churches gave attention to Jewish-Christian dialogue and finished the week by adopting a set of recommendations to their sending churches. In addition to these programs, CUE-M also conducted an interim urban experience for seminarians in the Twin Cities area and for students from Wartburg College.

Although everything seemed to be going well with a highly successful program that was proceeding with a balanced budget and continuing enrollment, Charles Lutz took the occasion of his resignation in June 1969 to challenge the Board of Directors of the Greater Urban Parish, which administered the program of CUE-M, to consider a different direction. He noted that the program had developed strength in "*sensitization* of middle and upper-middle class church members to the needs for and theological legitimation of major social change and the church's responsibility in such change," "*identification of resources* and methods for competently doing the sensitization job," and "*establishing some credibility* . . . with certain figures among the radical movements in the Twin Cities." He continued, "what CUE has not effectively done, and must begin to do if it is to grow, is to develop the *action* focus of the training we offer." In support of corporate action aimed at systemic change, he suggested CUE-M needed to emphasize "work at organizing the local churches for effective political action and, in neighborhood courses, strategizing for action around community issues and needs." [24]

In keeping with this recommendation, CUE-M chose William R. Grace, a White Presbyterian clergyman who had worked closely with Saul Alinsky during his previous service as presbytery director of urban work in the San Francisco Bay area. Grace shifted the objectives of the agency from training lay and clergy leaders for urban mission to training community organizers, consulting with community organizations and starting new organizations. Some of the orientation programs for church leaders and students were continued, but greater stress was placed on community organizing. Major attention was given to stimulating community organizing, both in the Twin Cities and in other parts of the country. Interns and trainees would come to the Twin Cities for a full year of experience in community organizing or a shorter exposure, and CUE-M staff would go out to consult with community organizations.

The results of this change began to show rather quickly in the Twin Cities. The Greater Metropolitan Federation was organized in the Twin Cities area and held its first convention using the Alinsky model in October 1971. By March 1971, the Minnesota Union of College Students held its organizing meeting, and November saw the Organization for a Better St. Paul hold a constituting convention for a new action federation involving 52 member organizations. On May 1, 1973, a full-time organizer began to bring together an organization in South Minneapolis. CUE-M did not set up any of these organizations directly, yet it is certain that they would never have been started if the organization had not taken a different direction and the churches had not seen mission to include the empowerment of people.

CUE-M's principal activity by 1975 was in developing and fulfilling organizational contracts with a variety of organizations and institutions in the Twin Cities area and elsewhere. Particularly important were consultation and training with organizers in Elizabeth and Paterson, New Jersey, in connection with the Mid Atlantic Training Institute, and with staff and leadership of organizations in Rochester and Corning, New York, through the National Center for Urban Ethnic Affairs. Individual training was offered for periods of one month to a year for students and persons already engaged in organizing. Courses, curriculum units and lectures in community organizing were offered at educational institutions in the Twin Cities area. CUE-M had thus become one of the most respected and effective trainers and consultants for community organizing in the country. Much of its work still involved churches, but now they were being urged to work in concert with other organizations and people in their communities. The Board of Directors still gave church support to the program, and denominational judicatories provided about half the budget.[25]

United Training Organization of Atlanta, Georgia: A group of denominational and seminary representatives met during 1967 to plan for a training agency to be called United Training Organization of Atlanta (UTOA). Its objective, as outlined in the original proposal, was "to provide training in mission in Atlanta as a pilot area for laymen, clergy, and seminary students in the context of specific urban problems and opportunities in Atlanta." They hoped by direct involvement "to coordinate and stimulate new missions through the local churches, seminaries, and community bases, seeking to do so across racial, economic and denominational lines." An Executive Committee was formed that included representatives of ten Protestant denominations (African Methodist Episcopal and Christian Methodist Episcopal among them), Roman Catholics and the "Jewish Community," as well as three seminaries in the Atlanta area—Candler School of Theology, Columbia Theological Seminary and the Interdenominational Theological Center. Training was to be directed to three groups: persons in mission, with priority to local church teams; churches in mission, including church volunteers, laity for mission at the ecumenical parish base (in coordination with the Ecumenical Institute of Chicago) and task forces; and seminary students.

Edgar M. Grider, a White Presbyterian U.S. clergyman who had served on the planning committee while associate pastor of Central Presbyterian Church, was chosen to be director and began work in January 1968. During the first year when the program was being designed, Grider and Robert N. Lynn, a White United Methodist seminary graduate who served as Associate in Community Development, conducted pilot programs in each of the agency's three areas of interest: a seminar in Urban Training for students from Columbia and Candler; an orientation to Atlanta for clergy and laity of four local churches, along with a Ghetto-Live-In Course that was taken by four White clergy; and skills training in community development with community leaders from five areas of the city. During the first year the staff discovered that an educational approach to white racism in suburban churches would not work.

Over the next two years the staff and Executive Committee decided that denominational grants would not furnish adequate financial base and moved to strengthen income from fees and training contracts, including those with the seminaries. Also, the staff was broadened to become interracial, first by using Andrew Young, who had returned in 1970 to work in

Atlanta after service on the staff of the Southern Christian Leadership Conference as its vice-president and principal aide to Martin Luther King, Jr., and later by naming as associate director Calvin E. Houston, a Presbyterian Black clergyman who had served as pastor of Rice Memorial Presbyterian Church. UTOA continued to offer the interseminary seminars in urban training, and several courses and other experiences for seminarians; to conduct training on social and institutional change and mission development with groups of local church leaders; and to expand its work with community groups. During 1969 Grider gave 1/3 of his time to staffing a Religious Resources Planning Committee for several denominations in Atlanta, and in 1971 UTOA gave staff services to a city-wide coalition of some 30 organizations concerned to develop a structure of citizens advisory groups within the Atlanta public school system.

Charles G. Helms, a White Presbyterian U.S. clergyman who had been active in community organizing, replaced Lynn as Associate in Community Development, and the community organizing activities of UTOA were increased. Helms had been active in the formation of the Bass Organization for Neighborhood Development (BOND) in an older inner-city neighborhood largely inhabited by poor whites, most of whom came from rural areas, as well as small numbers of Latin Americans, poor Blacks and people characterized as "quasi-hippies." The achievement of this community organization in changing city plans for highways and redevelopment, developing a low-income housing project, starting a Federal Credit Union, establishing a day care program, a neighborhood service center and a community crisis center, and publishing a community newspaper encouraged UTOA to expand its efforts in organizing.

In January 1973 the Board of Trustees adopted a proposal to establish an ongoing community development component in UTOA with the following purposes:

> 1. The restoration and redevelopment of selected close-in residential communities through the vehicle of Neighborhood Development Corporations based in local community organizations, and utilizing the planning procedures created by the new Atlanta City Charter.
> 2. Fostering the continued growth of central Atlanta using the principles of New Town-In-Town concepts with an emphasis on balancing the needs of the central business district with the needs of Atlanta's viable neighborhoods. [26]

Particular attention was to be given to continued work in the BOND community, consistent with its Neighborhood Development Plan and Neighborhood Development Corporation in two additional communities, work with the Virginia-Highland community and Community Foundation in the Kirkwood area, and enabling local churches to relate constructively to and identify with their immediate neighborhoods and communities in all these areas. The following principles were to be advocated for New Town-In-Town:

—rich diversity and healthy pluralism
—the attraction of middle and upper income residents into the core city
—the establishment of completely fair and adequate relocation plans and practices for any who might be dislocated by these developments[27]

In 1974, when Helms was elected to the Atlanta City Council, two banks cut off their financial support to UTOA's organizing efforts, prompting the Executive Committee to re-examine its assumption that business would support such efforts. The response was to strengthen the commitment to community development activities. UTOA had been working with other civic and community organizations, including the Virginia-Highlands Civic Association, South Atlantans for Neighborhood Development, the City-wide League of Neighborhoods, the Old Fourth Ward Neighborhood Council and the Association to Revive Grant Park.

UTOA continued to train seminary students and local church clergy and lay leaders, as well as to consult with denominational bodies, local churches and clusters of churches. But the main effort had shifted to the work for self-help and self-reliance by building self-directed and autonomous community organizations, which would not be indefinitely dependent upon its support, as had already happened in the Bass Neighborhood through BOND.[28]

Center of Metropolitan Mission In-Service Training, Los Angeles, California: In the late fall of 1965, following the Watts riots in 1964, the urban directors of six Protestant denominations based in Los Angeles began to meet for joint planning as Joint Action in Mission (JAM). They selected three geographical areas in the metropolitan region for priority action: southwest Los Angeles around the University of Southern California, the Pacoima-San Fernando area and East Hollywood. In addition to several councils of churches, there were already two ad hoc ecumenical structures established for specific tasks on a metropolitan basis— the Commission on Church and Race organized in 1962, and the Los Angeles Goals Project, formed in 1965. Representatives of the Methodist and Presbyterian denominations had already been talking about an urban training center for Los Angeles. Five denominations, with representatives of Claremont School of Theology, organized the Center of Metropolitan Mission In-Service Training (COMMIT) and called Robert E. Ryland, a White Presbyterian pastor, to be the first director as the program was being planned and the basic curriculum established.

The original purpose of COMMIT, as stated in its preliminary strategy and goals, was "to work with local congregations and their leaders to develop concern for a more human community and to plan for and carry out their mission together." This was later simplified to "training for mission in the urban community." Emphasis was to be placed on training for local congregations in the central metropolitan area ("urban") and those outside ("suburban") and for students and youth, as well as "to meet the needs of all concerned individuals who desire information and understanding of the current trends and problems of urban Los Angeles and the role the church could or should play in carrying out its mission."

In December 1967 Ryland was succeeded as director by Speed Leas, a White United Church of Christ clergyman who had been on the original Coordinating Drafting Committee for the center while serving a local church in the city. The staff was filled out during 1968 with the addition of Paul Kittlaus, a White United Church of Christ clergyman who had been serving in the Pacoima area, as Director of Theological Training; and Clifford Jones, a Black community organizer and trainer, as Director of Social Change Training.

The early training models concentrated on action training designs for local congregations, seminary courses on urban problems, and short-term courses on subjects like "Group Process Training," "Women: A New Self, Imaged by Style" and "Introducing Youth Groups to the City." In addition, COMMIT provided consultative services. Cliff Jones spent a good deal of his time with Black community organizations. By 1969 Arthur Holguin, a Chicano community organizer with experience in East Los Angeles, had joined the staff as Director of Community Organization Training, and Connie Leas was serving as Consultant on Women's Training. A grant from the Irwin-Sweeny-Miller Foundation to Claremont School of Theology for Project Understanding resulted in five years of consultation with this project to train seminarians to work against racism in congregations.

As the staff developed assurance in its training styles, the program of COMMIT proliferated in a tremendous variety of training, consulting and organizing contracts and experiences. For example, during 1969, exclusive of the program developed to assist with Methodist restructure, COMMIT fulfilled 43 different contracts with 3,442 participants. Six of these were one-day events, eight were over a weekend and 15 lasted from four days to three months, but 14 lasted from three to 12 months. They were with a great diversity of church and community groups, but the wide range of objectives fell into two primary categories: "(1) sensitization, exposure, and reflection on various issues confronting urban man, and organizations, and (2) the development of skills in organizational development and community organization." Jones was principally used to bring a strategy presence in training with interracial and suburban groups, but he served part of the year as executive director of the Los Angeles Brotherhood Crusade and organized a Black training firm, Institute for Training and Program

Development, which worked closely with COMMIT. By the following year he was insisting on more involvement with training in the Black community. Holguin was deeply involved with La Raza, a principal organization among Chicanos, and welfare rights in Los Angeles.

By 1971 it became clear to Leas and the Board of Directors that denominational grant income was going to remain at a steady level or even decline, while contract training was not paying for itself. At the end of June of that year, Leas reported that the four staff members principally engaged in training and consulting (Gail Thompson, Kittlaus, Connie Leas and himself) had during the preceding six months spent about 307 1/2 person-days on 69 projects that had taken from a part of a day through 32 days of staff time. Although there had been an increase in work with local churches, most of the sponsoring denominations were not using the program in proportion to their contribution. Yet, since the denominational grants were not covering the basic expenses of the organization, the contract income brought in by the trainers was needed to subsidize the community organizing and training done with Blacks and Chicanos by Jones and Holguin.

Based on the first five years of training experience, the staff proposed a distribution of staff time during 1972 that would give equal attention (30% each) to the following purposes: (1) training, education and effective social change in the Black and Brown communities with special attention to community organization; (2) the same approach to White suburban communities with special attention to community organization, clustering of churches, White racism, and motivation of clergy and laymen in social change; and (3) training, education and effective institutional involvement of the local church in its mission of service to its own members and service and action in the world. The other 10% would be devoted to training in conflict management, organizational development, community organization and group process for various organizations and groups. The emphasis on the institutional life of the local congregation had developed out of a staff research project on the Crisis in the Practice of Ministry during late 1970 which revealed that older and younger clergy had different paradigms or visions of their work, but that they found a purposelessness with local congregations, and their own sense of satisfaction as a profession had drastically decreased after 1968.

The denominations were unable to guarantee the proposed budget for 1972 and to undergird the priorities outlined in the staff proposal. Between the middle of 1972 and June 1974, there was a complete staff turnover and a gradual reordering of priorities. This change is described in a brief summary prepared by the new staff team in 1975:

> By 1972 it was evident that national and local judicatories were reducing their outlays for urban social change projects such as COMMIT. As denominational funding began to wane, an increasing dependence on organizational development and conflict manage-

ment contracts were necessary to subsidize full-time staff involvement in empowerment efforts related to minority, feminist and peace issues by COMMIT. . . .

Since 1974 COMMIT's primary emphasis had been on advocacy and community organizing for constituent groups struggling for social justice, rather than organizational development and conflict management for established groups. The staff receives basically one-third of its support from the denominations for this work and the rest of the work is funded through specific grants or contracts for individual projects. Sometimes the staff functions at partial salary. Administrative and executive functions are shared by staff.[29]

The staff by this time consisted of Rosalio Munoz, a Chicano community organizer and Episcopal layman; Grace Moore, a White United Church of Christ clergywoman who had originally joined the staff in a secretarial position and was responsible for feminist issues of empowerment in the Church arena; Louis Knowles, a White Presbyterian clergyman who was originally employed by the sponsoring denominations to do a report on COMMIT and its future direction, and was then assigned training responsibilities as well as emphasis on advocacy and empowerment.

The staff team stated the purpose of COMMIT in its new form as follows:

COMMIT sees itself as an ecumenical coalition of people finding mission through strategic witness in the struggle of new and changing communities to improve the inequality of life in our urban sprawl. The challenges we sekk (sic) to respond to are those involving social justice and societal inequities. Theologically, we are united in the conviction that liberation can best be achieved through the *self-determined* efforts of the constituencies that are victimized.[30]

What had begun as an attempt to stimulate mission through congregations to address the urban problems of Los Angeles was now principally committed to working through community organizations and those church people who would support their agenda. Although in the intervening years the staff of COMMIT, as an action-training agency, had spent all their time, skill and strength in a wide variety of effective and useful activities of training and consultation for denominations and local churches, they had not succeeded in getting them to adopt the agenda of social change, justice and peace. Therefore, a new staff with a new purpose moved to work with community groups, while still retaining the form of a non-profit corporation with a board and paid staff. The center closed down all activities in 1978.

Black Churchmen's Ecumenical Institute , Washington, D.C.: A group of Black clergy in Washington, related to the White-sponsored program of Metropolitan Ecumenical Training Center (METC) created a new agency in November 1968, out of a desire to have "maximum opportunity to develop their own leadership, base of economic and social power, dignity, style, corporate goals, strategy for development, and interpretation of Christian values in the light of their own experience and needs." The purposes of the training center were stated as follows in the initial proposal drafted by an all-Black steering committee:

> 1. To research, plan, administer and evaluate significant training events that will help the Black churches in the Washington area, to become better equipped to provide their unique kind of leadership and integrity on behalf of constructive community development through training programs . . .
> 2. To provide linkages with predominantly white training events aimed at relevant social issues.[31]

Thus, the Black Churchman's Ecumenical Training Facility (BCETF) was set up with one eye looking toward the Black churches and community, and the other toward the White church and community.

This split vision was a consequence of developing out of the middle of a White-dominated training organization in metropolitan Washington, where nearly 70% of the population in the District of Columbia was Black, and where there were approximately 1,000 Black or predominantly Black congregations. A consultation on Black-White cooperation, called by the Curriculum Committee of METC in the spring of 1968, resulted in a proposal for two parallel training efforts, one in the White community, which became the Race Institute of METC, and one in the Black community, which became BCETF. The first form of the proposal talked about working with other minority groups and churches, but an all-Black steering committee, chaired by Ernest R. Gibson, assistant director of programs for the Council of Churches of Greater Washington, who later became chairman of the board, decided to limit the program to the Black community and churches. The nucleus of support for the program came from the Council of Churches, 351 members of the Baptist Ministers Conference of D.C. and Vicinity, and Black caucus leadership in the United Methodist, Presbyterian and Roman Catholic denominations.

Although BCETF was conceived as a Black-controlled agency with a program directed toward the Black community and churches of Greater Washington, the principal source of funds was projected as the mission budgets and special "urban crisis" funds of the mainline White denominations. Eight national bodies or their local judicatories responded with some form of grant to BCETF, many of which were limited to three years. Requests to ecumenical funding agencies and foundations were all without concrete results. One participant in the process has pointed out that much of the denominational support was given after the assassination of Dr. Martin Luther King, Jr. (he calls it "guilt money") and has argued that this made the action-training agency, which was supposed to be Black-controlled, a "paternalistic puppet." Funds for BCETF were channeled through METC until it was incorporated, and the two action-training programs shared offices in the same building with the Council of Churches and other ecumenical agencies.

Rev. Charles W. Green, pastor of Pilgrim Baptist Church in Washington, was elected as the first executive director in November 1969 to serve on a part-time basis. After securing training requests and developing programs, Green began a series of events that paralleled METC's program with congregations and group ministries and also involved Black Baptists and storefront Pentecostals, as well as churches and clergy affiliated with mainline White communions. In the Spring of 1970 BCETF introduced a class of students at Howard School of Religion to urban problems in a weekly course on "Social Ethics in the World Order."

After BCETF was incorporated in early 1971, the Board of Directors conducted an evaluation of the part-time director and voted to dismiss him. Robert Pipes, a Black Baptist minister with community organizing experience, was called to fill the post in January 1972, when there was only a year's income left from the original denominational grants. He urged the Board of Directors to broaden the emphasis from training to community development, and to establish a corporation for economic development to sponsor a commercial center like the one established by Leon Sullivan in Philadelphia, so that the program could become self-sufficient. The name of the center was changed to "Black Churchmen's Ecumenical Institute" (BCEI) to signify this enlarged purpose.

Board meetings became less frequent as the grant funds ran out, and Pipes was left to support himself in early 1973 while shepherding the proposals for church-based programs in the Black community in Washington, D.C., through government, religious and private funding possibilities. However, the Board members, who were principally Black pastors of local churches and program administrators with the Council of Churches and mainline denominations, still supported the change of direction. In June 1973, the National Institute of Mental Health was prepared to make a grant for a church program to combat alcoholism in the Black community, but a lack of matching funds postponed approval of the grant. Finally, in 1975 the Department of Health, Education and Welfare approved a two-year program, Prevention of Alcohol Abuse, to be carried on by Robert Pipes through BCEI, with the funds channeled through Inter-met as a "stable" institution. Thus, BCEI was continuing in the same mode in which it had been set up—as a structure in the Black community which used money from predominantly White churches or the government to carry on its program with Black churchpeople. The program remained limited to that for which White sources were willing to pay, and it had not yet developed firm roots in the soil of the Black churches which it was designed to serve. Upon completion of the government grant, BCEI was closed.

EDUCATION

Center for Urban Education, Portland, Oregon: The Greater Portland Council of Churches organized the Center for Urban Encounter (CUE-P) in 1968 as a program unit of the Council for the purpose of "preparing men and women of the church to serve the city." Paul J. Schulze, a White clergyman on the Council's staff, was chosen as the original director. He was succeeded by Rodney I. Page, another clergyman, in 1970. CUE-P had three principal concerns: "(1) *Training* laymen and clergy for community service through urban encounter, reflection and action; (2) *Research* into the causes and cures for urban problems; and (3) *Experimentation* in the arts, liturgy and communication."[32]

Training was offered in METRO courses that met for six consecutive weeks on the same night. One series, METRO I, offered orientation to urban problems and ministry opportunities in four different locations around the metropolitan area. In addition, METRO II offered in 1970 a set of six-week courses on specific subjects—community organizing, institutional racism, the welfare dilemma, urban government, and national priorities in a world of conflict.

In July 1972 Page assumed other duties with the Council, and Stephen Schneider, a layman with educational background, became director on a part-time basis. A period of self-study by the CUE Commission resulted in adoption of a statement of "Guidelines and Objectives fo 1972-73," commitment to "education and involvement" as CUE's primary concern and change of the organization's name to "Center for Urban *Education*." Program priorities during the year were: land use, cable television, health care, criminal justice and alternatives to education.

This change in direction and focus was confirmed in a statement Schneider presented to the Board of Directors of Ecumenical Ministries of Oregon (which represented the reorganized Council of Churches) on December 14, 1974:

> The role of the Center for Urban Education is to provide to the religious community and to other concerned persons and groups assistance in discerning the shape of change, in determining what are the emergent social issues and public policy questions.[33]

He defined the uniqueness of CUE-P to lie "in making citizen participation more effective at the grass roots level by presenting perspectives that anticipate change." In January 1975 the Center was incorporated as a separate organization, still related to the Ecumenical Ministries of Oregon. Its principal activities for exploring public policy and social change were to be research, education, curriculum development and media. Funding no longer came from the sponsoring denominations, but from support by the ecumenical agency, and grants and contracts from other sources.

A grant from the United States Office of Education enabled CUE-P to extend its work in involvement learning methods in a program of Multi-Ethnic Heritage studies. The project was among 38 funded across the nation and was committed to produce a simulation game to introduce multi-ethnic heritage study, specific skill development modules to build upon skills introduced in the simulation, and a guide to provide detailed suggestions for organizing similar ethnic heritage study projects in other places. In addition to studies of specific ethnic groups in the Portland metropolitan area— Native Americans, European immigrants, Asian Americans, Blacks and Chicanos—CUE-P supported a film on the Thorne family, a pioneer Oregon family, from the days of nineteenth-century homesteading in Eastern Oregon to the present day.

In 1975 courses offered were Planning and the Citizen, Graphic Communications Workshop, and "Metro Up-Date," a successor to the METRO I course, as well as a two-day Clergy Orientation for new clergy and church professionals in the metropolitan area. In addition, the agency sponsored the New Theatre, where both the audience and the company "share in the creation of a dramatic event which we hope will reflect some aspect of MAN and his journey—what moves him, what amuses him, what inspires or defeats him, his glory and his tragedy."

A task force on the Status of Women in the Church produced a report and recommendations for local churches in the Portland area. Other reports were produced on Chicanos in Oregon, a survey of Asian-American schools and communities, and resources for citizen planners prepared for the course on citizen planning.

What had begun as a training program in urban mission and ministry for clergy and lay leaders had become by 1975 a flexible, creative educational agency using a wide variety of techniques and learning settings to address issues of social change in the greater Portland area. CUE-P retained its relationship to the ecumenical organization which had originally sponsored its program, but now had a full staff of professionals, augmented by other resource persons and researchers, to carry out its educational activities. Unlike most other action-training agencies, it used a variety of media techniques and the arts to involve people in changing their own images of society as well as working on specific public issues.[34]

"Ministry in Social Change" Graduate Program, St. Paul, Minnesota: Although theological seminaries shared in the development and sponsorship of several action-training agencies and programs, and most agencies conducted some form of program with seminary students, only "Ministry in Social Change" (MISC), the Twin City Graduate Program, was organized by seminaries solely as an academic program. After a planning year in

1968-69, five seminaries in the Twin Cities—Bethel Theological Seminary, Luther Theological Seminary, United Theological Seminary, Northwestern Theological Seminary and St. Paul Seminary—began operation in September 1969 of "an action training program in which constructive tension is maintained between the pastoral emphasis on individual needs and the social concern for the structures of political and economic power." Although principally designed as a one-year, full-time program for graduates of the five sponsoring seminaries, MISC also enrolled graduates of a number of other Protestant and Roman Catholic seminaries.

The format of the program included four different phases of curriculum: (1) input seminars on urban issues and aspects of ministry conducted by a wide variety of lay and clergy consultants recruited from local denominations, community councils, grassroots organizations, local, state and federal agencies, labor and industry, hospitals and clinics, colleges and universities; (2) 35 hours a week of supervised field engagements in two clinical settings, a church and a community organization; (3) three action-reflection papers, theologically and pastorally oriented; and (4) regular action-reflection seminars with other students in the program. The papers could be utilized in a major paper or thesis for the M.Th. or S.T.M. degree if the student desired.

MISC continued to offer this program through January 1975, when the faculties of the sponsoring seminaries decided that the D.Min. degree could be offered as an alternate track. This provided an action-training emphasis with social consciousness in the graduate professional education of clergy. Although the Action Training Coalition was doubtful about whether to enroll MISC as one of its members when the program first applied for membership in May 1970, the modest goals and format of this graduate program outlived the more grandiose goals and sophisticated methodology of many of the other agencies and programs. Unlike any of the others, it was academic and educational from the beginning, although concerned to use an action-reflection style for the development of skills in ministry.[35]

OTHER EMPHASES

Institute on the Church in Urban-Industrial Society, Chicago, Illinois: The Presbyterian Institute for Industrial Relations was organized in 1945 by Marshal Scott, a Presbyterian clergyman, as a training program to prepare clergy for mission with industrial workers. The program included seminars for clergy and some lay leaders in industrial areas, field placements for seminarians and a summer theological students-in-industry project, where seminarians had a chance to work in industry during the weekdays while sharing in evening and weekend seminars under Scott's leadership.

In 1966 the United Presbyterian Church in the U.S.A. and McCormick Theological Seminary, with the later collaboration of the Urban-Rural Mission Desk of the World Council of Churches, several national denominations and the Chicago Cluster of Theological Schools, organized the Institute on the Church in Urban-Industrial Society (ICUIS) as a resource and documentation center on the issues of urbanization and industrialization, and the mission programs, projects and activities being conducted around the world, as well as in the United States. The Institute had as its initial collection the books, periodicals and pamphlets on these subjects in the McCormick Seminary library, as well as materials collected through the years by Scott. Bobbi Wells, a United Presbyterian lay woman who had worked in the denomination's national missions office, came to ICUIS staff in 1968 and began to develop a more sophisticated system of information and documentation.

ICUIS was associated with PIIR until June 1973 when the two agencies were unified under the name of the Institute, with Richard P. Poethig, a White United Presbyterian who had returned from missionary service in the Philippines, as director. Since that time ICUIS has carried on a program of information and documentation that publishes a monthly *Abstract Service* on urban-industrial mission, which was sponsored until 1982 by the World Council of Churches office, and *Justice Ministries*, a quarterly on U.S. urban mission, as well as occasional papers. In keeping with the PIIR program ICUIS also offered courses and seminars in the Chicago Cluster of Theological Schools and conducted summer seminars and projects for seminary students. Visiting scholars and persons engaged in ministry and mission were able to use the resources of ICUIS, as well as to give lectures, briefings and courses for the seminaries and the Chicago community. While the Urban Training Center for Christian Mission was active, ICUIS assisted with its documentation and conducted some joint conferences. The Institute also engaged in some action and educational projects with denominational bodies and action organizations like the Chicago Committee on Human Rights in Asia. The use of seminary students in staff work for ICUIS also provided another avenue of education and training in urban-industrial mission in a world context.

When the Action Training Coalition began to consider the possibility of a joint information service, it hoped to be able to use the computer resources of the Department of Ministry of the National Council of Churches, based in New York City. However, this proved to be too expensive and too difficult to achieve. Therefore, when an Information Service Committee was organized during Consultation IV in Cincinnati, Bobbi Wells of ICUIS was chosen as a member of the committee, and agreed to serve as its liaison and reference person. When the Council of ATC voted to participate in the Information Service, beginning in December 1969, the National Council and

ICUIS were designated as the agencies for documentation storage. An ATC Index was created, and it was recommended that there be a category of classified information that would only be shared among ATC member agencies and programs. Subscriptions were to be solicited from the general public, libraries and institutions, with ATC picking up any deficit. Although this arrangement was to run a full year in 1970 before being evaluated and considered for renewal, the financial condition of the Coalition dictated a limited 60-day extension of the service for July and August, during which period attempts were made to sell it to other institutions and to promote it at the New Orleans meeting of librarians associated with the American Association of Theological Schools.

A study by the Information Services Committee in July 1970 showed that staff had received "amazingly little feedback from ATC directors," although member agencies had made specific requests. The committee's report was received by the National Delegate Assembly of ATC at Atlanta in October 1970 and the Council voted to continue the relationship on the basis of the report's recommendations: that the relationship with the National Council of Churches be renegotiated, that the system be seen as a cooperative one between ICUIS and ATC, and that it be viewed as "a non-profit self-supporting operation." ICUIS continued to operate an ATC Information System as part of its wider operation of information storage and documentation until the final ATC Consultation XII in Chicago in April 1973, and to receive the balances earned from the system. Following the dissolution of ATC, ICUIS files and abstracts became the chief reference source on the action-training movement, while the agency continued many of the processes developed in cooperation with ATC as well as some of the training responsibilities inherited from PIIR.[36]

Berkeley Center for Human Interaction, Berkeley, California: When the property that had been used for a national Episcopal training center for deaconesses in Berkeley became available, Episcopalians in the Bay Area organized the Berkeley Center for Human Interaction (BCHI) The purpose of the center was "to enable persons and institutions to face and respond creatively to change." The program of BCHI covered a wide span of training, as shown by the following summary of activity in 1968-69: personal growth (marathons, psychodrama, therapy groups, art dynamics, dance groups, art exhibits, Esalen programs), professional training (clergy musicians, seminarians, lay education, Navy and Air Force chaplains, interfaith fellowship on mysticism, clergy moving into new roles, sex education for professionals), organizational change and consultation with 14 different groups, community action (aging, community development, Alamo church Clergy, No Crap Movement, Blackstone Rangers, Saul Alinsky) and current issues (including racism, the Black church, the Resistance, dissent, Rhodesia, technology, image of women, new university, drugs). This yeasty combination was both a sign of the eclectic nature of the center's definition of "change" and the climate of Berkeley during the late 1960's.

Director of BCHI was Trevor Hoy, a White Episcopal clergyman, who was joined in the program by a network of consultants and resource persons, each of whom was encouraged to "do their own thing" and include it in the program. Hoy kept the facilities in constant use with a wide variety of short-term courses, workshops and programs. In addition, he and other staff members were able to provide consultant services in team building and organizational development.

BCHI was represented at all the national consultations of ATC from May 1968 through October 1969. However, when member agencies were asked in mid-1969 to provide papers describing the "particular action training philosophy and methodology" of their agency, the paper from BCHI was far broader and less committed to social change than that of any other member. During discussion of the Social Goal and Operational Goals of ATC during Consultation V in St. Louis in October 1969, Hoy argued for a definition of action training and a set of goals that would be broad enough to include all the activities carried on by the Berkeley Center. The results of that discussion were clearly in favor of a narrower definition of the purpose of action training that was focused on social, rather than personal, change. Consequently Hoy wrote to the officers withdrawing from membership in ATC.

BCHI (now called the Strong Center) continued its broad purposes and diverse programs. Having been part of the action-training movement for a short period, it continued to call its training for community action and on current issues by the title "action-training." However, its basic approaches were those of human relations, group dynamics and psychotherapy.[37]

Ecumenical Metropolitan Ministry, Seattle, Washington: At the time that the Ecumenical Metropolitan Ministry (EMM) was organized in Seattle as an interdenominational coalition in addition to the existing councils of churches, the seven denominations involved in the planning included "training" as one of the functions of the newly formed ecumenical agency. EMM was designed to bring together the separate urban ministry efforts of the sponsoring denominations, to produce greater economy of resources and to provide quick response to crisis situations.

Creation of an urban training center as part of EMM was stimulated by a study made by the Washington-Alaska Synod of the United Presbyterian Church in the U.S.A. in the fall of 1969. Half of the proposed budget of

$20,000 for an additional member of EMM staff was sought from the Board of National Missions of the UPC-USA, and the rest was to be provided by the synod, three presbyteries in the Seattle area and other denominations supporting EMM. Bryce Little, a White Presbyterian clergyman with overseas experience, began his service with EMM in August 1970, and the agency was represented at the ATC's Consultation VIII in Puerto Rico in March 1971. In line with EMM's priorities on resourcing local church action groups and developing lay empowerment, Little concentrated his attention on researching issues in the Seattle area, meeting with local congregations and clusters of churches, and training volunteers for Neighbors-in-Need, a food bank program developed by local clusters of churches to meet the needs of the "new poor," families that were unemployed as a result of the slowdown of production at Boeing Aircraft.

In June 1971 a "Pugetopolis Cluster Workshop" was held to encourage the development of local church clusters for ministry and mission. An international dimension was given to ecumenical mission in Seattle by the receipt of gifts of rice from Japanese churches for the Neighbors-in-Need food banks and the visit of Sadao Ozawa, a Japanese clergyman, made possible by the World Council of Churches. In the fall of 1972 Trinidad Herrera, president of the ZOTO community organization in the Tondo squatter area of Manila, gave two weeks to research the needs of the Filipino community in Seattle and to make contacts for EMM ministry. By 1973 the program of EMM had diversified to include churches in transition, revenue sharing, Skid Row, health issues, alcoholism, and support for the Trail of Broken Treaties campaign sponsored by Native Americans. Work continued with Neighbors-in-Need and local church clusters.

Action training for EMM was always a function carried on as part of a wider program of ecumenical mission and community organizing. Al Ward, an EMM staff member, described the agency's role as follows in 1973: "We have to be low visibility consultants to the poor, trainers of the church folk, and brokers or catalysts to put them together on particular efforts." Even after the United Presbyterian grant funds were ended and Little had left the staff, EMM continued to use training as one of the tools to resource churches and community groups for mission. All activities of EMM were a response to the charge to stay close to the poor. Its mandate was "to closely associate the agency with the community of the poor and the disadvantaged, in order to accurately convey the needs and feelings of that community to the church, the corporate community and all others who feel called to be responsive to both the need and the scriptural commands to do so."[38]

TWO ACTION-TRAINING AGENCIES THAT
TOOK A DIFFERENT COURSE

Two programs outside the Continental United States—CUT in Canada and PRISA in Puerto Rico— each took a different course than those already described. Each is still in operation, adapting its approach to new realities. CUT (Canadian Urban Training Project for Christian Service) had the advantage of being a national training center that continued to have the support of the three major Protestant denominations in Canada—Anglicans, Presbyterians and United Church—along with significant groups in the Roman Catholic Church. Regional training efforts have been organized under its umbrella, in collaboration with regional collectives of CUT graduates and other activists. PRISA (Programa de Renovacion y Investigacion Social para Adiestramiento en la Mision Cristiana) abandoned the attempt to be a training center or ecumenical agency, and became an ecumenical movement of Christian social activists concerned for economic, political and social justice in Puerto Rico. The movement continues to receive denominational and ecumenical financial support for its projects, but its members remain rooted in their own vocations, both inside and outside church structures. Although each was quite different and related to the particular situation in which it developed, the story of CUT and PRISA may be helpful both in understanding what happened to a part of the Action Training Coalition and in indicating something about future directions in urban mission strategy and training.[39]

Canadian Urban Training Project for Christian Service, Toronto, Canada: Three major denominations in Canada—Anglican Church of Canada, Presbyterian Church in Canada and United Church of Canada—brought together a group of people in Toronto in the spring of 1965 to discuss formation of a national urban training project for Canada, modeled on UTC in Chicago. After determining to go ahead with such a project on an experimental basis, these denominations provided funds to call a single staff member, Edgar F. File, a White United Church of Canada clergyman who had served both as an urban pastor and director of a church neighborhood center. File began service in September 1965, a year before the first training programs were to start. He conducted a two-week "reconnoitre" at UTC in Chicago during February 1966, corresponded with other programs in urban mission and training, and worked with a Curriculum Committee to develop a training pattern and style.

The purposes of CUT, according to its interim constitution adopted in May 1966, were as follows:

> To train and equip Christian clergy and laity to relate the work of the Christian church to the life of metropolitan areas.
> 2. To establish courses of study and training programs to the end that clergy and laity may better understand the urban culture and interpret the Christian faith within such culture.
> 3. To gather information concerning the life and problems of metropolitan areas, such as planning, urban renewal, slum clearance and the like, as this information relates to the work of the Christian Church and to make this information widely available.
> 4. To evoke new forms and patterns for Christian service, within existing church structures wherever possible.[40]

The structure provided both for members ("Christian churches which take official action to accept the Constitution and appoint Directors") and non-member participants ("Christian churches which take official action to appoint participant observers to the Board of Directors"), as well as for additional directors to represent groups like Woodgreen Neighborhood House, Ecumenical Institute of Canada, Canadian Council of Churches, the Social Planning Council of Metropolitan Toronto and the University of Toronto. Members in the first year were the three original sponsors plus the Ontario and Quebec Convention of Baptists. The Lutheran Council in Canada and the Canadian Friends Service Committee had observer status, and Roman Catholics were represented by at-large directors.

Training for the first program year in 1966-67 was described as follows:

> The basic *focus* of the project is upon the mission of the church to the metropolitan area and the kind of training needed for this mission. The unit of concern for training is the urban metropolis, not just the inner city, the suburbs, etc. The *task* through supervised in-service training and research, is to evoke new forms and patterns of Christian service within existing church structures wherever possible. The *method* of training is that of involvement, [sic], engagement with Urban society and reflection upon this involvement.[41]

Two patterns were planned for the year, both limited to clergy with five years of pastoral experience—two sessions in October-November and February-March of the short-term training program (called 6+2, because it included a six-week introduction to urban mission in Toronto, followed by a two-week recall program after six months of disciplined study and research in the trainee's home situation), and a long-term training for the whole year that would involve up to three trainees in a part-time supervised in-service placement in an area of specialized urban ministry, as well as taking part in the 6+2. The two short-term sessions were limited to ten each in the first year, and training sessions were held at Woodgreen Neighborhood House. A brief Urban Plunge on the UTC model was included as part of the orientation, and emphasis was placed on learning an action-training approach that could be evaluated during the recall.

An additional program element added during the summer of 1967 was a 12-week Summer Student Training Program, principally designed for seminary and social service students, that began with a two-week live-in and orientation, followed by weekly half-day sessions while the trainees had a summer job or volunteer involvement in community work and social action. The summer sessions closed with a three-day recall at the end of the period.

This basic pattern was followed in CUT training until 1970, when the first regional program of Community Action Training was held on-site in Winnipeg, Manitoba, after CUT had hired two additional staff trainers, Glynn Firth and Wally Brant, to assist in the program. The model adopted was a shortened version of the 6 + 2 which began with a two-week live-in devoted to residential training in analysis, strategizing and theological/value reflection, followed by a final week of residential training 2-4 months later (which came to be called the 2 + 1). Similar programs have been held yearly since that time. Being both shorter in duration and held in various locations across Canada, these programs have been able to enroll many persons who would not have come to Toronto for a longer period of time away from their own place of work.

A major shift in CUT's approach to training developed in 1973 when the Parish Action Training program was initiated after the first overall recall of CUT graduates from across Canada. The graduates saw themselves as part of the CUT network and wanted to share in the conduct of training in their own parts of the country. In addition, they were concerned that training be directed to action groups at the local level, including both church-related leaders and other community activists with whom they shared a common agenda. As a result of this opinion from the graduates, and a review process that included input from board members and supporting denominations, Canada was divided into five regions. Sister Noël O'Neill was hired half-time to coordinate the project and give leadership in Toronto, while quarter-time coordinators were retained in Halifax, Nova Scotia; Montreal, Quebec; Winnipeg, Manitoba; and Vancouver, British Columbia. Funding for this approach was made possible by two of the supporting denominations, the Anglicans and United Church, who had joined with other national church groups in 1972 to say, "We want CUT to take on an important further task of action training for laity and congregational committees who want to be better equipped for social action programs." As this idea developed, the development of training in Parish Action Training was in the hands of regional "collectives" of CUT graduates and associates, who received at least $1,500 annually, plus the services of national staff. In addition, continuing education funds of the supporting denominations were available for individual trainees. The collectives were accountable for their use of this funding to the CUT Board through the national staff.

A second national recall in 1976 was devoted to the question of information sharing. (The subject of the first one had been ministries in Skid Row areas.) With consultation from ICUIS in Chicago, the participants developed a Canadian Information Sharing Service (CISS), which developed the structure and policies for a national information network, under the title CONNEXIONS. The network published a monthly resource summary of organizations, materials and publications on Canadian and world issues. This project described itself as follows:

> CONNEXIONS is an independent project which supports networks of grassroots organizations and individuals across Canada who are working to create a just, human and equitable society. It provides a forum for socially active people to communicate through a regular publication summarizing their work. Consultations around specific issues complement this process. Although the impetus and major support come from Church organizations, CONNEXIONS strives to service a broader constituency. CONNEXIONS is made possible through subscriptions, church grants and the volunteer labour of a collective of about twelve people. French language documentation is usually presented in French.[42]

In a directory compiled in January 1979, CUT was able to identify 568 persons who had been part of its community action mobilization network since its founding in 1965. 110 were present and former Board members. The rest had taken part in training programs as follows:

Year-Long Internship (1966-78)	16
6+2 Training (1966-77)	94
2+1 Community Action Training (1970-78)	126
Summer Student Training Program (1967-78)	125
Supervised Field Education, Toronto School of Theology (1973-77)	23
Other Courses (1967-70, 1972, 1976-78)	74
	458

The majority of these persons were church professionals, lay leaders and local activists across the nation, but there have also been participants from Latin America, the Caribbean, United States, Africa, Japan, Korea and New Zealand. CUT also developed a significant group of persons who were related to actions for justice both inside and outside the churches. CUT continued to be used by the national mission boards of its sponsoring denominations in consultation and program development for their activities. A recent example of this was the development of a process and workbook for the emphasis of the Division of Mission in Canada of the United Church on "Mission and Ministry in the Metropolitan Core."

At a Board Retreat in September 1978, the following agenda items were identified and discussed: (1) shifts in the assumptions, style and design of CUT; (2) tensions in action training/pastoral care/social ministry training in education for ministry; (3) support of regional collectives and national CUT role; (4) false dichotomy between urban and rural; (5) making CUT resources more widely available; and (6) what CUT can do about movement of society in a totalitarian direction. Further discussion of these issues at the Annual General Meeting on March 15, 1979, resulted in the following resolution:

> Whereas: (1) There are now five hundred people spread across the country who have participated in CUT related activities—400 Grads and 100 Board Members; (2) There are now identifiable CUT related groups in at least six Canadian provinces; (3) Some members of these groups have expressed a strong desire to participate more fully in shaping the policy and curriculum of CUT; (4) It has come to our attention that many CUT graduates have burned themselves out due in part to lack of local social, psychological and spiritual support. Therefore be it RESOLVED that the Board of C.U.T. facilitate a three year consultative process to develop a new structure and a new mode of operating so that the wider C.U.T. constituency can participate fully in policy-making and curriculum design and can in effect "take over" and "own" the C.U.T. network.

This three-year process began with circulation of a working paper that outlined underlying values and principles, delineated some goals "hopefully to be achieved by the Consultative Process," and raised 14 questions "to Stimulate Discussion and Involve you More in this Process." This document was responded to by present Board members, regional groups and contacts, and selected grads. In September 1980 a consultation with representatives from regional groups and others solicited by national staff discussed the responses to this document and developed ideas for future direction.

The CUT Board continued to have strong representation from the three original national sponsors—Anglicans, Presbyterians and United Church —along with representatives of Toronto School of Theology, Canadian Religious Conference of Ontario, a Roman Catholic group, and Ecumenical Forum. Therefore, this consultative process was seeking to develop a way in which what continued to be a national project with strong support from national denominations could move from a centralized form of organization to a more participatory format in which trainees and regional collectives could help to shape the policy and curriculum. This present stage was reached as a result of experience in a variety of programs that maintained the church relationships and focus that were envisaged at the beginning of the project in 1965.

PRISA (Programa de Renovacion y Investigacion Social para Adiestramiento en la Mision Cristiana), Puerto Rico: In Spanish the word "prisa" means "in a hurry." Since the word "training" translates to *adiestramiento*, it is easy to understand why the acronym chosen for this pilot project in training on the island of Puerto Rico survived better than its full title or the original idea of being an urban training center. Like other agencies and programs already described, PRISA grew out of the Pilot Diocese Program of the Episcopal Church. Along with Mision Industrial de Puerto Rico (Puerto Rico Industrial Mission), with which it often collaborates, PRISA was created in 1968 as a proposal for specialized ministry by Thomas Anthony, a Canadian Anglican priest who was coordinator of the Pilot Diocese Program for the Diocese of Puerto Rico. Anthony had full support for his efforts from Francisco Reus Froylan, bishop of the Episcopal Diocese of Puerto Rico, and both the planning phases and the first two years of operation received both national and diocesan funds under the Pilot Diocese Program.

The initial process of forming and operating an urban training center in Puerto Rico represented the attempt to investigate whether a model that was being developed on the mainland could be imported to *La Isla*. The Episcopal diocese began its effort by hiring a Puerto Rican clergyman of the Evangelicos Unidos (a Puerto Rican denomination related to both the United Church of Christ and the Evangelical United Brethren in the United States), Alfonso A. Roman, to conduct a feasibility study during 1968. With the help of an Ad Hoc Committee, Roman planned a cafeteria of training programs in 1969—laymen and clergy in a housing project in the San Juan area, programs of social awareness with university student work organizations, short seminars on social issues and post-graduate training for theological seminary graduates. This grew to a more developed curriculum in 1970, prepared by a two-person professional staff assisted by a full-time administrative secretary.

Two parallel processes were initiated by Roman and Anthony both to assist in planning the program and to secure denominational and financial support. The first was the formation of the Ad Hoc Committee, which included representatives of the Episcopal Diocese, the Baptists, the Lutherans, the Roman Catholics, the Bible Society, and an assortment of Christian laymen and women who taught social sciences at the university level or were involved in government or community programs. George D. Younger, who was still a consultant in evaluation for MUST in New York City, was brought to Puerto Rico twice during 1968 to consult with Roman and the Ad Hoc Committee, as well as to visit with Evangelical and Roman Catholic leaders. On July 10-11, 1969, a group of denominational leaders gathered at the Institute for Community Organization Training in Cayey, along with a group of clergy who were preparing to attend UTC in Chicago in the fall. The denominational leaders were polite, and a couple agreed to join the Ad Hoc Committee. However, they continued to consider the training program to be an Episcopal project and gave no direct support from their own budgets. Other denominations were willing to have their clergy and lay leaders involved in PRISA training, and they permitted national urban mission funds to be spent for projects associated with PRISA, but the

Episcopalians' hope that PRISA would become ecumenical on the basis of official denominational sponsorship and support did not materialize.

The second process, which had far greater influence on the future of PRISA, was the recruitment of a group of 18 Evangelical and Roman Catholic clergy and women workers to attend the Urban Training Center for Christian Mission in Chicago during the fall of 1968. Carl Siegenthaler and Father Victor Nazario, a Puerto Rican Roman Catholic priest associated with CIDOC in Cuernavaca, Mexico, came to Puerto Rico in July to conduct a week of orientation for those planning to be in the training group. The group took part in a four-day urban plunge in San Juan before going to Chicago for a cold ten weeks as part of the regular 4-3-3 sequence in September-December 1968. Each participant worked on a project in ministry for their own situation in Puerto Rico, while Roman, who accompanied the group, was developing the final proposal for PRISA as a training program. Siegenthaler and Nazario worked with the group in Spanish while they were at UTC, and each person was asked to gather a reflection group in their own situation to assist in evaluation and other planning. One result of the UTC training was a variety of local projects in mission, as well as a network of communication among those conducting them. Another result was development of a mutual interest between Roman and PRISA, and the local projects. Several of the UTC alumni joined the PRISA Board. As the official denominational representatives drew farther away from PRISA, those who were related to local projects increasingly became both the policy-makers and the support.

When Younger consulted with Roman and others interested in the establishment of PRISA during 1968, he stressed over and over again that urban training was a United States model that would need to take indigenous form in Puerto Rico. The same emphasis was made by UTC staff during the training in Chicago. Although the form of the initial proposal and the method of operation during 1968-70 was in the style of mainland bureaucracies, the colonial situation of denominational bodies still tied to United States denominations and the political status of Puerto Rico in relation to the United States government were pressing for both a different definition of the situation addressed and a different kind of organization to serve the churches and their leaders.

The contemporary question of "status" for Puerto Rico began when the United States acquired the island from Spain in 1898 following the Spanish-American War. Although the U.S. was not one of the historic European colonial powers and had actually gained its own independence in an anti-colonial Revolutionary War, it was willing to assume political and military control of Puerto Rico, which had already, in the words of Irvin Torres, survived "the Caribe Indians, Spanish totalitarianism; French, Dutch, and British pirate attacks; periodic hurricanes," to which it added "economic exploitation and cultural aggression and assorted other calamities."[43]

Although Puerto Ricans received United States citizenship in 1917 by vote of the United States Congress, enabling them to be drafted and serve in the armed forces, the question of self-government was not raised until 1950, when Congress granted permission to draft a constitution which would then be approved by the United States. In 1952 Puerto Rico became a *Libre Estado Asociado* (" Free Associated State," which is usually called in the United States a "Commonwealth"), maintaining many of the economic advantages of a colonial dependent while gaining a measure of political independence. Since that time the major issue of political life in Puerto Rico has been the question of "status" —whether the island should maintain its present relation with the United States, be wholly integrated into the U.S. system as a 51st state or gain its independence as a separate nation. Socialist and nationalist parties and organizations in Puerto Rico favor the course of independence, and are thus called *independentistas*. The other major political parties, which have ties to both the Democratic and Republican Parties on the mainland, are either committed to maintaining *status quo* or statehood. Although *independentistas* have only a minority of the population as members and have not won the majority either in elections or referenda on Puerto Rico's status, they represent a large sentiment among the people.[44]

Christianity in Puerto Rico is intimately involved in the island's colonial history, for Roman Catholicism was brought by the Spaniards and Evangelical Christianity by the United States. Although Protestant missionaries took their Gospel to the poor, who had been largely ignored by Catholicism, they taught the work ethic and encouraged middle-class aspirations. As they moved away from the colonial pattern of missionary control, which had originally divided the island into six geographical districts of denominational influence, the mainland denominations set up a pattern of "decentralization," in which Puerto Rican leaders who had been trained by Americans and favored continued relationship with U.S. denominational structures were established in positions of executive responsibility. However, this pattern of turning over control to Puerto Rican executives and church bodies did not bring freedom from colonial dependence on financial support from the United States or from the slavish maintenance of theological and political positions taught by missionaries. Thus, when mainland denominations consulted with Puerto Rican church leaders or permitted them to decide their own policies and programs, they were actually hearing the echo of their own voice. Interestingly enough, PRISA itself as a project established on a North American model with financial support from the United States, proved to be a prime example of this kind of liberal "anti-colonialism" at the time of its inception.

In April 1970, with the Episcopal grant coming to the end of its three-year guarantee for a "feasibility study" and a "pilot project," PRISA had been unsuccessful both in efforts to arrange training with the major denominations on the island or to secure their financial support and steady membership on the Board. Instead, its staff and Board were finding greater response from the members of the UTC training group and other pro-*independentista* clergy and laity in both Evangelical and Roman Catholic churches, as well as their politically oriented collaborators and the urban and rural poor with whom they all were working. A decision was made to continue to maintain a staff on a subsistence basis, while trying to secure financing for both PRISA and the various local projects in which PRISA's supporters were engaged. During this period, in the words of one of the UTC alumni who has continued to play a strong role in PRISA, the group moved from "ideological naivete" through a period of "politicization" in which they searched for a new ideological perspective to a stance as a movement that saw itself as "an arm of the workers in the struggle for liberation."

During 1970-71, while PRISA was working with ATC to be recognized as the Third World Caucus, the process of politicization was beginning, although the church workers in PRISA still held hopes for change through a ministry of presence and service. At the time that PRISA served as host for the ATC at Assembly VIII on March 22-24, 1971, this duality was evident. Background statements were made by Puerto Rican and Dominican Republic political activists committed to anti-colonialism and socialism, who saw the churches and their people as potential allies in the liberation struggle. Then, on field trips designed to point out the extent of United States imperialism and neo-colonialism, the participants were taken to El Cano Martin Pena in Metropolitan San Juan and to Comerio, where the Methodist Church and Dominican fathers at the Roman Catholic parish had organized a community development project. In addition, fishermen fighting against the U.S. Navy's use of the island of Culebra for target practice brought their testimony to the group. In the next several years the optimism and naivete of the church activists was challenged as they faced active opposition from the Evangelical Council, which was in the hands of virulent anti-Communists, indifference from most church officials, and a concerted attack from political forces opposed to independence. Within a short time the Methodist and Roman Catholic clergy leaders had to leave Comerio, and PRISA began to move to a more activist stance as a movement of Christians committed to political struggle in Puerto Rico.

PRISA has described itself as "a coalition of diverse ecumenical projects which are involved in the search for alternatives and liberating structures, which may produce the changes necessary in Puerto Rico's economic, political and social milieu, so that equitable development may really occur." The movement operates with a minimal staff composed of a national coordinator and secretary, who are concerned for coordination, assistance and communication for the local projects, as well as publications. All persons actively involved in the projects that are part of the coalition compose the national assembly, which meets annually to establish priorities, evaluate achievements, and engage in sharing and analysis. The assembly elects the

Junta (Board), which establishes secretariats or working groups as necessary and elects a committee of coordination to work closely with the national coordinator.

The heart of PRISA has been in the local projects which make up the coalition, all of which include both church and non-church participants. The fishing project "Victor Rojas" attempted to develop a new approach to that industry and form a new generation of fishermen. The Ecumenical Agricultural Projects of Lares in the central area of the island tried to develop a new form of *fincas* (family farms) to make Puerto Rico more self-sufficient for food and fiber. The Ecumenical Communications Workshop produced three weekly programs heard over eleven radio stations. The Citizens Committee Against Pollution was an environmental project rallying citizens against the damage created by the petrochemical and pharmaceutical industries and other sources of pollution in the northern sector of the island. The handicrafts workshop "Guasabara" in Bayamon and the "El Seco" Workshop for graphic arts in the central region both gave attention to preserving cultural roots of the Taino Indians, African Blacks and Spaniards, and expressing the protests of the poor and oppressed. In addition to organizational work in poor communities and squatter areas concentrated on consciousness raising and leadership development, projects in the coalition were also trying to collaborate in labor organizing through the Trade Union Project, in promoting sports as a means of national expression through the Sports Project, and in reaching university students through the Students-Center Project.

Although continuing to face opposition both within the churches and from the wider society, the activists in the PRISA coalition remained loyal to the Christian faith, while working closely with non-Christians, and maintained a commitment to political, economic, social and cultural change. They worked closely with the Puerto Rico Industrial Mission in holding church-sponsored hearings to call attention to the ecological and social damage that would result from copper mining. In collaboration with the National Council of Churches in the United States, they called attention to the colonial situation of *La Isla* and took a vital role in both the Commission on Justice, Liberation and Human Fulfillment and the Theology in the Americas Project. Most of PRISA's active leaders retained their church appointments or lived on a subsistence basis in relation to the communities and projects where they are working. PRISA has been closely related to the struggle of fishermen on the island of Vieques against the U.S. Navy, which uses its beaches and coastal waters for maneuvers and target practice. While most of those in PRISA have been associated with one of the *independentista* political parties (which also identify themselves as socialists), they have tried to maintain a stance in which they are not a front for any party or political group but keep their closest relationship with the people in local communities, for whom they serve as a bridge to the churches, the political parties and the international community. PRISA can truly be called an "ecumenical movement," both in its ability to bring diverse groups of Christians together and in its commitment to the kind of "secular ecumenism" in which all who work for human liberation make common cause.

The following represent important contributions which both CUT and PRISA made in the development of action training.

(1) *Both programs showed a willingness to adapt to their national reality.* Although urban training had developed out of a particular period in urban mission in the churches in the United States, both Canadian and Puerto Rican action-training programs tried from the start to keep in touch with the realities of their own national situation and to make sure that their training would meet the needs of their people. In CUT this meant a slower pace of development that tried to be sure of its grasp of Canadian issues, and that spread across the same continental distance as in the United States over a longer period of time. Where regional and metropolitan training was developing in the United States within a year after UTC began its first training program, CUT did not develop a regional program until four years after its start. With PRISA the whole bureaucratic model of an agency with full-time staff and a cadre of trainees was abandoned for a collective leadership with subsistence staff and a coalition of local programs as collaborators. The pace and direction of program development since that time has been determined from the bottom up and the outside in, rather than coming from a training "center." The major issue for all activity has been the status of Puerto Rico in relation to the United States, rather than "mission" agendas set by denominations still related in a colonial manner to the United States.

(2) *Both programs chose to decentralize as a result of challenges from trainees.* It is instructive that the principal—and first—national urban training program in the United States called itself the "Urban Training Center." This placed initiative with staff and sponsors from the beginning, and placed all trainees—and other centers, as they developed—in the position of being "local," "regional," "in the field" and away from the center. Both CUT and PRISA have permitted themselves to be challenged by those whom they trained and with whom they felt themselves linked in common action, so that they decentralized both decision-making and activity to the local communities where action occurs. This was not a natural development in either case, but the national program was willing to respond to the challenge with serious structural change.

(3) *Both programs maintained the tension between their commitment to action and social change and the institutional stance of the churches.* Although the common allegation is that specialized ministries formed during the 1960's (including agencies that were part of ATC) abandoned the institutional church in favor of social activism, neither CUT nor PRISA was willing to let go of either pole of this dialectic. Because their commitment to the Gospel was sincere, they were willing to continue to confront the church

structures in their country while maintaining fellowship, even when others tried to cut them off or deny what they were saying and doing. Yet each program succeeded in keeping faith with communities and social activists among oppressed groups in their country. PRISA has seen its role as a "bridge;" CUT was ready to be "taken over" and "owned" by those in whose cause it labored.

(4) *Both programs adopted an ecumenical stance, both within the community of faith and with those outside it.* Although both Canada and Puerto Rico had official ecumenical organizations, CUT and PRISA brought together a wider diversity of religious leaders and groups around people's issues than they had done. In fact, PRISA did so against the embittered opposition of the Evangelical Council. Neither stopped with the Faith and Order definition of Christian unity and ecumenism as joint action of Christian bodies. Instead, they went on to practice a "secular ecumenism" in which all who shared a common concern for social justice were able to make common cause in common action. Neither was able to work out all the theological consequences of this position in their reflection, but each shared the same quality of ideological commitment.

OTHER TRAINING PROGRAMS ORGANIZED OR PROPOSED

Fourteen urban training programs were organized or proposed in the period between 1964 and 1968, thirteen of which belonged at one time or another to the Action Training Coalition. The great majority of these, like those which survived, were developed under ecumenical sponsorship. Three which had purposes that included action training were developed by denominational agencies, while CHART in Cincinnati was unique in having university sponsorship throughout its career. Many of the agencies whose history is recounted in this section made important contributions to the development of action training and to the Action Training Coalition, but they did not survive the serious cutbacks of the early 1970's.

ECUMENICAL SPONSORSHIP

Commission on Ecumenical Education, Greater Cleveland Council of Churches, Cleveland, Ohio: As part of the reorganization of the Greater Cleveland Council of Churches in 1965, Rev. William Voelkel, a White clergyman of the United Church of Christ who had served ten years in that city in the interdenominational Inner City Protestant Parish, joined the Council staff as director of its Commission on Ecumenical Education (CEE). Voelkel proposed organization of "an Institute for Metropolitan Ministries," which would provide "an intermediary setting between practical experience and a formal academic process" for different functional vocational groups. The training proposed included orientation to urban mission for both laity and clergy; training for two groups of volunteers—those serving in ongoing institutional programs and those working in groups organized around community needs and action; training for professionals engaged in service in the metropolitan community in fields like education, social work, medicine, law and government; and education for seminary interns assigned to urban posts in the metropolitan area. The main purpose was "to help equip the 'people of God' (meaning here both unordained and clergy) for ministries in the urban community."

In his proposal, as well as in the title of the commission that directed the program, Voelkel avoided the word "training" because it "implies a course of instruction that offers methods and skills that are directly applicable to one's defined role." He saw the focus of CEE programs to be "largely analytical and integrative, helping its students in the midst of practical experience to analyze and evaluate the urban ethos in which they live and move and have their being and to search out with them a meaningful theological framework for their decision making."

The program began in the fall of 1965 and lasted for three years through the fall of 1968, when Voelkel joined the staff of the Cleveland Internship Program (CIP), where he was later instrumental in helping to organize Action Training Network of Ohio (ATN). The Commission on Ecumenical Education had official representatives from the following denominational bodies that were members of the Greater Cleveland Council of Churches: African Methodist Episcopal, American Baptist, National Baptist Convention in the USA, Inc., Disciples of Christ, Evangelical United Brethren, Lutheran Church in America, American Lutheran Church, Methodist, Protestant Episcopal, United Church of Christ, and United Presbyterian. Associate relationships were maintained with Greek Orthodox, Inner City Protestant Parish, University Christian Movement and Church Women United.

During its three years CEE offered a wide variety of programs; a seminar for suburban parents serving as Friendly Town hosts, a seminar for church executives on issues of justice and power, retreats for Christian educators, a seminar for new clergy, a seminar for summer service students, and a series of training sessions or retreats with ecumenical groups or local churches in the Cleveland area. A luncheon series on "Ethical Problems in Decision Making," was held with business men in the downtown area. A forum on "Technology and Community Vitality" was sponsored in March 1967 for community and religious leaders. In cooperation with CIP, lay leaders from ten congregations, including six whose pastors were enrolled in the CIP program, participated in 1966-67 in Training of Laity for Mission in a Metropolitan Community, where they were exposed to central city problems, given a model of urban analysis and then divided into three teams to plan a strategy for mission in relation to the problem area.

In cooperation with the Protestant Ministry to Poverty, sponsored by the Council's Commission on Metropolitan Affairs, CEE conducted a workshop in the fall of 1966 for speakers who would interpret the home mission study theme, "Poverty and Affluence," in local churches. In April 1967 a Workshop on Communication Network in Cleveland's Racial Crisis briefed key people from the city and the suburbs who had been involved in the civil rights and poverty struggles, and took the first steps in organizing a network of suburban support groups and starting a newsletter for interpretation in the face of potential ghetto violence.

CEE built on existing relationships in the Cleveland metropolitan area and used the Greater Cleveland Council of Churches as its organizational base. When its programs could no longer be supported by the Council budget, Voelkel moved to CIP and took along the experience gained in three years of urban education and training in Greater Cleveland.

Proposed West Coast Urban Training Center, Bay Area, California: Only one of the many urban training agencies or projects proposed during the 1960's was abandoned after the planning phase. This was the proposed West Coast Urban Training Center (WCUTC) considered by denominational, ecumenical and foundation executives in the San Francisco Bay Area of California. The interest of the Ford Foundation, expressed in May 1965, resulted in drafting a proposal and formation of a board. Further discussion of a possible national training organization, in cooperation with the Urban Training Center for Christian Mission in Chicago, resulted in clear indications that Ford assistance was unlikely and national denominations would only support a more local effort.

In January 1966, Francis Geddes, a White United Church of Christ minister, was hired as full-time coordinator to continue coordination of planning efforts and to pursue funding possibilities. The proposal saw the purpose of WCUTC to be assisting churches to be a "force for transformation and creation in our cities." Training programs would include clergy and lay leaders and would provide for interns to spend three months to two years working with urban institutions, including local churches, to have a chance for complete involvement in some segment of urban society.

Original support was promised by Methodists, United Church of Christ and American Baptists, as well as the Methodist-related Glide Foundation. Other groups that participated in the planning included: Disciples of Christ, Episcopalians and Presbyterians; all the major ecumenical organizations in the Bay Area (San Francisco, Oakland, Berkeley Area and Santa Clara Council of Churches); the Laymen's School of Religion; and the seminaries related to the Graduate Theological Union. Links were also sought with COMMIT, the urban training program organized in the Los Angeles area.

During the last six months of 1966 a Job Development Project was conducted in Marin City following street violence in that ghetto housing project. A Job Workshop was held for youth, and orientation was given to lay persons seeking job leads. In February through May 1967 eight Urban Exploration and Action Seminars were held with nine congregations in Berkeley, but a Community Action Institute planned for June in Oakland had to be cancelled for lack of sufficient registration.

After exploring linkage with institutions in the Bay Area—Berkeley Center for Human Interaction, the Laymen's School of Religion, Graduate Theological Union and Glide Urban Center—the Board decided in April, 1967, to phase out the proposal for an urban training center in June of that year. Principal reasons given were:

1. lack of cooperative urban policy, or structure necessary for the development of a training center among the several denominations
2. lack of funds regionally and nationally from both denominations and foundations

Although seeing a real need for the proposed center, Geddes concluded in his final report that "there is no willingness on the part of denominations to pool existing or future resources for training or agree on a common urban work policy or strategy." Without the necessary cooperation from the denominations, an ecumenical program was impossible.

Midwest Training Network, Kansas City, Missouri: Few action-training programs had as solid a base in ecumenical and denominational mission agencies and area theological seminaries as did the Midwest Training Network in Kansas City. The development of the training agency, which was originally called Training for Ecumenical Action and Ministry (TEAM), came after almost two years of planning by an experienced team of persons who were already heavily involved in urban mission in the Kansas City metropolitan area. Richard Nesmith, a White Methodist clergyman with background in church planning and research, was a member of the faculty of St. Paul School of Theology, while also serving as consultant for the local ecumenical agency, Metropolitan Inter Church Agency (MICA). Others who contributed heavily to planning for the training program were Vann Anderson, also a White Methodist clergyman who was on the staff of the Methodists' Inner-City Parish; Kenneth Waterman, a White Presbyterian clegyman serving an inner-city church; William Case, who was director of the Center for Renewal of St. Paul School of Theology; and Maurice Culver, who was director of the local unit of Project Equality, an interfaith program to secure affirmative action in employment from suppliers of goods and services for religious institutions and churches.

St. Paul School of Theology already had experience with training seminary students for inner-city mission, using both some of its own faculty members, and inner-city clergy and other adjunct faculty. Out of this background they hoped to develop a broader front of denominational support, as well as to provide resources for efforts at action and teaching in metropolitan Kansas City. This was largely sparked by W. Paul Jones, a White professor of theology at the seminary.

The program began in the fall of 1967 with a series of orientation programs for inner-city activists and lay leaders, combined with seminars at St. Paul. When Nesmith left the seminary for a position with the Methodist denomination nationally, his successor was not as committed to action training or the coalition that had been developed to support the TEAM program. The Board was reorganized in 1969 to establish the Midwest Training Network (MTN), which still had strong support from St. Paul but included only those denominations that were interested in action training. Robert Beech, a White United Presbyterian clergyman, was called to serve as its director, with a mandate to develop training programs not only in metropolitan Kansas City but in other parts of the Midwest.

Although Beech and his staff worked diligently to develop training contracts and continued to cooperate with St. Paul and other area seminaries, some of those who had worked hardest from its earliest days to develop TEAM and MTN left the area. In addition, a series of explosive racial incidents in the Kansas City area led denominational leaders to be more cautious about involvement with mission programs that were active in issues of race and poverty or that fostered advocacy rather than service. The agency ran out of funding at the close of 1970, the staff members were released, and, for all intents and purposes, action training in the metropolitan Kansas City area stopped at that point, except in the St. Paul curriculum. Jones, who had been active in ATC from its earliest days as chairman of the Clergy Education Task Force, retained an interest in the Coalition and continued membership for Community 33, a small residential community which he had organized for community organization activity in the city. However, this also dissolved by December 1971, bringing the action-training experience to a close.

Strategy Training in Renewal, Rochester, New York: The action-training program in Rochester, New York, grew out of ecumenical planning that was attempting to give a new face to the Council of Churches in that city, and was intimately connected with the organization of FIGHT by Saul Alinsky's Industrial Areas Foundation after the urban riots of the summer of 1964. When the Rochester Area Council of Churches was reorganized in 1961, its Committee on the Inner City, along with the interdenominational Inner

City Pastors Fellowship, established an Inner City Board. In 1964 Herbert W. White, a White Presbyterian Church in the U.S.A. clergyman, was hired as director of the Board for Urban Ministry of the Council. After the riots BUM was responsible for establishing a contract with Industrial Areas Foundation to bring in Ed Chambers as the organizer of a Black inner-city community organization, which named itself FIGHT. From September 1966 through April 1967 FIGHT was engaged in a struggle with the Eastman Kodak Company over the hiring of Black workers.

During the first months of 1967 White and the members of BUM, which had been sponsoring an Urban Seminar for students at Colgate Rochester Divinity School, joined with others to begin planning a joint urban training program for students at CRDS and St. Bernard's Seminary, the Roman Catholic diocesan seminary. The planning group included William R. Nelson, a White American Baptist clergyman who was both Teaching Minister of the Lake Avenue Baptist Church and a lecturer at CRDS, and P. David Finks, who had just been named by Fulton J. Sheen, the Roman Catholic bishop, as his Episcopal Vicar for Urban Ministry. This program, which was called Strategy Training for Renewal (STIR), enrolled 15 Protestant and 15 Roman Catholic students for the 1967-68 academic year. The students met every other week with urban specialists in an ongoing seminar. In addition, they spent up to 20 hours each week in field work under the direction of pastoral or community supervisors in churches and community programs in three sectors of the city—Northwest, Southeast and Southwest. In March the students and staff took a three-day field trip to visit churches, community organizations and ecumenical programs in Chicago.

BUM had been an exclusively Protestant operation as part of the Council of Churches. Its principal participation and support came from Presbyterians, Episcopalians, Methodists, Reformed Church in America, United Church of Christ and American Baptists. In order to involve Roman Catholics, who were becoming more heavily devoted to ecumenical efforts in the inner city, the Joint Office for Urban Ministry was organized to include the Roman Catholic diocese. An Ecumenical Lay Seminar on Urban Issues, which also involved Jewish participation, was held for 45 adults during 1967-68 and expanded to 75 participants in 1968-69. In addition, RISK, a loosely organized coalition of the city's ecumenical youth ministries, sponsored a ten-week seminar for staff members in the fall of 1968 under the auspices of Nazareth College.

By the spring of 1969 JOUM was receiving many requests for consultation and training. The participants had already learned that training needed to be more than information sessions and should include practical development of analytical techniques combined with better understanding of group dynamics. The evaluation of the first year of STIR training had also recommended "giving priority in training for mission to the continuing education of laity and resident clergy." At this point JOUM considered a proposal to hire a full-time staff member for lay and clergy training.

Larry Coppard, a White Roman Catholic layman who had been serving as community minister in a local parish involved in STIR, was chosen to start a pilot program in training in June 1969, along with assistance from several women religious and other staff members working in inner-city situations. In the fall of 1969 Coppard and his associates developed Metropolitan Action Training, a five-session orientation program for persons seeking ways to meet the metropolitan crisis, which focused on analysis of the Rochester situation and ways of developing strategy for social change. In addition, they prepared a model for training with White congregations to deal with issues of institutional racism.

Early in 1970 the ecumenical framework that had developed the STIR training for seminarians, supported the organization of FIGHT and a variety of ecumenical strategies in urban mission, and cooperated in JOUM came apart. The Council of Churches reorganized its Board for Urban Ministry into the service-oriented Genesee Ecumenical Ministries (GEM), while Roman Catholics pulled back from JOUM to a diocesan Office for Human Development. Coppard, Sr. Barbara Steinwachs and others who had participated in the training efforts organized Urbex Affiliates to continue the training and consultation contracts that were still coming from Roman Catholic parishes, but this effort ended sometime in late 1971 or early 1972.

Ministry of Urban Concerns, Denver, Colorado: In 1967 four denominations decided to unify their existing inner-city ministries in Denver under the title Core City Ministries. A. MacRaven Warner, a White Disciples of Christ minister who had been executive of the Manhattan Division of the Council of Churches of New York City, was called to serve as executive. The program was attached to the Denver Area Council of Churches by its sponsors, Disciples of Christ, United Church of Christ, Methodists and United Presbyterians.

In 1968 the Denver Area Council of Churches was merged with the Colorado Council of Churches. Under the umbrella of a newly formed Metropolitan Division, Core City Ministries joined with the former Department of Social Services to furnish ministry in the city, especially among the poor and with Black and Hispanic minorities.

The Ministry of Urban Concerns (MUC) of Core City Ministries was established to interest clergy and laity of suburban churches in inner-city problems. Because it planned to conduct orientation and training as part of this program, MUC applied for membership in the Action Training Coalition when it was organized in 1968.

Warner and the Cabinet of Executives were in conflict over the direction to be taken by MUC. In addition to urban training, the agency was active in organizing the Model Cities Residents Participation program and boycotts to support California lettuce workers and Colorado carnation workers. The position of director of MUC was terminated in June 1969, and the basic program of church ministry to the inner-city was turned over to Church Community Service.

Taskforce for Research, Urban Strategy and Training, Richmond, Virginia: At the initiative of several local clergy and lay persons, the Church Extension Committee of Hanover Presbytery of Richmond, Virginia requested experimental funds from the Board of National Ministries of the Presbyterian Church U.S. to begin an urban strategy project in 1967. The proposed name was to be Center for Urban Strategy and Training in Mission. An interim board was set up, with both funding and representatives from the following denominations: African Methodist Episcopal, African Methodist Episcopal Zion, Episcopal, National Baptist Convention, Southern Baptist Convention, United Church of Christ, United Methodist, United Presbyterian Church in the U.S.A. and the Roman Catholic Diocese of Richmond. The board also had representatives from Union Theological Seminary, Presbyterian School of Christian Education, Graduate School of Religion of Virginia Union University, Virginia Institute of Pastoral Care and Virginia Council of Churches.

The organization was incorporated as the Taskforce for Renewal, Urban Strategy and Training, but the word "Renewal" was quickly changed to "Research" to reflect the functions to be performed. The chief objectives of the program were defined as follows:

> 1. To search into the distinctive needs of the metropolitan citizen and the resources of the church and community available to meet these needs.
> 2. To develop strategies by which the whole church can fulfill its mission to meet the needs of the whole person in the urban community; and
> 3. To offer specialized training for clergy and laity and to offer consultant services to boards, agencies, congregations and denominations.[45]

Richard F. Perkins, a White Presbyterian Church U.S. clergyman who had assisted in developing the proposal while pastor of Bon Air Presbyterian Church, was called as executive director, assisted by Irving R. Stubbs, a White clergyman who had been ordained in the United Church of Christ and had served Presbyterian Church U.S. congregations in Virginia and North Carolina. Both men had received NTL training and were active in evangelism and church development efforts of the denomination.

During the pilot year the staff was active in research into urban needs and resources in metropolitan Richmond and served as consultants to a variety of local programs and denominational units. Several training programs were also conducted during 1967-68: a Technopolitan Mission Seminar, in cooperation with the Board of National Ministries of the Presbyterian Church U.S., using Marshal L. Scott of the Presbyterian Institute of Industrial Relations, Chicago; classes in denominational leadership schools; four courses on various aspects of the church and the city at Union Theological Seminary and the Presbyterian School of Christian Education; two training programs in human relations with Neighborhood Advisory Councils and the staff of the Richmond Redevelopment and Housing Authority; and summer training for two groups of church workers in Richmond.

The program was trying to work with an interracial situation both in the churches and in the community. Therefore, in 1968 TRUST added a Black staff member, Milton A. Reid, pastor of Trinity Baptist Church, Norfolk, Virginia, who was also active in community development activities in that city. Emmanuel Last was used with the staff as a consultant for its own development. Cooperative relationships were established with the Southern regional training program being organized as ACTS of Memphis, Tennessee, and with METC of Washington, D.C., for which TRUST provided consultation in organizational development and board training.

At the close of its first year of operation TRUST reexamined the work it had been doing in urban strategy and training. Its goal had been shortened to the following "capsulization" :

> TRUST seeks to relate church and metropolis in ways that will encourage the development of an urban community in which persons may live and mature according to the purposes of God.[46]

Increased emphasis was to be given to work with an Advisory Council of denominational staff persons responsible for urban mission activity, consulting with denominational groups and churches, and giving more attention to reinforcing the Neighborhood Advisory Council that had been set up in Richmond's poverty communities as part of the federally funded Community Action Program (CAP). TRUST saw its role with denominations, local churches and community groups to be one of "connector, communicator and coordinator."

However, in the next couple of years denominational interest in coordinated ecumenical strategy slackened, and TRUST was called in more often as the paid consultant for denominational programs. In addition, the federally funded programs began to wane, but the agency had already established its expertise with government and voluntary agencies. In response to these trends, TRUST gave up its attempt to be a coordinating agency for urban mission, and moved into the private sector as a consultant in organizational development and human relations. Although it never formally withdrew from the Action Training Coalition, it ceased to be active in the national organization after the middle of 1971. In 1979

TRUST, Inc. was formally dissolved, to be succeeded by Organizational Development Consultants, Inc.

Inter-religious Center for Urban Affairs, St. Louis, Missouri: The experience of William H. Mead and Stanley F. Rodgers, two White Episcopal clergymen who were dean and canon of Christ Church Cathedral in St. Louis, at Chicago's Urban Training Center for Christian Mission in 1966 was responsible for the development of a training center in St. Louis. When they returned from Chicago, they drew together an organizing committee composed of Episcopalians, United Presbyterians, Missouri Synod Lutherans, African Methodist Episcopal and Roman Catholics, as well as representatives of Eden Theological Seminary, Metropolitan Church Federation, Lutheran Mission Association and Experimental Campus Ministry. Their proposal for a Center for Urban Affairs was developed with the purpose of starting "a cooperative ministry for the Metropolitan community with enough support, authority, resources and competence to enable them to respond to the challenges and opportunities of the urban scene."

Because St. Louis was part of the Pilot Diocese Program of the Episcopal Church, Mead and Rodgers hoped that it would be possible to secure national church funds to get the Center started. However, when that request was delayed, the United Presbyterian Church in the U.S.A. was able to assign John L. Quigley, Jr., a White seminary graduate, to get the program started in September 1967.

During the pilot year of 1967-68 the Center developed its rationale and program. Because it involved Jewish as well as Christian groups, the title was expanded to Inter-religious Center for Urban Affairs. Much of the program consisted of training: a three-day program of Community Leadership Training for indigenous community leaders; an intensive four-week urban training program in mission planning for clergy, which was also to involve lay leaders of their churches; a series of eight seminars for clergy, students and social service workers on Power and Decision Making in St. Louis; and a seminary course on Urban Issue Analysis for students at Concordia Seminary, Eden Seminary and the Divinity School of St. Louis University. The first three programs were administered jointly with the Center for Community and Metropolitan Studies of the University of Missouri-St. Louis. In addition, ICUA served as planning consultant to the New Dimensions Committee of Church Women United and co-sponsored a series of conferences on the housing issue in St. Louis with the American Jewish Committee and the Urban Housing Program of Washington University. Proposals were being developed with other St. Louis organizations for a Metropolitan Data Bank and a joint center for Urban Studies that would pull together university resources.

The program was all set to go in the Fall of 1968, but the Episcopal funding was still not forthcoming. Only a promise of three-year grants from the

United Thank Offering of Episcopal Church Women, which needed to be matched by funds from the local diocese, and from joint funds of JSAC was available to get the program off the ground. Smaller grants from other local denominations and foundations made it possible to piece together the program through 1971.

ICUA gave particular attention to housing as an issue in the St. Louis area. Paul F. Mittlestadt, a program assistant for housing, produced a special research report recommending formation of a housing development corporation. An Ecumenical Housing Fund raised loans and grants of $280,000 for assistance to non-profit housing. Metropolitan mission planning was encouraged both on the ecumenical level and by denominations, with ICUA serving as both participant and consultant. Both the data bank and the urban studies proposals had to be dropped for lack of sufficient funds.

In the field of training ICUA began to give particular attention to two areas. White racism was addressed with a program design that was used for two weekend sessions with local congregations and a summer program on "Metropolitan Problems and Potential." This emphasis on "the White problem" was terminated as a major program involvement in September 1969. However, ICUA was able in 1970 to add a Black staff member, Buck Jones, a United Church of Christ minister who had been leader of a long, successful public housing rent strike the previous year. Simulation games (known technically as "heuristic games") became a special feature of ICUA training through use of the Community Land Use Game (CLUG). In cooperation with the Center for Simulation Studies of Washington University, ICUA developed and used a computerized method of keeping score in this simulation, which divided participants into teams representing various income levels of the metropolitan area. After 1970 this program was given completely to the university's center.

As ICUA approached the end of its three-year period, the board and staff began to seek ways to continue the program over the long run. Denominational units in metropolitan St. Louis felt they could not support the parallel ecumenical programs of the 50-year-old Metropolitan Church Federation and of ICUA. Therefore, plans were made to merge the two organizations into an Inter Church Association that would carry on the principal emphases of both. Program priorities were set in the areas of housing, public education, public welfare, church ministries to institutions, and planning and research. The newly formed ICA also committed itself to continuing to try to develop a Joint Urban Staff among participating denominations, a project that ICUA had been working at for three years, to organize a middle-class organization to work on metropolitan issues, and to study the feasibility of an action-training component that would:

1. Develop lay participation in urban issues of concern to religious groups;

2. Give strategy development training to indigenous groups (e.g. NWRO or Operation Live)

3. Conduct analysis and training within a major institution on such subjects as New Roles for the Corporation in the City, Human Values in Corporate Planning, and Institutional Racism.[47]

Within six months most of the ICUA staff members who had joined the new organization were no longer working for ICA, and the training emphasis was submerged in the other service and advocacy programs that were continued from the previous year.

Columbus Action Training Associates, Columbus, Ohio: Action training began in Columbus as the result of a request from Methesco, the United Methodist seminary in Delaware, Ohio, for urban involvement for their students during the winter inter-session in 1969. Jon Brown, a White United Methodist clergyman on the conference staff of that denomination, and Don Huey, a White United Presbyterian clergyman on the presbytery staff, pulled in Tom Duffy, a White Roman Catholic inner-city priest, and Marlene Wilson, a Black community worker, to assist in the program. They repeated the training for students from Evangelical Lutheran Seminary as well as Methesco in 1970 and 1971.

As a result of conversation with the Cleveland Intern Program and CHART in Cincinnati, the Columbus group joined in the formation of Action Training Network of Ohio. In addition to conducting local training with church and community groups in Columbus, they were influential in developing the Intra Systems Change Model in a training program with the Presbytery of Columbus during early 1971.

Ecumenical Training Council, Boise, Idaho: As part of the Episcopal Pilot Diocese Program, the Episcopal diocese in Idaho developed a training proposal. The research for carrying on training was to be an ecumenical council funded both locally and out of national Episcopal funds. This group expressed interest in joining the Action Training Coalition, but did not hold together until ATC was organized in 1968.

Ecumenical Academy of Webster Groves, Webster Groves, Missouri: Local clergy who had experience with the Ecumenical Institute of Chicago organized the Ecumenical Academy of Webster Groves during the mid-1960's. The program was concerned with church renewal in local congregations. The group sought membership in ATC when it was organized, but never sent representatives to the meeting or took further part in the development of action training.

DENOMINATIONAL SPONSORSHIP

Metropolitan Associates of Philadelphia, Pennsylvania: Metropolitan Associates of Philadelphia was organized in 1965 by Jitsuo Morikawa, a Japanese-American clergyman who was serving as director of the Division of Evangelism of the American Baptist Convention, as an experiment in missionary engagement in the modern metropolis. The project grew out of the World Council of Churches study on "The Missionary Structure of the Congregation," initiated at the New Delhi assembly in 1961, and the concern of American Baptists during the program of the Baptist Jubilee Advance from 1959 through 1964 for reaching into the structures of urban life.

MAP began with direct assistance assured by the American Baptist Home Mission Societies, which provided funds and freed Morikawa and two of his staff members, Richard M. Jones and Richard E. Broholm, both White American Baptist clergy, to be part of the organizing group. The Episcopal Diocese of Philadelphia, the United Church of Christ and the Lutheran Church-Missouri Synod gave staff and funds. The National Council of Churches provided a staff member.

The format of the project was based both on theological insights growing out of the World Council study and a social analysis suggested by Robert C. Hoover, chairman of the Graduate Department of Urban Planning at the University of Cincinnati. The purpose was stated, "to engage in experimental missionary action in the city of Philadelphia, for the sake of common witness to, and participation in, Christ's work of renewal in metropolis." The program was defined initially as consisting of "research on the character of the church's influence and witness in the public, holistic, productive, and secularized spheres of industrialized society" through lay presence, and "experiments in missionary action across the major sectors of the metropolis."

Using a typology of the sectors of metropolitan society furnished by Hoover, MAP was committed to looking at all parts of the common life — art, culture and education, medicine and health, social organizations, politics and government, business and industry, and physical development. The church as an institution was seen as belonging to the cultural and educational area, which Hoover considered to be "soft" (voluntary, flexible, without compulsion), but also as "mission" permeating the whole continuum.

MAP wished to engage in disciplined reflection on the involvement of lay persons in all parts of the metropolis. To effect both research and experimental mission engagement, the project planned to rely on three categories of persons: worker-ministers, who would be theologically trained clergy taking secular jobs; lay associates, who would be theologically sensitive lay persons already involved in secular occupations; and urban agents, who would be theologically competent clergy and laity seeking to serve as researchers and reporters for events occurring within the sectors. Between 1965 and 1968 Jones served as urban agent for Arts and Education, and Broholm for Business and Industry. Paul Goetting, a White Missouri Synod Lutheran clergyman, joined the staff as urban agent for Social Organizations, followed by Robert McCloskey, a White Episcopal priest, who served a similar function for Medicine and Health. Steven Yale and Richard T. Snyder served as urban agents for Politics and Government, and Physical Development. Worker-ministers were recruited to work in various positions throughout the city, and a core group of lay associates was developed out of persons who joined the sector reflection groups.

In 1967 MAP rejected the proposal of Theodore Erickson, a White United Church of Christ clergyman serving as a worker-minister in a city department, for a congregational development project that would try to gather clusters of local churches to work on issues in the metropolitan area, as well as in their own communities. At this point MAP was committed to working beyond local congregations rather than through them. As a result, Erickson went to MUST in New York City, where the project was sponsored for two years before he joined the staff of the Board for Homeland Ministries of the United Church of Christ.

From July 1966, through July 1967, Hoover joined the staff of MAP while on sabbatical. During this period he developed an elaborate action-research proposal for investigating more deeply the nature of lay involvement and the direction that missionary engagement should take if it was to result in significant social change. This resulted in production of a manual for action research, known as "The Style Manual," to assist lay associates and urban agents in analyzing their institutions and preparing for significant action for change.

Although MAP had declared itself from the beginning to be uninterested in training because it was still engaged in research and would not know what to train about, the staff began in December 1966 to consider the need for an education and training component, as they began to move from decentralization in sectors toward integration of what was being learned about the style of missionary engagement. Education and training would begin with finding ways of "sharing the insights of MAP action-research" through exploratory efforts in lay training and education. These could later be refined as "training and educational techniques in order that other institutions might be able to make effective use of these insights." It was on the basis of this interest in future training, as well as consideration of the creation of a Division of Parish Development in mid-1968, that MAP was included in the original membership group of the Action Training Coalition. However, after Consultation IV defined ATC membership more tightly in terms of agencies engaged in action training, MAP withdrew from membership by October 1969.

By the early 1970's MAP was itself engaged in training, both through its own parish development project and in association with TEAM, which had been formed as a training agency in Philadelphia and was an ATC member. At ATC Consultation XI in Philadelphia MAP staff, in cooperation with TEAM, presented the MAP model of lay ministry for organizational change that had grown out of the experience of its lay associates, worker-ministers and urban agents, and the refinement of the Hoover research using the Style Manual. This material, published as "A Strategy for Hope," reversed the original MAP model. Instead of starting with engagement in metropolis, it began with study groups in local churches, followed by support groups in local congregations, which would eventually send their members to develop support groups in the work place. In addition, MAP shared with the other ATC programs its experience in the use of closed-circuit television for group evaluation and feedback. As a result of this exposure, several ATC agencies joined MAP in preparing a proposal for a pilot program on lay ministry for organizational change.

MAP continued its creative engagement in Philadelphia through the end of 1974, when the American Baptist Home Mission Societies pulled one staff member who had been sent to the Philadelphia project back into denominational service and also reduced the funds available to MAP. Other sponsoring denominations were finding it more difficult to secure funds and personnel, and the primary learnings of the program were already being applied by lay associates, clergy staff who had been associated with the program, and staff of the sponsoring denominations who had followed the project closely.

Urban Young Adult Action, New York, New York: In June 1968 the Board of Evangelism of the United Methodist Church decided to release the staff who had been working on a special project to study the patterns of young adult life and to develop means of reaching them with the Christian Gospel. At this point Earl R. Barr, a White United Methodist clergyman who had been director of the project, and some of those who had been associated with him when it was supported by the Board from its base in Nashville, Tennessee, organized Urban Young Adult Action (UYAA) to offer consulting and training services about young adults and issues to denominations, campus ministries and local congregations. They received a wide base of support not only within the United Methodist Church (from the Board of Evangelism, the Board of Laity and the National Division of the Board of Global Ministries) but also from the Episcopal Church, the United Presbyterian Church in the U.S.A., the Presbyterian Church U.S. and the United Church of Christ.

Setting up offices in New York City, Barr and other associates travelled around the country holding conferences and training sessions for persons interested in young adult ministry. They also published notebooks on aspects of young adult ministry and resource books on young adults and on drugs and the young. In addition, they provided resource packets on issues affecting young adults.

UYAA joined ATC in October 1969 and remained active until the program closed for lack of funding in June 1972.

Glide Urban Center, San Francisco, California: Glide Urban Center was created by the Glide Memorial Church and the Glide Foundation as a means of extending their urban ministry in the San Francisco Bay Area and beyond. Glide Church is a local, interracial congregation belonging to the United Methodist Church. As a result of gifts through the years and income from property which the church owned in downtown San Francisco, the Glide Foundation, under the leadership of Lewis Durham, a White United Methodist clergyman, was able in the early 1960's to play a significant role in civil rights, poverty issues and other problems facing that urban area.

The Glide Urban Center was created as a way of disseminating some of the learnings made by both the church and the foundation during the period. When Ted McIlvenna, also a White United Methodist clergyman, took over the work of the Center in 1968, he perceived a common interest with the urban training programs that had formed ATC. Therefore, he brought the center into ATC membership in April 1969. However, in the succeeding period his interests—and the Center's program—moved more into the field of human sexuality. Therefore, in October 1970 the Glide Urban Center withdrew from ATC.

UNIVERSITY SPONSORSHIP

Center for Human Action, Research and Training, Cincinnati, Ohio: Dr. Robert Hoover, director of the Department of Community Planning at the University of Cincinnati, played a role in the organization of two agencies that were part of the Action Training Coalition—Metropolitan Associates of Philadelphia (MAP) and CHART in his home base of Cincinnati. The catalyst was a consultation in May 1967 sponsored by the Basin Ministry, an inner-city church mission program, and United Campus Ministries, the ecumenical outreach to university campuses in the city. During a follow-up seminar on metropolitan lay ministries, the idea of a metropolitan urban training center for lay people in Cincinnati was brought forward. As a result, Hoover offered a proposal that the ecumenical organizations and the University of Cincinnati join in sponsoring a model of urban training, which he titled "Indigenous Non-Professional Teams for Planned Community Change in the Cincinnati Metropolitan area" (a title that completely defied becoming an acronym).

After further discussion in early 1968, two ecumenical sponsors joined the University of Cincinnati's Graduate Department of Community Planning in a program that would go beyond the customary forms of lay training and involve both denomination and community leaders in organizing their own communities. The church sponsors were the Ecumenical Center for Continuing Education and the United Campus Ministries at the University of Cincinnati, both of them staffed by Paul Buckwalter, a White Episcopal priest who had extended the concept of campus ministry beyond the academic community. The purpose of the program would be to train teams of local citizens for planned community change. Funding came from a grant that the university department had from the Federal government under Section 749 of the U.S. Public Health Act to develop a curriculum for the training of community health planning personnel (one form of "indigenous non-professional") and from the Episcopal Church nationally, as well as from the Diocese of Southern Ohio.

The original format of the program provided for ten-week courses in both inner-city and suburban neighborhoods that would provide one evening of formal instruction and one evening of consultation each week. The design provided for reaching one inner-city and one suburban neighborhood in each cycle. The faculty of the program would include members of the graduate department, staff especially hired for the program and graduate students. Paul Henry, a Black assistant professor, was appointed director, and Buckwalter assisted him in administration. As the program developed, some of the community residents who had been trained in earlier cycles became trainers and served on the training team.

Although the goal of the development was to recruit 18 students for each course, the program discovered it was having greater success in securing participation from Black residents in both inner-city and suburban communities. In addition, consultation did not end with the close of the ten-week course. As a result, the staff began to develop a continuing relationship with trainees and community organizations in communities where training had been completed, as well as picking up some new sites for training.

In 1968-69, the program's first year, three ten-week cycles were conducted in College Hill, a suburban area with eight neighboring communities, and in the Model Cities area of Over-the-Rhine, an inner-city neighborhood. In subsequent years the program spread to other communities, training leaders and developing community organizations, but CHART maintained a storefront center in Over-the-Rhine as the area of "highest social crisis" in the city. This served as a base for continuing training and consultation, as well as the office of the Upper Basin Council. By 1971-72 the agency had completed 15-18 training cycles in Cincinnati communities and produced a cadre of almost 200 persons who were involved in various types of community change.

The program had been designed to self-destruct. Training was not supposed to produce a need for more training and dependence on continuing consultation. Rather, the people and groups were to keep going on their own. The university department's five-year grant ran out, so that it could no longer devote as great an amount of faculty and graduate student time and effort to the program in the city's neighborhoods. Yet the program had its effect on the University of Cincinnati. Kenneth E. Corey, department chairman, reported in 1969 that CHART had the indirect effects of sensitizing faculty to the need to develop human resources and formulate action strategies and of bringing some of the CHART graduates into the department as faculty. CHART also helped in producing a bibliography for the training of citizen-agents of planned community change.

As already noted earlier, CHART played a key role in bringing together action-training programs in Cleveland, Columbus and Cincinnati to share efforts in the Action Training Network of Ohio (ATN). After CHART closed, some of its trainers continued to function as members of the ATN collective.

CHAPTER V

The Development and Abandonment of the Action Training Coalition

ESTABLISHING THE COALITION (1967-1969)

In late 1967, when there were already ten action-training agencies in operation (and another in the planning stage), steps were taken to call together representatives of the "urban training centers" to share information and look into the possibility of forming a national association of centers similar to National Industrial Mission, which had been established by industrial mission projects in 1966. Representatives of seven programs, (ACTS, CUE-M, METC, MUST, TEAM-Kansas City, TRUST, UTC) met on the evening of October 3, 1967, during the 50th Anniversary convention of the American Institute of Planners to consider this question. They were joined by persons from the national mission programs of the Episcopal Church, Disciples of Christ and Methodist Church, along with the Ministry Studies Board and Roanridge Center of Kansas City.

Several considerations led to the joining of the training centers at this time. (1) Since December 7, 1965, when Rev. Joseph Merchant of the United Church of Christ, as president of the Board of Directors of the Urban Training Center for Christian Mission in Chicago, had called together a meeting in his office to discuss the formation of MUST and other regional training centers, the UTC Board had been concerned about the problem of the "proliferation" of centers. The original design of the founders of UTC had been to regionalize at a later time, but centers were being formed without their initiative. Also, UTC staff had been under pressure from its Board for a couple of years to conduct programs in areas outside Chicago. (2) The two largest centers, UTC and MUST, together with the Cleveland Internship Program, had already begun to have some common experience in the Research on Training in Metropolitan Ministry (RTMM) evaluation research project. These centers, along with several others, were also scheduled to meet at the invitation of UTC for a conference on theological reflection. (3) Smaller centers and those still in the process of formation were feeling the need for staff training and technical assistance as they began their programs. (4) National mission boards had already seen in the formation of National Industrial Mission (NIM) an example of a group of programs, which they had played a role in forming and which laid claim on them for support, going to seek outside funding from foundations and other sources, as well as playing a role in moderating each other's claims for church support. The example of NIM was very much in their minds at the meeting with training centers in Washington.

A committee of five, including one each from UTC and MUST, was chosen to plan the meeting. In addition to planning the purposes, schedule and personnel for the first meeting of those already doing or planning to conduct urban training, this committee considered two other areas that were to be critical for ATC—membership and types of linkage between centers.

The committee suggested the following as a beginning definition of an "urban training center," using the main features of the programs already in existence:

> A national, regional or metropolitan ecumenical network of resources to provide an arena for confrontation, reflection, commitment, skills training and strategy in action to enable the church to perform its mission in an urbanizing society.[1]

This definition caught up the ecumenical sponsorship and the action-reflection methodology which were to appear in ATC's final definition of membership. The distinction between "national" and other programs was important to UTC, which wished to preserve its status as the only national center in the United States. The definition of the purpose of action training was far more church and mission-oriented than ATC's social and operational goals, which were developed later.

The committee also suggested the following means of linkage between training centers: (1) yearly meetings for "exchange" between directors, (2) special consultation on particular problems, (3) staff and/or board visits to other centers, (4) joint staff training sessions, (5) joint research, and (6) mail distribution of important program materials. They suggested that centers begin to share some materials by mail immediately, and joint research was already underway in the RTMM project. The other four means of linkage were to be features of the succeeding ATC consultations, with the programs of Consultations V through VIII between 1969 and 1971 including all four.

Fifteen of the 21 training centers then in existence attended the National Consultation of Urban Training Centers at Chevy Chase, Maryland, February 9-11, 1968. They were joined by persons from four other training programs that did not join ATC, and representatives of five national mission boards and the National Council of Churches. Purposes of the meeting were to explore common problems and issues and to develop means of working at these together, both within the consultation and in the future. George D. Younger, a staff member of the American Baptist Home Mission Societies who was directing evaluation for MUST, served as a neutral but interested convenor of the sessions, and Edgar W. Mills, director of the Ministry Studies Board, served as process consultant. This set a pattern for the use of outside consultants at many of the ATC consultations.

The main issues which arose in the discussion were summarized by Mills as follows: (1) effective Black-Brown participation in training systems, (2) institutional development questions in the creation of a training organization, (3) training whom for what, (4) relation of seminaries and the continuing education movement, and (5) relationship of training process to urban mission strategy. Mills noted that a great deal of information was exchanged among participants—which was only natural with three of the programs present still in the planning phase and another five in their first year of operation. He also remarked on the way in which the inclusion of race in the discussion changed both its quality and the outcome; the stratification between the larger centers with more experienced program staffs and the newer and smaller centers, with the former accorded higher status; and the threatening nature of the subject of funding.

The consensus of the first consultation was to hold another to go farther with the questions of developing and funding centers, methodology of training, reformation of theological and continuing education, urban unrest, and the kind of vehicle needed to further the urban training movement. A committee composed of directors and one board member (including two Blacks, one Puerto Rican and one Canadian) was appointed to plan Consultation II, which was held in Kansas City on May 24-26, 1968, as the National Consultation of Urban Training Centers and Networks.

Consultation II moved "from psychology to politics," according to Robert H. Bonthius of CIP, who wrote the report of ideational development that corresponded to Mills' consultant's report of the first meeting. At this meeting it was decided to drop the term "urban" because it made people think of the inner city and to form the Action Training Coalition with Randolph Nugent, the Black director of MUST, as chairman and Bonthius as vice-chairman. Seventeen of the 22 training centers then in existence were represented at the meeting, along with three other training programs, representatives of four national mission boards, the American Association of Theological Schools (AATS), the Society for the Advancement of Continuing Education for Ministry (SACEM), the Department of Ministry of the National Council of Churches and the Interreligious Foundation for Community Organization (IFCO).

The consultation used papers prepared out of the experience of the two largest centers to focus discussion. George W. Webber, director of academic programs at MUST, who had been its first director, presented the picture in relation to seminary and continuing education, where action training was seen as an implicit judgment on and competition for existing programs and institutions, in spite of the basic fact of considerable cooperation. Archie Hargraves, director of mission strategy at UTC, developed the theme of urban unrest, using the Black Consortium in Chicago as a model for dealing with issues of White power and the Black condition. A paper by George Younger, "Do Training Centers Know What They Mean by 'Training'?" with a critical review by Carl Siegenthaler of UTC, served as the starting point for discussion of curriculum and methodology.

However, the main thrust of the meetings was toward action to form an ongoing relationship as a coalition. This coalition was described by Bonthius as "more like a covenant than anything else," with no dictation of policy from the coalition to its member organizations. The form of decision-making used was to present results of the discussions to the directors of the training centers present at the consultation, who in their turn reported back to the assembly what they had decided. Action between the Kansas City session and the next consultation was to be carried forward by ad hoc task forces, in which all centers could participate (even though the budgets of smaller centers might not support such participation), and by individual representatives to agencies and organizations with which it was felt to be important to maintain contact.

Task forces were established for the following: Clergy Education, to consider relationships to theological seminaries and continuing education; Curriculum and Evaluation, to consider uses of evaluation instruments and sharing of currriculum; Institutional Racism, to design training programs to combat racism; and Long Range Development, to confer on regional development of training networks, and possible specialization among centers and networks. Representatives were named to SACEM and AATS meetings in St. Louis in June to present ATC's resources to seminary and continuing educators, to IFCO, to the Board and Training Committee of JSAC, and to the Continuing Education Committee of the Department of Ministry of the National Council of Churches. Thus, major relationships were established with those denominations that had played a major role in bringing the centers into being, with seminaries and continuing education programs that were engaged in similar pursuits, and with church-supported community organizing efforts. It was also agreed to look into the possibility of joining the NCC Communications System through the Department of Ministry.

According to Bonthius's summary of the Kansas City Consultation, "K.C. saw the politics come out," since action training people "tend to be political animals."

It was arranged to have key guests present. The centers and networks themselves were well represented. The kind of coalition was decided upon which guaranteed control of policy by the directors themselves. . . . The feeling was that the organization could represent the interests of all and that it could make definite impressions upon boards and agencies which might otherwise be making fateful decisions about action training without the trainers. There was even a touch of messianism about Kansas City. The reformation of the seminaries was envisioned: Awaking the Church to its mission in metropolis was dreamed of! The Action Training Coalition was born in an atmosphere of hope for church and world as well as hope for action training centers and networks.[2]

From the beginning, the Coalition was planned with as much attention to those whom it was intended to affect—denominational executives, seminary faculties, continuing educators, Black community organizers—as to those whom it was organized to serve in the training centers and networks themselves.

Consultation III was to focus on the question of institutional racism. Originally scheduled for the fall of 1968, it was finally held in Cleveland on January 2-5, 1969. The original planning committee designated for the meeting was the Institutional Racism Task Force, with Archie Hargraves as convenor and other Black trainers in ATC as members. When Hargraves's health did not permit his carrying out this responsibility, the task of planning the sessions was passed to an all-White committee, convened by Speed Leas of COMMIT. The committee developed by mail and phone a schedule of presentations on the theme, "The Black Situation and White Racism," that tried to move more in the direction of "liberation" for Black, White and Brown people, and asked Carl A. Fields, a Black psychologist on the staff of Princeton University who had been serving as training consultant at MUST, to be the outside process consultant.

Fourteen of the action training centers out of a total of 27 that were in existence by then attended the sessions, and CHART of Cincinnati was added to the original founding group of 19. The training component started calmly with presentations by a panel of Black activists from the Cleveland area. The second session on strategic options presented a wide variety of persons: Burt Gardner, a member of Mayor Carl Stokes's staff in Cleveland; Eliazar Risco, editor of *La Raza* of Los Angeles, C T Vivian of UTC; Dr. Grace Boggs, a Marxist from Detroit, Alvin Pitcher, from the Committee for One Society; and Stanley Hallett, from the Commons, both Whites from Chicago.

The training session for staff became a confrontation between White and Black participants, which was useful in underscoring the extent to which racial differences were a factor in the internal operation of the training centers as well as in the situations they were addressing. It also brought forward the extent of difference there was among trainers and agencies as to the kind of social changes that were being sought and the extent to which racism needed to be addressed. Both Fields as consultant and Nugent as ATC chairman were helpful in sorting out these differences.

As noted by Paul Kittlaus of COMMIT, who served as editor and recorder of the process of the training of trainers, the group moved to a different style of operation when the business session began, with much of the conflict being replaced by harmony, and "real enthusiasm and zest."

> This says to me that this particular group of people are much more at home at planning power strategies than they are in trying to deal either with their own gut level racism, as some wanted to do, or at spending time looking at a variety of conceptual models.[3]

Major areas in which decisions were made during the business sessions included the internal matters of membership and decision making and further development of relations with AATS, SACEM and JSAC. The only addition to the membership definition suggested by the planning committee for Consultation I was the requirement that a center "has successfully completed one training program." Although a committee report recommended that "only directors and staff members" be eligible to vote at ATC meetings, this was changed to permit voting by "not more than four delegates from each ATC member organization," changing the decision-making from the directors to representatives, and curbing the ability of larger centers to send more delegates to ATC sessions.

Upon recommendation of the Clergy Education Task Force, the Consultation took several actions regarding relationships with theological education: to reproduce and distribute the ATC statement presented by Bonthius to the June 1969 meeting of AATS; to participate in a 1970 issue of *Theological Education*; to study methods of consulting with theological seminaries and publicizing the resources of ATC agencies; and to seek membership in SACEM. In regard to denominational funding through JSAC, the following action was taken:

> ATC makes this recommendation to the JSAC Training Committee on funding: that JSAC and its member denominations recognize ATC as a primary instrumentality to be consulted for JSAC decisions on action training, and to be fully utilized as the agency through which JSAC and its member denominations arrange for services to be provided by ATC members.[4]

To this action was added a note explaining, "It was understood that the main point of this recommendation is that we expect JSAC to deal with centers and networks not in isolation from one another but in relation to each other, and that each center will deal with JSAC not unilaterally but in collaboration with ATC." Thus, the group had begun to deal with one of the critical issues between the centers, their competition for national funding, although it still left untouched the question of the relation of all the other centers to UTC, which already had all the JSAC denominations and many others on its Board.

Consultation IV, which was held just three months later at a retreat center in Erlanger, Kentucky, from March 30 through April 3, 1969, went much farther in discussing common business between the centers and possibilities for collaboration. There was no outside consultant this time, but the absence was noted and action taken to have a process observer for Consultation V. Fourteen out of 27 training agencies which were eligible for participation in ATC were represented at this meeting. A committee of five, chaired by Ted McEachern of ACTS, had conducted an agenda search before the meeting and presented the following priority areas for discussion: funding, functions of ATC and constituencies.

On funding the decision was to leave responsibility for "the development and broadening of local funding sources" with each center, but to consult on all negotiations with national funding sources (e.g. individual denominations, JSAC, National and World Councils of Churches, "foundations of national and international scope," IFCO, National Institute of Mental Health, Southern Christian Leadership Conference) and to seek common funding for training on "issues of critical priority." This protected local initiative, while striving to cut down competition for national funding. ATC representatives were named to handle discussions with potential funding sources, and a Funding Development and Advisory Panel was set, consisting of staff persons from UTC, CIP and MUST, the three programs with the largest budgets and longest experience, in order to provide technical assistance in preparing proposals and advocacy for presenting them to funding sources.

The discussion of functions of ATC consisted of answering a prior question, "Will ATC organize a national training network?" Then the group turned to questions of membership, constituencies, collaboration and specialization. The action on membership assumed a positive answer to the basic question of a national training network and went still farther in defining how the Coalition members saw action training:

ATC is a membership coalition
—composed of action training agencies, primarily but not exclusively rooted in the Judeo-Christian tradition
—offering engagement/reflection action training to enable groups and individuals in society to effect institutional and community change for humanization and justice.
The purpose of ATC is to establish and maintain high standards for action training, to procure adequate funding and other resources, and to develop common strategies for social change.[5]

By this action the member agencies enlarged the scope of ATC beyond being church-related and concerned for the church's mission in society and added the purposes of maintaining standards and developing common strategies to their previous purposes of learning from each other and having an effect on their sponsoring church bodies and theological education.

This enlarged purpose was also reflected in the constituencies which ATC was itself serving. "Top priority in all ATC training will be given to developing agents of systemic change," and the constituencies named include seminaries and continuing education, policy makers and change agents in religious systems, and policy makers and change agents in secular systems. Several items decided under the heading of collaboration were intended to govern relations between UTC as a national center and all the other centers, as well as between centers: a national organization working in a local area "will do so in relationship with the regional or metropolitan centers (or not at all)"; "when a member agency is recruiting in an area, the center or centers in that area will be contacted"; member agencies should collaborate with one another on "training events and issues considered critical for that region"; resources to deal with national issues considered critical by ATC shall be coalesced; and ATC should operate a referential system to pass trainees from program to program. Specific programs were established to contract with NCC for an Information Service, to produce national publicity materials and to write up research findings, looking toward a central research and evaluation unit.

All centers were encouraged to develop a core of activities, including the following: values systems confrontation on social change issues; skills development, including systems analysis, environmental analysis, group process, organizational planning, community organization, theologizing and action-research; and institutional consultative services. Specialization of two kinds was projected: training resources development (such as gaming at ICUA and curriculum at UTC) and locale-related issues (like Federal issues at METC, youth culture at Glide and Caribbean issues at PRISA). In a move to stimulate greater participation, the member agencies were divided into five regions.

By the end of Consultation IV, after one and a half years of joint effort, ATC had developed a loose national policy for the action-training centers to operate within, a clear sense of membership and decision-making, some common enterprises in the area of theological education, information and publicity, and a united front toward national funding sources. In addition, a shift had occurred in the centers' statement of purpose from equipping the churches for their mission in urbanizing society to developing agents of systemic change, whether in church-related or secular institutions. The organizational phase of the coalition had been completed, and the next period was to bring elaboration and testing of the relationships that had been established.

DEVELOPING A NATIONAL STRATEGY (1969-71)

Over the spring and summer of 1969 the Training Planning Committee of ATC developed a contract with UTC giving that national center a function of identifying critical national issues and developing curriculum resources for training on those issues. This contract was developed while James P. Morton was on sabbatical leave and Siegenthaler was serving as acting director of UTC. In the course of the negotiations, it became clear that UTC's Board of Directors had never been adequately informed of the nature of ATC or UTC's membership in the coalition. Thus, for the first period of formation UTC had at one and the same time been continuing to develop its own unilateral efforts in national training while appearing to cooperate in the effort to create a multilateral instrument. Many of the national denominations represented in UTC were committed to the support of a single program, while some, like the Episcopal Church, United Church of Christ, United Methodist Church and United Presbyterian Church in the U.S.A., were actively engaged in supporting the development of other centers as well as UTC.

Consultation V, held on October 5-8, 1969, in St. Louis, marked a high-water mark of participation by training agencies in the coalition. Twenty-one out of the 27 centers eligible for participation in ATC were present for the deliberations, as well as representatives of three centers that were in the process of formation—Center for Ecumenical Action Training of Detroit, Houston Metro Ministry and METRO of Indianapolis. Nugent, who was still serving as ATC chairman, was in the chair, and Fields was again acting as process observer.

The intent of Consultation V was to tighten up the ability of ATC to operate as a national training network. However, in retrospect this seems to be the point at which ATC began to over-organize itself for the amount of common business that the member agencies were willing and able to do with each other, and great amounts of talk about common program started to outweigh the relatively small amount of joint effort that ATC was able to generate.

The two principal results of the St. Louis discussions were adoption of a Social Goal and Operational Goals for ATC and the creation of a representative body, originally called the Priority Strategy Council and composed of two representatives from each of the five regions, to develop policy and administer ATC program between consultations. Also, "in order to become an acceptable channel for foundation and other financial resources," it was decided that ATC should be incorporated.

The Social Goal confirmed the direction of training change agents for society, not only equipping the church for its mission in society, which had been set in Cincinnati:

> The Social Goal of this coalition is to use and create resources and to employ action train-
> ing to develop the power of those who are participating in the liberation of society, such as
> those who are Black, Brown, Red or poor White; alienated youth and women; and disaf-
> fected decision-makers within the institutions of society.[6]

Operational Goals were identified in two categories: (1) work for systemic
change (social revolution), and (2) work for alternate value systems
(cultural revolution). Most ATC agencies were principally concerned for
the former, but there were several staff members and a couple of agencies
who linked this with the latter or were more concerned for changes in life
styles. The irony of this Social Goal is that it was adopted by a group of
agency representatives who were almost all White, male and ordained
clergy, and whose agencies were still largely engaged in training church staff
and constituents for participation in social change.

A report session by the Training Planning Committee during the meetings
contrasted the way in which UTC had dealt with the Black Manifesto by
making it an Issue Seminar with UTC students and denominational officials; while MUST had given active support to James Forman and BEDC
in presenting the Manifesto to denominations, published its materials and
then done training with its own Board and several other groups. Existing
task forces and committees reported on their activity and asked for more
time at the next consultation to discuss their business. All agencies agreed to
send their definitions of "action training" to the Presbyterian Institute on Industrial Relations in Chicago, for inclusion in the ATC Information Service.
However, most issues of ongoing importance for ATC were referred to the
first Council meeting in December.

In a memo sent to persons interested in ATC on October 28, 1969, Neal
Fisher, a staff member of the National Division of the United Methodist
Church and chairman of the JSAC Training Committee, wrote that the St.
Louis meeting "demonstrated that the task forces and machinery established
at last spring's consultation had functioned through the summer and that
the ATC is well on the way to becoming a major force in training for mission." He called on JSAC member denominations "to collaborate on their
own priorities in training and to fit action-training into a comprehensive
picture of national mission." He added:

> The development of a strong coalition of action-trainers can represent a resourceful partner
> in mission strategy and training for the denominational mission agencies. Such a coalition
> provides an arena for the improvement of training skills and the sharing of resources which
> can strengthen the entire training movement.[7]

Thus, ATC agencies, which had been largely created under denominational
auspices, had now achieved through ATC sufficient distance from their

sponsors to be regarded as allies and collaborators, not only as creatures. This had been an important dynamic in the creation of ATC, but it needed to be balanced by a continuing interest on the part of the denominations and not give the appearance of too great a distance from their concerns. In the light of this tension, it is possible to understand that the Social Goal was principally intended to stake out territory that action-training agencies hoped to fill and that could be useful to the churches, rather than to go beyond the original focus of enabling the mission of the church.

The first meeting of the ATC Council on December 19-20, 1969, in Chicago gave primary attention to codifying what had been decided in St. Louis. Functions were divided among the member agencies, regions, Council and National Delegate Assembly, which was to meet during each national consultation no less than once a year. ATC finances, which had been growing in importance, now became critical in order to pay the expenses of Council meetings. In addition, finances were needed for expansion of the ATC Information Service and the proposal to have a half-time National Coordinator. The training planning function was taken on by the Council itself, and plans were firmed up for ATC participation in the UTC Issue Seminar on "Community Development, Federal Programs, and Church Response," which was scheduled for January 19-26, 1970. The Working Agreement with UTC was reaffirmed, and Ted McEachern, ATC vice-chairman, was assigned the role of coordinator. Plans were made to draft a Constitution and By-Laws in connection with incorporation in the State of Missouri. Hopes for national funding were developing with negotiations by Nugent with the Ford Foundation and by Bonthius with JSAC.

In the period between Consultations V and VI other forms of collaboration were developing among the centers. The centers in Ohio, including CIP, which was reaching the end of its Federal funding from NIMH, CATA and CHART, were forming a common strategy through the Action Training Network of Ohio. Nugent and Younger of MUST were retained to produce a feasibility study of the network proposal for the Ohio centers, under a grant from the Department of Ministry of the NCC. In the Southeast, as part of the regionalization of ATC, ACTS, which had been established as a region-wide training center, worked out some reciprocal understandings with TRUST and UTOA.

Most significant of the joint training efforts were the Model Cities training event at UTC, which had been designed under the ATC-UTC contract, and the anti-racism training performed under the Fund for the Americas of the Church of the Brethren. A number of local community leaders and ATC training center staff members took part in the "ATC caucus" at UTC during the week of January 19-26, under the direction of Milton Reid of TRUST. This provided a substantial additional group of Model Cities citizens for the program, but underscored the difficulties of participating on a collaborative basis in the multi-ring circus of interconstituency training at UTC. The

Church of the Brethren used the Race Institute of METC for its original planning sessions for the Fund for the Americas program, which was to include both fund-raising for minority empowerment and anti-racism training for the largely rural and almost exclusively White constituency of the Church of the Brethren. UTC, METC, MUST, ATN and COMMIT all conducted weekend training sessions with groups in various districts across the country, with Siegenthaler of UTC serving as coordinator. The programs were principally sensitization of Whites to racial issues, although in a couple of areas plans were made for action on racism by the district. At the Toronto consultation it was agreed that 5% of the fees received by centers from the Church of the Brethren would be rebated to the ATC general account. Also a charge by MTN that MUST had worked with the Brethren district in Western Kansas on its home base territory without consultation and used an MTN staff person without adequate compensation was acted on by the Delegate Assembly in Toronto and arbitrated by an ATC committee which met with the two centers during the meeting. National training, then, was already becoming an accomplished fact, although it had many problems and weaknesses.

Consultation VI, which was held in Toronto, Ontario, Canada, March 20-25, 1970, was attended by 21 of the centers eligible to participate. However, that number had declined to 25 with the withdrawal of BCHI and MAP from the coalition after the St. Louis meeting. Like the two preceding consultations, this meeting was largely a business session for further development of the coalition. The only other program was a presentation on fund-raising by Leonard Styche of Styche Associates of New York, who stated that action training and action training centers were "out of vogue" and "have no constituency." He warned that "the more effective you are the harder it is to get funded" because others will coopt successful programs. This was an accurate description of the situation which the centers had already reached with their principal sponsors in major Protestant denominations. UTC was still coasting on a Ford Foundation grant renewal but MUST had been informed by the United Methodist Church that it was withdrawing its substantive support, and all the centers which had processed grant applications through JSAC were finding that additional funds were not forthcoming.

At Toronto the pluralistic nature of action training came to heightened visibility with actions by both a Black Caucus and an International Caucus (Puerto Rico and Canada) to secure representation on the Council and various committees, as well as ATC support for their own priorities. The Black Caucus was principally concerned about the long-standing issue of centers having no Black staff to sensitize and inform White trainees rather than to work with Black groups and issues, as well as the possibility of funding through the Ford Foundation. On the issue of Black staff, it was agreed to use predominantly Black and/or Brown training teams on future programs with the Church of the Brethren, and the Black Caucus offered to raise a task force to help any center concerned about Black programming, staff relations or input. The Ford Foundation issue was stickier, because UTC was in the process of seeking further extension of its program for Black clergy, while Nugent had been negotiating on behalf of ATC for a national grant that would include the work of several centers, and TRUST was working through Milton Reid in Norfolk to secure a large grant for racism training in Virginia. Although in each case the grant would pass through the treasury of and be administered by a White-controlled center, the Black Caucus discussed and fought over these competing grants as if they would be Black-controlled. At Toronto the ATC Council voted to endorse the TRUST Racism proposal and heard a report from Nugent on his efforts with Ford.

The International Caucus first became visible in meetings of the Northeast Region, which included both CUT and PRISA, which had concerns that were affected by but not limited to the United States. At first the region tried to handle the differences by appointing at least one of its two representatives from outside the U.S. mainland. When the Black Caucus asked for separate representation by two persons on the Council, the International Caucus was formed and asked for the same. In addition, a strong priority statement was adopted on international program priorities in which ATC pledged itself "to collaborate with initiatives forms of [sic] third world revolutionaries in any way we can, commensurate with our goals and committment [sic] for human liberation." Three possible forms of action outlined in the paper were: mutual sharing of workable training designs; a catalytic function of bringing ministries together with groups clearly working for social transformation; and making consultative skills available to community leaders and decision makers.

A great deal of time was spent at Toronto on organizational matters with the adoption of by-laws. Nugent resigned as chairman, to be succeeded by Bonthius, another original officer. The treasurer's report showed that in the first year of operation a dues system based on 0.5% of a member center's total budget, cash receipts had been $3,385.35 and in-kind contributions of expenses $3,129.32. Nugent had served as coordinator as well as chairman, without additional remuneration, but the cost of holding Council meetings was almost as much as the net cost of holding a Consultation and Delegate Assembly. The Clergy Education Committee recommended that its name be changed to Theological Education Committee, and its priority and focus be shifted from "theological education in relation to seminaries to the theological aspect of reflection in the action-reflection mode." The experience of ATC centers with seminaries had been negative enough that the committee recommended in the future that there be faculty training where possible, that attention be shifted from "fringe courses and field experiences" to attempts "to shift the policies and curricula of the seminaries," and that "ATC agencies seriously consider a parallel structure strategy in relation to theological education." Participation in the ATC Information Service was continued, and the Research and Evaluation Committee raised the question of the extent of interest of centers in significant evaluation. As part of the Membership Committee's process of biennial evaluation of ATC member agencies, a goal was set of evaluating ten centers within the following year.

The Council met in St. Louis on May 28-29, 1970, and it required 20 pages of double-spaced typescript to record its discussion and actions. The shift to a representative government from the earlier consensus style was questioned in a discussion "noting particularly the loss of energy from some of the Directors within the ATC network in relationship to ATC who were not now 'on board' with ATC action." Membership evaluation procedures were firmed up, plans were made for the next consultation, and possibilities were discussed for training with the YWCA in institutional racism, with Model Cities citizens organizations and welfare recipients in the National Welfare Rights Organization. Specific attention was given to the funding process in JSAC, resulting in a decision to do a "power structure analysis of funds being spent by JSAC denominations in all categories."

Consultation VII in Atlanta from October 26-28, 1970, represented the most consistent attempt to share experience and reach agreement on the core of "action training" as a discipline. Nineteen of the 25 centers eligible to participate were represented at the sessions, which had been planned by member agencies in the Southeast. Workshops were held in the following areas considered to be essential to action-training methodology: sensitization, analysis, strategy, theological reflection and evaluation. Input for the discussion in each workshop came both from the experience of the centers represented and from a group of persons from the Atlanta area who had taken part in training with UTOA. Unfortunately, the reports of these workshops were never collected and compiled, as had been planned; as a result, the final fruits of this experience are available only in the way it has affected the practice of those who participated. This in itself may be a parable of action training, for its prime results have more often been in the experience of the trainees than in printed reports or evaluation of the training.

Third World concerns, as brought forward by the delegation from PRISA, dominated much of the business sessions. The International Caucus was dissolved, to be replaced by one delegate from Canada and one from Puerto Rico, "as the establishment of a Third World component in ATC which would open the door to establish closer relationships with Latin America." The Council was instructed "to frame a top priority agenda vis a vis ATC and the Third World," the Information Service was asked to establish an agreement with CSIC (Centro de Socialisacion de Informacion del Caribe), all training with Puerto Ricans or Dominicans was to be planned and executed "in the closest collaboration possible with PRISA," and — perhaps most important for its effect on ATC — Consultation VIII was to be held in Puerto Rico in the spring of 1971.

Another allied concern was the "white elitist male leadership and style of ATC." In addition to the Third World challenge to this dominance, Susan Halverstadt of MTN raised questions concerning the hiring of women trainers in ATC and the selection processes for delegates to Consultations, and the Black Caucus moved that ATC apportion $500 per center by November 30, 1970, to be paid to the Black Caucus of ATC for the training of Black trainers. The women's issue was disposed of by giving time and agenda to Halverstadt to pursue her questions, while the Black Caucus motion was passed by a vote of 18-7, with several centers that voted "No" indicating they would refuse to pay the assessment.

Although nothing much had come from efforts to develop national training by ATC since the May Council meeting, the suggestion was made to explore with the Department of Agriculture the possibility of training on racism by ATC agencies, similar to that which MUST was developing with the Food and Nutrition Service in the Northeast. The Training Planning Committee reported on the development of training designs and resources on the health services issue at UTC, and completion of the Church of the Brethren training, which would be carried in the future by the denomination's own staff.

The ATC Council meeting in St. Louis on February 19, 1971, was conducted in an atmosphere of crisis over institutional survival of many of the centers. This was mirrored in the local situation reports:

All centers are suffering from both cut backs in original grants from denominations and from the scheduled phasing out of national seed money grants. Some centers face severe if not fatal crisis in the immediate future. High commitment to continued training and organizing on behalf of social change was expressed. Also important action is in various stages of development in many areas. Hope, morale and commitment are high although drastic changes in style and form are required by the financial realities.[8]

The Council was seeking to keep a national structure going and formulate its direction at the same time as the base on which ATC was organized, the local centers, was eroding.

Against a goal of ten biennial evaluations of ATC agencies, by April 1971 only three had been completed (at COMMIT, MUST and CATS). Contributions for the Black Caucus fund to train Black trainers had been received from CATA, CATS, MUST and PRISA, and pledges from ACTS, CHART, UTOA and TEAM, representing only eight of the centers that had voted for the motion in Atlanta. Another motion stated that unless input and use of the Information Service increased before the Delegate Assembly in Puerto Rico, "the Council will recommend that participation be discontinued." Several of the centers which participated in the Church of the Brethren training did not pay the 5% levy to the ATC treasury.

On the external relations front, affairs seemed mixed but hopeful. AATS had refused the request for ATC representation on each standing committee but was ready to use selected ATC leadership as resource persons at a series of regional gatherings of key seminary personnel, financed by the Mellon Foundation. NWRO had written asking ATC to collaborate in the development of training for its national leadership. The Missionary Orientation Center at Stony Point, New York, had written about possible membership in ATC or passing its work over to ATC. SACEM was making use of ATC resource persons and techniques in its own think-tank on continuing education. However, the Ford Foundation had slowed down in processing the TRUST proposal, and the Black Caucus of ATC was developing a larger national proposal including other centers with TRUST.

Consultation VIII, held at the Colegio Episcopal in San Justo, Puerto Rico, from March 21 to 24, 1971, was both the last of the consultations devoted to building and developing the national coalition and the first of the consultations devoted to a specific issue that might be useful in action training. Only 13 of the 25 eligible centers had representatives present, but five others (ACTS, CUE-M, ICUA, Community 33 and UTC) sent their regrets at not being able to afford the increased expense of participation. A travel pool arrangement considered by the Council had to be turned down "because so many member agencies are in financial straits and cannot afford to put additional monies into a pool much as they would like to do so," and attempts to get foundation help for travel were unsuccessful. In addition to the four days in Puerto Rico, some delegates took advantage of PRISA's invitation to go on to the Dominican Republic for four more days of exposure to the Caribbean *realidad.*

The PRISA group had set up a schedule designed to make the consultation "an exposure to the Caribbean as representative of the Third World in general and not just a field trip to Puerto Rico." Most sessions were conducted in Spanish, with those who did not understand the language having to rely on shorter periods of translation or the summaries given by those who did. Presentations by informed university personnel and political activists were made to live by field trips around metropolitan San Juan, to Taller El Alacran, a visual arts workshop, and to the ecumenical action project of Methodists and Dominicans in Comerio. The claims of Puerto Rican independence from United States colonialism were underscored by the testimony of a fisherman from the island of Culebra, which was being used as a firing range by the U.S. Navy.

Although it had been hoped that Consultation VIII would provide concrete suggestions for a Third World agenda in ATC, the principal effect was to replace the Yanqui chairman, Bonthius of CATS, with Irvin Torres of PRISA. The report of the Council's Nominating Committee had brought in a slate of Paul Buckwalter of CHART for chairman and Robert Washington of MUST for vice-chairman. However, the Black Caucus submitted a substitute slate of Torres as chairman and Buckwalter as vice-chairman, which was adopted with one opposing vote and one abstention. Torres subsequently attended only one Council meeting and did little organizing work between Consultations. Thus, a liberal-oriented vote to place ATC under Third World leadership, at the urging of the Black Caucus, had the effect of assisting the gradual dissolution of ATC.

The scaling down of the national organization was very much in line with the priorities for ATC that developed when the National Delegate Assembly discussed the question, "What, if any, joint actions should ATC be about?" The three areas for which there was greatest support were: informal relationships and sharing; national and international strategies (including common projects and social analysis); and training of trainers (including Consultations). Other areas receiving some interest and support were: affecting denominational funding; developing and managing national contracts; credibility (national legitimacy); member agency information on development; evaluation; and Information Service. In other words, most of the activities to which attention had been given since Consultation V and the supporting organization to accomplish them were no longer wanted by the member agencies, as the Coalition became secondary to their own survival needs. Suggestions for future consultations were all in the area of training of trainers or developing perspective on issues of social change, including farm workers organizing, low-cost housing in suburbia, welfare rights and Black Caucus agenda. It was agreed that the next consultation would be under the sponsorship of the Black Caucus.

The only national projects still underway at the time of the National Delegate Assembly in Puerto Rico were the training of Black trainers and the Information Service. Washington reported that $2,600 had been received from agencies for the Black Caucus fund, and that a training event was scheduled for the end of April. Bobbi Wells of ICUIS spoke of the difficulties in getting both information input and finance from ATC and the centers for the Information Service, as well as the need to withdraw from the NCC computer services and bring all activities to Chicago. The Council voted to continue the relationship "with further active exploration of its use" until the next Council meeting.

A survey, "Working Relationships among ATC Centers in 1970," conducted by Younger for the Research and Evaluation Committee following the Puerto Rico meeting, showed that a good deal of interaction was occurring between ATC members in this period, even though national cooperation was becoming more limited. Seventeen of 22 centers reported a total of 108 relationships with other centers, and only ACTS, BCETF, Community 33, PRISA and UTC did not reply. By far the largest pattern of interaction was in the state of Ohio, where the three agencies that were working together as ATN had 45 relationships reported, and in the Eastern region, where 24 were listed. The following types of working relationships were mentioned most frequently: joint sponsorship of training (22), cooperation in Brethren racism training (18), use of staff to lead simulation games in training event (15), consultation (12) and joint proposal development (9). Other cooperation included: staff visits, referral of trainees to training events, joint planning, use of staff as trainers, staff involved as trainees, evaluation, use of reports or materials, and joint research project. Younger commented on the data, "On the whole, those centers which reach out and try to cooperate with others are the ones which are reported as having the greatest number of working relationships."

RETRENCHMENT (1971-73)

The last separate Council meeting was held on June 1, 1971, in St. Louis. Most of its actions were devoted to restricting national operation of ATC and tightening up its limited budget. William Ramsden of TEAM, as Membership Committee chairman, was instructed to "sound out centre directors on the self-interest of their centres in being evaluated, and that no evaluation be conducted until after his report at the next council meeting." Delegates to other organizations were no longer to have their expenses paid for representing ATC. Regional representatives were to contact ATC members to secure 1971 dues. The Information Service relationship with ICUIS was to be continued, and its expenses were given top priority for payment. Later in 1971 the ATC Information Service was amalgamated into ICUIS's own Abstract Service and ceased to need separate funding. The collapse of ICUA resulted in one of its staff members who was remaining in Missouri, Robert Spencer, being named as the corporation's registered agent in the state. The only positive action was to initiate action research among members on the issues raised by Robert Hermanson's paper, "Abandoned Offspring," which reported to JSAC concerning the danger that ATC centers would go out of existence without further denominational support.

Although the Council was still expecting the Black Caucus to take charge of Consultation X, that group became even more badly divided than the White agencies they served as a result of failure to secure a Ford grant for a unified training proposal. One meeting was held by the Caucus, but it was never able to achieve its own training event for Black staff, let alone to organize one for the entire Coalition. Planning of Consultation IX was placed in the hands of COMMIT, which set up a program around issues represented by the United Farm Workers Organizing Committee on October 3-6, 1971, in Delano and Los Angeles, California. The number of centers eligible to attend had declined to 22, but only 12 were represented at the sessions, marking the beginning of a decline in interest in getting together as ATC.

Leaders of the United Farm Workers Organizing Committee and the National Farm Worker Ministry developed the history of the struggle in the fields and showed the work of their institutions at La Paz. Then the participants moved back to Los Angeles, where they took part in boycott picketing of chain stores and discussed future strategy of support for the farm workers.

Only the National Delegate Assembly met during Consultation IX. The national committees were dismantled and their functions given to designated individuals. Relationships were confirmed with the following organizations: JSAC, IFCO, AATS, Division of Overseas Ministries of NCC, SCLC and UTC Board. Evaluation was to be reserved in the future for agencies applying for ATC membership and any ATC agencies desiring it. Dues would continue to be assessed and collected to support the Information Service, Council meetings and representatives, as well as a new ATC Director for publicity purposes. The only area for possible national cooperation was training in connection with the Fund for the Self-Development of Peoples of the United Presbyterian Church in the U.S.A. This represented a recognition that funding by national mission agencies was declining or non-existent, and the only possible sources of national support were the crisis funds set up by national denominations.

Consultation X was planned for Chicago on March 19-22, 1972, with the main content being issues of health services, as developed at UTC. Only ten of 20 eligible centers were represented, participating in two days of a four-day UTC conference on "Our Collapsing Health System." The Medical Committee on Human Rights, the National Free Clinic Council, the American Hospital Association, and the Joint Health Venture of Los Angeles presented their points of view, and the program ended with a discussion of possibilities for ATC linkage.

ATC Council members present at the Consultation met at odd times during the training sessions under the leadership of Buckwalter of CHART, who had become chairman when Torres resigned as a symbol of the withdrawal of "Third World solidarity" with ATC. They agreed on a limited set of functions for ATC in the future year—communication network, staff development and legitimation. This confirmed two of the priorities adopted a year before in Puerto Rico, but substituted legitimation through such means as publishing a brochure (the only item for which budget was to be spent), biennial review, admission standards, peer consultation and ties to other organizations for the more ambitious development of national and international strategies, which was not happening anyway. Ramsden of TEAM was elected as the new chairman, with Mance Jackson of ACTS as vice-chairman. Affairs of ATC were placed in the hands of the four officers, instead of the Council. This direction was ratified by the National Delegate Assembly, and the Coalition was now returned to its original state of a skeleton directorate to operate between consultations, when any major decisions on direction would be taken.

Consultation XI on the theme of training church-related laity for systemic change in secular institutions was held in Philadelphia on October 15-18, 1972. Only nine of the 17 ATC agencies still operating were present for a program presented by MAP on its training design for lay ministry for organizational change. Although MAP had earlier withdrawn from ATC, TEAM in Philadelphia had been conducting a great deal of its own training with MAP staff. The program consisted of an introduction to the resource packet, "A Strategy of Hope," and use of videotape recording as a means of group self-evaluation. Interest in this subject was so great among those attending that a Task Force on Lay Ministry for Organizational Change was formed with representatives from TEAM, COMMIT, EMM and other interested centers.

Seven centers were still present for deliberations of the National Delegate Assembly at the close of the Consultation. They agreed to continue the looser structure set up in Chicago and to ask for member centers to reaffirm their ATC membership. The chairman was asked to issue a periodic newsletter to keep centers informed of what was happening. A survey of linkages showed that, through the work of individual centers, ATC was related to the Third World, ARABS (Association for Religion and Behavioral Sciences), JSAC, Lay Ministry for Organizational Change Coalition, NCBC (National Committee of Black Churchmen), BITF (Black Interreligious Task Force), Chicanos and other Latins, Native Peoples and health care groups. Discussion of the ARABS relationship centered on a mutual concern for accreditation of trainers, which was to be pursued further. Speed Leas of COMMIT had already written a paper for the Accreditation Committee of ARABS, in which he had suggested that "action training" be reserved to describe what ATC had been doing and that action trainers wishing ARABS accreditation go through whatever process and standards were set up by that group (which has since become the Association for Creative Change). He underscored that ATC was a network of agencies, not individual trainers, and that its accreditation processes were only for agency programs not their staffs.

Consultation XII was scheduled by the Delegate Assembly to be held at ICUIS in Chicago the following spring on corporate responsibility and power structure research. A core group of six centers which had been at the Philadelphia session (CUT, EMM, ICUIS, TEAM, UTC, UTOA), was in attendance for the sessions on April 1-4, 1973, along with three others interested in subjects on the program (ACTS, COMMIT, CUE-M). Thus, in the course of a year 12 of the 16 centers still in existence had been represented at Coalition meetings, even though there was a diminished national agenda to be pursued.

Power structure research was presented by the Corporate Intelligence Alliance of Chicago, ACTS and UTOA, while corporate responsibility was covered by the Council of Corporate Review from Minneapolis (connected with CUE-M), Corporate Information Center, Citizens Action Program of Chicago, Clergy and Laity Concerned's Honeywell Campaign, CUT and Interfaith Committee on Social Responsibility in Investments. Although very little had happened in the way of common action on lay ministry for organizational change since the Philadelphia meeting, a good deal of time was taken in discussion of priorities for ATC action on corporate responsibility for the next six months and possibilities for liaison through ATC members with groups involved in actions with corporations. It was promised to collect data "on the way in which centers work or do not work" with these priorities over the following six months, so that Consultation XIII could evaluate what had happened.

Apart from the discussion of ways to follow up on the issue of corporate responsibility, the business session of the National Delegate Assembly was very brief. The four officers were reelected; Bryce Little of EMM, treasurer, reminded the group that dues for 1972 and 1973 were due; Leas reported there was "no need of further action in relation to the organization formerly called ARABS"; and the body voted to accept the invitation of EMM to come to Seattle for Consultation XIII on October 14-16, 1973, for sessions that would examine the issues of Native Peoples (Trail of Broken Treaties) and hunger.

Thus ended the final official meeting of the Action Training Coalition. When EMM as hosts and Ramsden as chairman tried to check on registration for Consultation XIII, they found so few planning to come that the meeting was cancelled. Ramsden subsequently wrote in his last letter as chairman to ATC members:

> I am sure the low rate of paying ATC dues in 1973 and the low rate of registrations for the Fall Consultation reflect both ATC's present low profile and the funding difficulties all of us are facing. I wonder, though, if it does not reflect more basically a waning of self interest of the Centers in ATC (and as I see it, a coalition is by definition based on mutual self interest).[9]

Others, however, had seen this pattern earlier, although they attributed it not only to a change in the centers but to the climate in which they were operating. Bonthius had written after Consultation X:

> I really did have a sense of grief by the time the Consultation was over. Somehow I found myself associating action training centers with the civil rights era and wondered whether what I was experiencing was a decade gone—the Sixties. In any case, the oppression has

moved in—the sky *is* falling—and the struggle is a good deal less clear, more complicated, and much longer than the charismatics of yesterday suggested.[10]

In summary, the six-year history of the Action Training Coalition divides neatly into thirds, each one spanning four consultations. Stage 1 was concerned with finding each other and organizing the coalition, and lasted from the first exploratory meeting in October 1967 through Consultation IV in April 1969. Stage 2 was marked by attempts to develop a national strategy for action and the creation of a larger form of organization to carry it out. This period began with Consultation V in St. Louis in October 1969 and ended after Consultation VIII in Puerto Rico in March 1971. Stage 3 was a period of retrenchment, in which many centers were closing and those that remained were principally interested in using ATC for communication, staff development and legitimation. Stage 3 can be said to have closed in October 1973, when Consultation XIII was called off for lack of registrations.

EVALUATION

How are we to interpret the end of ATC? Ramsden attributed it to the survival difficulties being faced by the centers and their lack of mutual self interest in meeting or working together; yet the centers that survived into 1974 were mostly doing a better job of sustaining themselves than earlier. Bonthius felt it was part of the end of the civil rights era and the tightening of oppression in the wider society; yet the centers which were still operating had a stronger base of support for the kind of activity in which they were engaged than was true at the time of ATC's formation.

When the record is examined as a whole, the end of ATC appears to be more a case of abandonment than anything else. First, the coalition was abandoned by those who had encouraged its formation in the first place—the national mission boards of the major Protestant denominations—and by those whom it had hoped to influence—those same mission boards, the theological seminaries and a variety of national groups interested in issues of social change. Although his study was superficial, Hermanson had been accurate in describing the action-training centers as "abandoned offsprings" in March 1971. But even those who have been abandoned can find some community in their estrangement and alienation. What ended the coalition was not the abandonment of ATC by the national church bodies and other groups, but the abandonment by the training centers themselves. As they found their survival and continued vitality to depend more on their own efforts and responsiveness to more local constituencies, there was not only a decline of interest in national strategies but a decreasing desire to meet together or even to remain in communication. The touch of messianism that Bonthius had noted at Kansas City in 1968, concerned for the formation of the seminaries and awakening the church to its mission in metropolis, had completely petered out by the time the surviving centers received their invitation to Consultation XIII in 1973. What the training centers had brought together and organized in 1968, they themselves abandoned in 1973.

On balance, the strengths of ATC during its period of operation seem to have outweighed its weaknesses. Among those strengths were the following:

1. ATC gave technical assistance and support to developing centers. At the time of its organization, most of the centers had been in existence less than two years and some had only begun to engage in training. In a highly competitive situation, ATC was able to encourage cooperation and sharing.
2. ATC, in both its consultations and its other organized activities, created a participatory forum for a wide variety of centers with different programs and constituencies. Its diversity was a strength so long as there were some areas of common interest among the centers.
3. ATC enlisted a great amount of participation in its consultations and a surprisingly high degree of budget support from struggling institutions. There was still a balance of $1,946.92 in its bank account after Consultation XIII was cancelled.
4. ATC made good use of task forces of interested persons and representatives with natural ties to the institutions which it wished to affect.
5. ATC nurtured the development of the Information Service, which ICUIS later expanded into a wider operation. Although it was never used to its fullest potential, either in input or use of materials, the Information Service continued to receive top priority for ATC financial support even when there was grave doubt that the necessary funds could be raised.
6. ATC was able to make a far greater unified impact on some institutions like AATS, SACEM and JSAC than any center could have made by itself. Theological seminaries still saw "action training" as a formidable opponent seven years after the first lightning raid on an AATS meeting. The national denominations in JSAC gave training centers a far greater role in setting criteria and screening proposals than was given to any other category of mission projects.
7. ATC was willing to practice what it preached. Consultants and action-training methodology were used in ATC consultations and meetings. In spite of its own strongly held objectives, the coalition was open to new issues and unfamiliar constituencies.
8. ATC remained unwilling, despite efforts of others to reduce action training to a methodology, to separate the activity of training from the question of who was being trained for what. As a coalition it remained loyal to a concern for the powerless, for minorities and for international issues, especially in the Third World.

The weaknesses of ATC were in some cases a result of its origins and in others a result of its high aspirations or lack of performance.

1. ATC discussions about funding action training were always looking for a pot of gold either among the national denominations affiliated with JSAC or from one of the national foundations. This had been encouraged by national denomination support for the organization of ATC and was only dropped as local sources began to prove to be the firmest basis for sustaining the centers.
2. ATC was always gingerly about its relationship to the one national center in the U.S.—UTC, which had on its Board most of the major national denominations and was engaged in spending $147,000 to $603,000 per year during the life of ATC. UTC's own realization that it needed the other centers in ATC came too late for their joint efforts to

be supported out of UTC resources; prior to that time UTC participation in ATC was less than wholehearted.

3. ATC meetings and activities were principally composed of staff members of the training agencies. Attempts to secure agency representation of board members and other involved persons in the earlier stages of the coalition had settled down to programs of staff training by the time of Consultation IX.

4. ATC was largely under the control of White male clergy, even though Randy Nugent, a Black Methodist clergyman, was its chairman for over one-third of its career.

5. ATC overorganized itself, with the adoption of an elaborate system of representative national government, and was never able to set or enforce standards for member centers, although membership procedures kept moving in that direction.

6. ATC's Social Goal represented a solid commitment to liberation in the society, but it assumed that the churches were also willing and able to back that kind of purpose. However, at the time the Social Goal was adopted, a large share of the training being done by the centers was in more prosaic areas of church organization or sensitizing church people to societal issues.

7. ATC depended on its caucuses—Black, International and Third World—to carry it into new areas of training connected with liberation, but those groups were poorly organized and did not follow through on their intentions when given the initiative.

8. ATC was not able to realize its major effort to develop national programs and contracts that would involve the local centers on a sustained basis.

CHAPTER VI
Learnings and Conclusions

To make sense out of a confusing time and a multi-faceted group of projects that arose during that time, it would be easiest to choose a single interpretation by focusing on one aspect of this development to the exclusion of all the others. This is what is now occurring as many in both the wider society and the churches use their own understanding and interpretation of "the Sixties" to justify both what they reject and what they choose to continue. At one time in this study I set down a quick list of "hypotheses -stated as extremes" to remind myself that, depending on what aspect of action training one chose to emphasize, the whole development could appear quite differently. The following list illustrates how this can happen:

Racial - group of White guys kicked out of ghetto looking for way to remain in control of strategy

Vocational - group of inner-city clergy trying to "make it" in new form of specialized ministry

Bureaucratic - group of denominational executives trying to be like industry, and have own training and R & D arm

Educational - group of rebels against theological education trying to develop more practical form

Ecumenical - group of ecumenically oriented clergy trying to get beyond straitjacket of denominationalism

Political - group of liberal clergy trying to build larger power base in metropolitan areas

Cultural - group of dissatisfied clergy trying to find way into counter-cultural stance

Social Sciences - group of urban oriented clergy trying to engage in action-research and behavioral science-based training

Financial - group of denominational executives engaging in "boondoggle" with surplus national funds

Responsive - group of reformist ("renewal") clergy trying to create church equivalents of (a) NTL training in organizational development, (b) management training, or (c) poverty program training

U.S. Institutional Crisis - group of aware clergy feeling way toward new forms for church and metropolitan society

There are data in the records of the Action Training Coalition and its member agencies to support all these hypotheses — and many more. Yet a balanced interpretation should both take these people at face value in what they have said they were trying to do and note those patterns of behavior which were characteristic enough to be distinctive. What follows is an attempt to explain both what these agencies and programs were, and to draw learnings and conclusions for the next phase in urban mission on the North American continent.

A SUMMARY DEFINITION

The definition of an "urban training center" used to develop the invitation list for the first National Consultation at Chevy Chase, Maryland, in 1968 already picked up some of the most important characteristics of the agencies and programs that were to define themselves as engaged in action training:

> A national, regional or metropolitan network of resources to provide an arena for confrontation, reflection, commitment, skills training and strategy in action to enable the church to perform its mission in an urbanizing society.[1]

The original purpose of all the ATC agencies (except CHART in Cincinnati) was to train clergy and laity (and, in many cases, theological and other students) for urban mission. As this study has already described, most of the programs worked largely with a church constituency.

The theological point of view with which most of the founders and staffs were operating was the "mission theology" that had developed in ecumenical circles through the leadership of Hans Hoekendijk and others in the World Council of Churches following World War II. This perspective already assumed the historical-critical approach to the Bible, a kerygmatic or so-called "Neo-Orthodox" statement of theology and a willingness to see the church as one of the institutions in society, with the ability both to influence and be influenced by the life of its times. However, in contrast to much of the churchly and confessional theology of the post-war period, which could be summarized in the slogan, "Let the church be the church," this approach took seriously the Johannine statement that "God so loved the world..." Therefore, it placed great importance on the church's secular involvement. Some of its proponents summarized their views in the slogan, "Let the world set the agenda," although the glasses through which they read that agenda were those of Biblical faith. The mission to which they saw the church called was not only the calling of persons into the Christian community but the identification of God's work in human history outside the church. The church was to stand alongside the rest of humanity both in proclaiming that work and assisting in carrying out its purposes. *Heilsgeschichte* transcended church history, and the mission of God was being brought to fulfillment in the history of the whole world in which Christians also share. There was a strong identification with the prophetic tradition and an emphasis on either a realized eschatology or a coming Kingdom that shows itself in first-fruits in the present time.

Connected with this theological perspective were some other assumptions that helped to undergird the kinds of programs that were developed and those forms of action that were promoted. (1) Most of those connected with support for or development of action training shared the liberal assumption that both society and the church needed only to be "renewed." Another name for "mission theology," especially when its principal focus was on the life of the church, was "renewal theology." Although the radically eschatological claims of the Gospel were kept in the forefront, they were usually connected with a call for forms of action, both in society and in the church, that were basically reformist. (2) The pragmatic and practical nature of Christianity that has been emphasized in North American society and theology since the early nineteenth century (a strain that is well represented in Horace Bushnell) caused the leaders of these programs to place their emphasis on ways in which the Gospel would produce "projects," "programs" or "actions." This was an activist Christianity for an activist civilization. (3) Based on the reading that the Gospel is particularly addressed to the poor and oppressed, the approach used in these programs was tipped toward the minorities and the underdogs of society. A major share of the urban mission effort from the East Harlem Parish days on had been among the urban poor in ghetto areas. Therefore, it was not surprising that race and poverty, which were two dominant issues in the United States during this period, were also major concerns for the action-training centers. (4) It was not incidental that one of the defining characteristics of an "urban training center" was that it should be "ecumenical." Not only had their theological point of view developed out of the ecumenical movement, but it was also informed by some of the mission approaches that had been made by Roman Catholics, especially the French worker priests. As already noted, the emphasis of mission theology on the action of God in the world led many to affirm a "secular ecumenism" which discerned redemptive action in movements, groups and events outside the churches.

In addition to these theological assumptions and practical corollaries, there were several operational assumptions in action training that helped to determine the tools that were used. First — and in many ways most important, although seldom explicitly acknowledged — was the reliance on the methodology of social science research. Essentially inductive, this approach is concerned to gather and examine the data connected with any historical or social situation before arriving at conclusions about the forms of action to adopt. Even when social scientists were not directly connected with a training agency, the training staff made heavy use of the research findings of social scientists and encouraged trainees to research the details of their own social situation or any other in which they anticipated taking action. Second, as has already been noted in the discussion of the origins of "training," these centers made use of many behavioral models and techniques that had been developed in applied psychology. Although many of their staff members and the groups with which they were allied were suspicious of personal counseling and some of the ways in which group dynamics methods were being used in the churches, they also accepted the assumption that behavioral patterns are acquired and can be changed. This meant that they were willing to try some of the technology that had been developed in applied psychology. Finally, the principal mode of training that was used in action training was so-called "action/reflection," or what National Training Laboratories dubbed the action-research model. Much of the reflection in this church-sponsored training used theological language and images, but it built on the inductive approach of the social sciences and the behavioral concern of applied psychology.

This examination of the history of the development of urban training has made it plain that the principal actors in bringing action training into being were the national urban mission offices of the mainline White Protestant denominations. These executives were concerned both that the experience of urban mission that had developed in the preceding 15 years be transmitted to a new generation of missioners and lay leaders and that new models be developed for both the churches and metropolitan society. Across the nation, in both the United States and in Canada, they were aware of a network of urban projects being sponsored by their several denominations, a wide variety of community programs and civil actions that were being supported with both involvement and funds, and a cadre of denominational and ecumenical metropolitan mission executives and clergy.

The action-training centers, then, were both a repository of experience and a place for sustained research and development ("R and D"). The experience upon which they relied was principally that of post-war urban mission among the largely White mainline denominations, although in time it came to include the experience of the Black churches that came forward in the civil rights movement and of urban activists in the Roman Catholic Church after Vatican II. Trainees were not only brought in touch with the learnings from past experience; they were also encouraged to study the needs of the current situation, and to develop "models" of action and strategies that would help to alleviate injustice, meet human needs and change social structures. At times the centers were engaged in true "experiments" with new situations in an attempt to devise new patterns of action, but their principal function for the churches was to serve as a sensitive barometer of social change, a kind of Distant Early Warning system of what was to come in the future.

Although it was not required by their sponsors, those who set up the action-training agencies and programs usually adopted a bureaucratic form of organization in which there were staffs, arranged on a hierarchical salary grid. Programs and budgets were arrayed in the form of "proposals." And it was felt necessary to form some sort of board of directors to set policy. In part, this was made necessary by the United States tax laws, which were ready to grant exemption to any form of religious or non-profit activity that was properly organized. As a result, many of the action-training centers — like other specialized ministries — were incorporated and had their certificate of tax exemption before they had clear plans for the kinds of training they were going to carry on.

Finally, the experience of many of the sponsors in developing support for urban mission and of many of the original planners in working on urban issues had led them to rely on strategies of coalition. According to the dictionary definition, a coalition is "a combination or alliance, especially a temporary one, between persons, factions, parties, states, etc." In a coalition, various self-interests (or organizational interests) come together to work in a common cause or action. Where the parties coalescing have a base of organization and support other than the cause around which they are gathered, it is possible to combine and recombine in a variety of patterns while still maintaining their own identity. This made it possible for the church to remain true to its own values and patterns of organization, while joining with those of different values and structure. However, coalition did not furnish an adequate basis for the reconstruction of community, either in society or in the church. And, in the case of organizations as dependent as the action-training agencies, coalition was able to achieve quick gains without lasting results.

The sources of the crises that caused many of the action-training agencies to terminate operations and others to change their programs and structure were manifold. Some stress the rise of the movements of cultural identity (Black, Brown/Hispanic, Red/Native American, Yellow/Asian American and other "ethnics") and sexual protest (women and homosexuals) as being the principal cause, because they challenged the liberal consensus and its attempt to create movements of unity across lines of division in society. Others would point to the disquieting effects of the Vietnam War. Still others stress the change in the financial situation of the major national mission boards, which could no longer depend on both interest and capital gains from invested funds. However, some of the causes must be sought in the action-training agencies themselves. Most had experienced great difficulty in sharpening their own goals and were overextended in a variety of directions. Because they were "tertiary" organizations in church structures that depended for their financial support upon the "secondary" organizations of denominations at the national and regional level, they were cut off from the sources of support available to local congregations as "primary" organizations. In addition, their training activities principally enrolled professionals and had been unable, in most cases, to build a significant lay constituency. Thus, they were also cut off from the largest group of potential trainees, the members of congregations.

ASSUMPTIONS

Change - Although the initial definition of the purpose of action-training agencies like the Urban Training Center for Christian Mission in Chicago and of the Action Training Coalition itself was centered on the concept of "mission," by 1968 the principal word used to define their position was "change." A whole cluster of assumptions accompanied this shift.

(1) *The meaning of "change," for action-training agencies, remained ambivalent, covering the whole range from revolution and radical change to institutional reform and cultural fulfillment.* As action training began to ask sharper questions about what constituted the mission of the church in an urban society, the need to challenge the status quo became clearer. However, there was no clear agreement about the goals for which Christians should be working in society. The beginning definition used by the Organizing Committee for the National Consultation of Urban Training Centers in February 1968 spoke of their purpose as enabling "the church to perform its mission in an urbanizing society." At Consultation IV of the Action Training Coalition in March 1969 this was changed to enabling "groups and individuals in society to effect institutional and community change for humanization and justice."

What action-training agencies meant by "change" covered a wide range of purposes. Some Black revolutionaries and Marxist thinkers who were used as resource persons in training were working for replacement of the political and economic institutions of the society. Most of those engaged in action training were committed to reform of the existing institutions by a variety of strategies. A great deal of attention was given to "community organizing," usually along the lines taught by Saul Alinsky, who was attempting to assist groups of people to work to change those issues that were hurting them most in their communities. However, for many the principal issues of "change" were those of institutional reform, especially within the church itself. And some, under the influence of the human potential movement, were particularly interested in personal and cultural fulfillment through the "humanization" of institutions and society.

In this stress on change, action trainers were following the lead of much of the theory and literature on group dynamics, developed out of applied psychology and sociology. The techniques of group dynamics, planned change and organizational development had been developed by the ruling elites of the United States, using the resources of universities, military research and a growing group of consultants (both firms and individuals), with some support from foundations. Even though they continually used the language of "change," these techniques had been developed for the use of elites and on behalf of the dominant large institutions of American society and carried with them a strong ideological overtone of social control. Action training did not proceed far enough with answering the question of "Change for what?" to be able to have agreement about the nature of the change being sought.

(2) *The focus of change moved from the society as a whole to institutions within the society.* A primary component of the vision that brought most of the action-training agencies into being was the understanding that urban society is an interaction of systems, and that change was needed for the whole as well as the parts. Most of the orientation and analysis which they included in their training programs used specific issues and institutions as examples of the way in which the whole society was operating in an unjust fashion toward racial minorities and the poor. However, as the persons needing training and the groups willing to pay for training were increasingly limited to those who were part of institutions, especially the religious institution, the focus was limited to institutional change.

A good example of this is found in an analysis of the programs conducted by agencies connected with Action Training Network of Ohio (ATN) between 1966 and 1974.[2] In the beginning of their training most attention was focused on strategies of external change, and the major targets were social issues that affected other institutions in society. Between 1966 and 1974, 123 of 226 training programs were directed to external change, and another 20 worked at both external and internal change. However, programs devoted exclusively to internal change and organizational development went from only one program before 1970 to 61 in the period between 1970 and 1974.

When the programs are examined more closely, two factors were responsible for the shift from an almost exclusive emphasis on external change to greater emphasis on internal change. (1) Programs concerned with anti-racism training within the church were necessarily focused on how to produce change within that system. ATN conducted several programs of this kind between 1970 and 1972. (2) Programs on social change with community groups increasingly began to emphasize how a group could change its own way of working in order to have greater impact on other institutions in society. Thus, when the issues of social change had to be faced within religious institutions or a group needed to organize itself better to produce external change, the training groups associated with ATN began to emphasize internal change and develop a new emphasis on what they called "intra-systems change."

(3) *Action training worked with a mood of optimism that assumed change would be relatively easy.* In the spirit of the administrations of John F. Kennedy and Lyndon B. Johnson in which they were born, the action-training agencies and their denominational sponsors assumed that, if they

had a proper analysis of the problems of the cities, reasonable proposals for
their solution, and the ability to bring together enough of the victims and
persons of good will ready to support them, significant and lasting changes
could be made in the structure of American society. Although they were
quite aware of the realistic appraisal of social structures of sin made popular
by Reinhold Niebuhr, they worked with a doctrine of "realized
eschatology" that saw each issue and each struggle to secure change as a
manifestation of the Kingdom in contemporary life. Although they knew in
great detail the degradation of human life by urban systems, they trusted in
the goodness of human nature — and the exercise of organized power — to
improve conditions for all, but especially for those at the bottom of the
social system.

Power - There was far greater agreement among action-training agencies on
what needed to be changed and the principal means by which such change
would occur. Each training program was concerned for analyzing the way
in which power was organized and institutionalized in urban society and for
teaching ways in which it might be utilized to produce change.

(1) *Action-training agencies operated on an understanding of injustice
that saw it to be a web of institutionalized policies and practices that maintained the power of some persons and groups, while denying it to others.*
Urban systems were not understood as impersonal machines that could be
used for the benefit of some or for the benefit of all. Rather, they were seen
as the organized means by which a limited group in society maintained their
power and privilege and continued to dominate the lives of the rest of
society.

Most of the action-training agencies sharpened their understanding of this
dynamic of domination and deprivation by giving particular attention to
the operation of racism in urban society. By using the factor of skin color as
a major indicator of inferiority, White-dominated institutions were able to
maintain their oppression of Blacks, Hispanics and other non-White
minorities, and to deny members of those groups a fair share of the
economic, social and political power in the community.

(2) *Organizing group power was taught as a principal means of affecting
the behavior of unjust systems and overcoming the dominance of others.*
Again, the "community organizing" approach of Saul Alinsky, with its
assumption that power must be opposed by power, provided a strategy that
seemed adequate to reorder the unjust systems that affected jobs, education,
housing, health and all the other issues that plagued the lives of urban
citizens. This strategy had the advantage, on the one hand, of affirming the
democratic values of citizenship and popular action, while, on the other
hand, avoiding the difficult question of violence or taking up means of

physical force to change the status quo. Instead, it tried to focus anger and apathy toward changing the specific situations that people wanted to have changed, while hoping that this would produce significant alterations in the structures of power that maintained injustice. For Christian churches and agencies sponsored by those churches, this was an approach that took account of social sin, but also proposed social means to change it.

(3) *The principal strategy, apart from organizing groups of the oppressed in their own interest, was to be the formation of coalitions between such groups and institutions, including the churches.* Rather than seeking to organize new political parties or organizations with an ideological base, action-training agencies gave their primary attention to ways in which coalitions of interest might be formed on various issues that affected the lives of city-dwellers. They believed that Christians and others drawn from a variety of backgrounds could acquire skills and coalesce new centers of power that would be able to challenge and change the existing structures.

Thus both structural and institutional analysis gave a realistic understanding of the ways in which power is actually organized in American urban society. However, rather than proposing the overthrow of this system or the erection of an alternative, most training programs chose different issues or institutions around which to organize opposition, in the hope that, if a large enough constituency could be organized to work for change, the institutions — or hopefully, the system as a whole — would have to give in and take a different course. The proposal to oppose power with power was in accordance with the analysis that had been made; but the attempt to do this with community organizations and actions that had limited targets overlooked that part of the analysis which said that injustice is systemic. If the desire of dominant groups to maintain their position would not be sufficient to guarantee continuation of the status quo, then the satisfaction of limited goals or the ability to gain limited power would stop the momentum for change that was generated.

For religious institutions, coalition was a particularly favored tactic at this time, because it only required a limited commitment to limited objectives without in any way challenging the nature of the religious institutions themselves. Churches and synagogues, along with most of the other institutions of society, could enlist in campaigns to change government policies or the policies of other institutions, while not needing to consider change in their own methods of operation or their own involvement in the patterns and structures of injustice. However, when their own institutions and resources were challenged, as when the Black Manifesto demanded $500 million in reparations from religious institutions, they were no longer so eager for change. Their power was then turned from support of and coalition with the oppressed to maintaining the survival of their own institutional base. Analysis and strategy that had been based on an understanding of the organized and institutionalized power operating to oppress others or to assist them in resisting oppression was then abandoned for the simpler understanding of institutional self-interest and survival.

Business Values - An irony of action training is that, although it often engaged in criticism of and opposition to the business systems that dominate so much of United States society, the centers discovered that the methods they had adopted were not value-free, but had their origins in business and industry, and that the managerial and entrepreneurial models of organization from the wider society influenced their own structures and operations.

(1) *The techniques of "training" were not value-free, because they had been originally developed as means of improving social control.* The development of training in the wider society has a history in which wars and social conflict have sharpened the desire of military, industrial and government agencies to have adequate means of indoctrination for administrators, supervisors and employees, and to produce "managed change" which would remain within their institutions' capacity to control. Both World War I and World War II resulted in quantum leaps in the application of the social sciences to human society, first within the military and war industry, then transferred to civilian life at the end of hostilities. Adoption of the National Labor Relations Act in 1935 made it necessary for management to deal with employees in groups rather than as isolated individuals. During the 1960's social unrest and rising expectations, especially in urban ghettos, produced a similar pressure for more sophisticated means of socialization and social control within the large institutions which hold most of the power in industrial society.

It is to the credit of action-training agencies that they were initially suspicious of many of the activities that went by the name of "training." Commitment to the dynamic of redemption or liberation for those enslaved or managed by the powers of urban-industrial society, especially Black and Hispanic Americans, caused many of them to discard or seriously modify a great many techniques that had been accepted as viable for producing organizational change and personal growth. No technique or method is value-free, and it is necessary to look carefully at their origins before accepting them as useful for the task to which an agency is committed.

(2) *For the most part, managerial and entrepreneurial models of organization were adopted by the action-training agencies.* Each agency was set up as a separate non-profit, tax-exempt corporation, and its table of organization provided for a director and other staff members in the customary bureaucratic pattern. The major exceptions to this pattern were PRISA in Puerto Rico, which moved quickly to being a collective of ecumenical Christians committed to independent status for their island, and those ecumenical agencies which added training as an activity to an already

diverse form of organization.

The pressures of limited funding from sponsoring denominations caused many action-training agencies to adopt an even more frankly entrepreneurial model as a group of "consultants" operating to fulfill training contracts with various groups of "clients." These agencies used this terminology unabashedly to describe the way in which they were seeking to serve the training interests and objectives of those who could afford to pay for their services. In many cases this moved them away from training with religious and community groups toward more work with business and with government agencies and programs. And it led to an almost exclusive emphasis on internal change and organizational development.

The need to be "in business" showed itself very strongly both in the development of each training center and of the Action Training Coalition itself. Each agency had both to "have a business" (know what it existed for and what it was trying to do) and to "do business" (have a set of reciprocal relationships with other groups or organizations for which it could do what it was equipped to do, and to receive substantial reward both in the form of economic return and satisfactory recognition). Attempts at cooperation among agencies in the Action Training Coalition tried to solve this problem collectively. Much of the time at ATC meetings was spent in addressing the question of whether the agencies "had a business" and what that business was. They showed much less disposition to "do business" together, except in a few attempts at joint efforts in training or developing curriculum resources. Finally, the need of each agency to be "in business" for itself overwhelmed the cooperative efforts. Some survived by seeking new constituencies or by giving their trainees what they were expecting, while others went out of business at a dramatic rate between 1972 and 1975.

(3) *The action-training agencies were highly dependent on the heated-up defense economy of the Vietnam Era and the cheap fuel available in the United States at that time.* Some have contended that specialized ministries and social change activities of the national and metropolitan offices of the mainline denominations during the 1960's were financed by channeling contributions from local churches into these efforts. However, a careful study of the budgets of the various action-training centers, together with an analysis of the budgets of the national denominations during this same period, shows that the money which went for their support came not from current contributions, but from the income out of past contributions that had been invested in endowment funds. Both high returns on these investments and capital gains in an economy that was making its profits on increased activity by the military-industrial complex provided the funds that were devoted to efforts for justice and liberation. Therefore, it was not a sudden slump in giving to such causes that made it difficult after 1968 to continue support at the same level. Rather, it was the drying up of some of those financial sources, as well as the way in which some national denominations, along with their regional counterparts, had overextended

themselves optimistically and then had to cut back. When national staffs were being cut back at denominational headquarters, it was no longer possible to continue new institutions that were highly dependent on them for financial support.

Another irony of the Action Training Coalition was that it depended on cheap petroleum fuel for the air travel that made it possible for national executives to travel freely from their offices to metropolitan areas all over the country, and for staff members of ATC agencies to gather frequently with one another at national consultations. The Board of the Urban Training Center for Christian Mission in Chicago included 11 denominations as full sponsors and 7 others represented by board members. From 1963 to 1972 they met from four to ten times each year in Chicago, although most of the members came from national offices in New York City and elsewhere. Between February 1968 and April 1973, the member agencies of ATC held 12 consultations, most of which were attended by at least 40 staff members in locations stretching from Pennsylvania and Maryland to Ohio, Missouri and Illinois. One session each was held in Toronto, Puerto Rico and California. This kind of gathering would not have been possible without the relatively inexpensive air fares made possible by the availability of cheap petroleum as fuel for planes. Although many thought this to be only the beginning of the emergence of the United States as a galaxy of four to seven megalopolises and the dawn of the era of the "global village," it has proven to be a momentary aberration in world history that was not so permanent as some assumed.

Metropolitan Focus - From the very beginning the action-training programs were committed to a metropolitan focus, which stressed the interrelatedness of urban society, while emphasizing the need to redress inner-city and minority injustice. UTC in Chicago, as the first of these centers, began with the purpose of training church workers for all parts of the metropolitan areas. Other programs kept a clear vision of the roots of the problems of the inner city that lay with institutions and people outside those blighted areas. This was not a popular emphasis, even at the height of the Civil Rights Movement and the War Against Poverty. Middle-class people, especially those living in suburban areas, preferred to see the residents of the inner city as responsible for their own plight and to treat them as objects of Christian service rather than the subjects of their own empowerment and liberation. Although there were many temptations to adapt to or adopt this reigning value system and faulty analysis, the action-training centers kept the kind of vision and emphasis that saw metropolitan areas and the whole urban society as an interrelated system in which most were victims, and only a few dominant institutions and members of the ruling power groups were able to control their own life and destiny. As their analysis of this situation deepened, action-training centers also began to appreciate the international dimensions of the situation, in which populations were not only joined with each other across local political boundaries and from metropolitan area to metropolitan area, but also across national boundaries between developed countries like the United States and Canada, and the poor nations of the so-called Third World.

Alternate Educational Institutions - While often using resources of existing educational institutions, action-training agencies saw themselves as alternate educational institutions. During the planning period for UTC, a conscious decision was made not to locate the Chicago center at any of the area's seminaries nor to enter into a direct relationship with any of them. Rather, the training program for clergy, lay leaders and theological students was itself chartered as an educational institution. Many of the other agencies, while not explicitly saying they were alternate institutions, took similar steps to distance themselves from the formal enterprises of theological education and lay leadership education supported by the churches. Most were self-consciously organized in a dialectical relationship with the education offered by theological seminaries. They stressed the need for "secular involvement," for non-academic methods of teaching/learning, and for theology taught in relation to concrete situations. Although some of the approaches and learnings of the action-training centers were built into innovative theological programs like Inter-met in Washington, D.C., and New York Theological Seminary, most of them are still not represented in the ways in which seminaries today try to engage in "contextual education" or to make use of "case studies" and field engagements.

ORGANIZATIONAL DEVELOPMENT

When national denominational mission executives and other regional and local church leaders first set out to create centers for urban training, they deliberately chose the strategy of institution building. They saw limited usefulness in the existing educational agencies of the major White Protestant denominations — theological seminaries and boards of Christian education. In making this choice, they took on a related pair of costs — psychological costs involved in developing new forms to serve existing or new constituencies and financial costs involved in creating new resources or diverting existing resources into the new institutions.

Church-Related Institutions - The action-training agencies, with few excep-
tions, retained their principal identification with religious institutions. As
already noted, action-training programs were established to train clergy,
lay leaders and seminary students for urban mission and ministry. The only
exception was CHART in Cincinnati, which combined the resources of
denominations with those of the University of Cincinnati to train community leaders in urban neighborhoods. Some training centers moved heavily into community organization as the way to broaden activity and their base of
support. TRUST in Richmond went completely into consulting for
organizational development with a wide variety of institutions and left
behind its religious identification, while the educational program that CUE
in Portland has developed in recent years has been financed by government
grants and directed to the whole community. Yet, on balance, whether
measured by the memberships on boards, the types of training programs
conducted, or the number of trainees and trainee-sessions involved, action-
training centers were church-related institutions not only in their origins but
throughout their history.

*Psychological Costs of Institution Building - In a sense, the newly formed
urban training centers that developed in the 1960's were not "the lengthened
shadow of one man," as the popular aphorism would have it, but "the
lengthened shadow of a group of men," the inner-city pastors who had
stayed in inner-city areas during the period after World War II when the
churches spent their principal energies on church extension in the burgeon-
ing suburbs that developed around the convenience of travel by
automobile, and those denominational urban executives who supported
their work. Their desire to pass on what had been learned out of more than
15 years of parish work, and to train clergy, seminarians and lay leaders
was the initiating spark in most of the action-training agencies.

(1) *One serious problem in the development of action training was the*
discovery that training could not be separated out as a function. Most of the
action-training centers were set up with the primary or sole purpose of
training others to carry on the urban mission. However, as they improved
their capacity to do the kinds of training required, they found that they
either had to organize some of the mission activity themselves or that they
needed to exist in some close relationship with those who were carrying it
out. "Training" furnished a convenient banner under which to organize the
various programs and agencies, but within a very short period of time it
proved to be inadequate as the means by which they could remain in existence.

(2) *The basically congregational form of church organization in the*
United States meant that the action-training agencies, like other forms of
specialized ministry and ecumenical mission structures founded in the same
period of time, were essentially "tertiary" institutions in the life of the

denominations. Local churches, the "primary" institutions of church life, were not only the most numerous forms of church life, but they also controlled most of the resources of people, leadership, local involvement and finance. In spite of confessional polities that often claim that the denominational structures — regional and national, like dioceses, presbyteries, synods, conferences and boards — are the principal seats of authority (or, to use the Reformed term that has become jargon nomenclature for all such bodies, the "judicatories"), these structures are really the "secondary" institutions of church life, able to claim such resources and authority as local congregations are willing to permit them to use. Like councils of churches and other ecumenical agencies, the action-training centers were "tertiary" institutions dependent upon the denominational structures, which were in turn dependent upon the local churches. Although they could be brought into being rather easily by decisions made at the secondary level, they could not claim the same access to the primary institutions, the local churches, and became at a later point competitors for the same resources with the very organizations that had brought them into being.

(3) *The Action Training Coalition, by joining the energies and interests of a wide variety of training institutions, assisted each one in both its organization and survival.* Between February, 1968, and March, 1971, the Action Training Coalition was organized and held eight consultations for staff and board members, along with interested denominational executives. During that period every action-training agency, including UTC in Chicago, which was the largest and the only one claiming to be a national center in the United States, gained both status and improved ability to carry out its own training by belonging to such a coalition. In fact, several years after ATC had ceased to meet, "action training" was still perceived by many in theological education and continuing education to be a separate enterprise that had its own validity. In this case, the whole was certainly greater than the sum of its parts. ATC was not able, however, to develop the same measure of financial support, in spite of several attempts to develop common funding.

Financial Costs of Institution Building — If the strategy for the development of training had continued in the direction originally taken in the late 1950's and early 1960's — use of existing educational institutions, or teams of resource people put together for particular training events or sequences by persons or agencies who served as either "brokers" or "contractors" — the overhead of institutional maintenance would have been a great deal less. However, the decision to create new institutions involved far greater financial costs than those who set up the action-training agencies had originally contemplated.

(1) *Institution building incurs heavy financial costs.* Those who worked to establish the action-training agencies had little ability to build on past loyalties or to make use of resources that had been brought together for

other purposes. In addition to the actual costs of training, those who sponsored these new institutions had to find ways to pay for capital costs, the cost of planning, exploration, research and development, and the basic support of staff. Instead of being responsible only for purchasing training with increments on the margin of existing overhead and personnel, institution building required the sponsors to provide the basic "nut" as well.

In 12 years of training operations UTC raised and spent over $ 3.33 million to serve 1983 trainees, an average of nearly $ 1680 per trainee. MUST in New York City spent more than $ 1.18 million in six years for 4185 trainees, an average of nearly $ 283 per trainee or almost $ 33 for each trainee-session. Other programs might have shown more modest figures, but in any case the financial costs of training persons in an institution specifically organized to provide that training were considerably higher than the costs of purchasing the same services from an existing institution.

(2) *No action-training agency was able to find a way to make training "pay for itself."* The heaviest mortality of action-training agencies established to train church people for urban mission was between 1970 and 1974 when, after being in existence for 2 to 12 years, they used up their original "seed money" or the available subsidies from denominational sponsors and were asked to become self-supporting. No other educational institution is able to "pay for itself," and action-training programs also needed subsidies and/or auxiliary income to survive. Those which moved to less expensive forms of organization or were able to attract support for ancillary activities were able to continue to do action training, but not as their principal activity. In effect, then, the financial costs of institution building made it impossible for these institutions to continue as single-purpose organizations devoted solely to training.

Research and Development Approach — In common with many business and government enterprises of the same period, action-training agencies were operating with an "R & D" (research and development) approach. Many of the projects they undertook were labeled as "experiments" or "pilot programs." UTC in Chicago, as a national agency, was most consistent in assembling large amounts of data about urban situations and what secular and religious agencies were doing there, as well as in encouraging trainees to develop innovative approaches to ministry. Although this approach was often criticized for not being related to the local congregation, it tried to take seriously the wide variety of situations in which the Christian Gospel was to be communicated in a complex society.

However, unlike industry, which is capable of taking the results of its "R & D" work and turning them into new sources of profit, the religious institution was too heavily committed to its existing programs and forms of organization to devote additional resources or to shift them to other ways of operation. Thus the experiments and pilot programs were not followed up with substantive changes in the ways in which churches conducted their mission.

Centralization or Decentralization — A key organizational question for action training from the very beginning was whether it would be a centralized or decentralized activity. In both the United States and Canada, as well as Puerto Rico, the original vision was of a "center" for training and innovation. However, developments over a longer period of time moved toward decentralization.

(1) *The idea of centralized training did not prove adequate to the variety of local situations.* Basic to the thinking of those who established the first national training centers — UTC in the United States and Canadian Urban Training (CUT) in Canada — was the assumption that the dynamics of urbanization were the same throughout North America, and even all over the world. Therefore, they felt that by bringing leaders from a variety of local situations to a "typical" urban metropolis, those trainees could learn to distinguish the patterns of urban problems and to replicate the forms of urban mission they found in the metropolitan "laboratory." Chicago and Toronto were ideal locations for this sort of strategy, except that it did not take into account the fact that local leadership would need to develop the programs and take responsibility for their execution. UTC tried to keep its focus on the "back-home" situation, but it was still perceived by many as "a Chicago operation." CUT has had a similar problem in Canada.

Within two years after UTC began training in the United States, 10 other training programs were being planned or were already in operation, many of them with support from the same denominations that had established UTC as a "national center." Although the UTC Board was concerned about this "proliferation" of regional and local centers, there was not much they could do to prevent or even to slow up the development of training in closer proximity to the places where urban mission was being conducted.

The process took longer in Canada, where CUT had full support from the national sponsoring denominations, which also had their headquarters in Toronto, where CUT was located. However, within four years the national training agency held its first on-site training program in Winnipeg, and CUT has now moved to seeing itself as a network of urban activists and trainers across the entire continent. In this way local initiative is respected while keeping a national vision, rather than seeing control to be located with the staff of the action-training agency at the "center."

(2) *As national support for action training weakened, the agencies needed to move to local bases of support.* METC in Washington, D.C., was one of the first action-training agencies to understand that national financial support was not only firmly committed to UTC in Chicago but was also reaching its limits. Therefore it would be necessary to develop support from those denominational agencies and other groups that were being served in the local metropolitan area. The same insight informed the training strategy

of COMMIT in Los Angeles, ACTS and UTOA in the Southeast, and ATN of Ohio as it began to reorganize. However, principal dependence on local support was neither a guarantee of survival nor assurance that such support would be wholehearted. Few agencies had stronger credentials from local denominational bodies and other institutions than TEAM in Kansas City (which later became Midwest Training Network) or Inter-religious Center for Urban Affairs (ICUA), which was the sole ecumenical agency in St. Louis; yet each found it difficult to maintain its existence past 1971.

Pace of Development — A slower pace of development has helped some of| *the training centers to develop adequate programs and survive in the long*|\ *run.* Because staff members were already brought together in denominational urban programs and in national groupings like the Department of Urban Church of the National Council of Churches of Christ in the U.S.A. and the Board of UTC in Chicago (not to mention metropolitan configurations of full-time denominational and ecumenical staff working with urban issues), it was relatively easy to organize training centers and other ecumenical agencies during the early and mid-1960's. A look at the boards of most agencies shows at their core a small group of national or metropolitan staff people. These groups were able over a relatively short time to put together the planning, the board structure, the proposals and pilot programs, and the seed money necessary to get an agency started. However, they were not able to guarantee the same amount of support and financing over the long run.

In addition, an atmosphere of optimism combined with a sense of *kairos* during the Kennedy and early Johnson years to give the impression that an all-out effort over a short period of time would redress the injustices of decades and redesign the nation's cities. Then the period of urban uprisings and the Vietnam War made the feeling of crisis even greater. Thus, in the United States those who were associated with urban mission in the mainline White Protestant denominations, as well as those in the Black Church who were part of the Civil Rights Movement, moved quickly in a wide variety of directions at the same time. To use agricultural imagery, they planted a lot of squash and pumpkins that covered a great deal of ground and ripened quickly, rather than trees that were able to bear fruit for a longer period of time but would take longer to mature.

The contrast between this pattern of rapid development and the slower, more organic pace taken by national denominations in Canada who were working across the same continental spread is particularly instructive. Less people have been trained over a longer period of time, and attempts at regionalization have been modest. Thus, 15 years after the organization of CUT the national training program was just beginning to develop a more sophisticated set of relationships with urban activists and churches all over Canada, and to become more decentralized. Many gaps still existed, but they remained to be filled in as it became more appropriate. Similarly, PRISA responded to its inability to gain denominational support, the strong opposition of the Evangelical Council, and repression from government and political parties by organizing on a subsistence basis for the long run. In this way it was not only able to preserve the unique programs its members already were fostering, but to spawn new ones and to be able to respond to crisis situations like the campaigns against the U.S. military in Culebra and Vieques.

Vocation and Career — A significant number of action-training staff members have continued to see training as their vocation and have made it their career, while many more have gone on to other positions. Yoshio Fukuyama has developed the thesis that a great many of the specialized ministries that arose in the late 1950's and 1960's represented the attempts of theologically trained and ordained clergy to develop new careers within their vocation to Christian ministry. Rather than leaving the religious institution, they tried to make a place for themselves within it by developing new organizations and jobs to be fulfilled.[3] This is in keeping with the insight that ultimately all history can be written as biography. Without a Saul of Tarsus and his conversion to Christ, no mission to the Gentiles; without a Martin Luther and his renunciation of Rome, no Reformation.

In most cases where action-training agencies have continued, they are still led by persons who came out of the urban church experience of the post-World War II period and have made action training, along with related activities, their career. In some cases action-training programs collapsed before their staff members gave up their activity as trainers. However, the inability to maintain institutional viability led many to return to other positions within the church, including seminary education or other forms of training. A few joined the exodus of significant numbers of clergy out of church-related vocations.

In 1972 ATC rejected the bid of the Association for Religion and Applied Behavioral Science (ARABS) to go the route of other forms of training by setting up an individual accreditation review process. Action training was declared to be a process carried on by agencies and training groups, not by individuals who made it their "profession." This stance ruled out individual careerism and professionalism. However, the example of those who have stuck to the task and of PRISA, which has become a collective of persons committed to common goals and joint effort, show that the elements of vocation and career have been needed to continue the effort.

MISSION STRATEGY

Experimental Ministries - As has already been noted, the action-training agencies were working from an "R & D" (research and development) stance.

This meant that they themselves were considered to be experimental ministries, as well as building on the experience of earlier experiments in urban mission and themselves sponsoring experimental approaches. In the project budgets and files of the sponsoring denominations, they were listed with other experimental ministries in urban mission, including the metropolitan ecumenical agencies that were often their sponsors and the local mission projects whose staffs and constituencies supplied many of their trainees and requests for consultation. In their own files could be found proposals and reports of urban experiments from all over the nation and many other parts of the world.

In a number of cases the action-training agencies became umbrellas for the sponsorship of other experimental ministries. In Chicago UTC played a strong role in organizing the West Side Organization, the Black Strategy Center and the Committee for One Society, all of which gave their trainees field experience but also received funds through the training agency. CIP in Cleveland and METC in Washington both developed Black action-training programs or agencies. Several centers sponsored community organizations in different parts of the metropolitan area in which they were located. And those which were the ecumenical coordinating agency in their metropolitan area — like CUE-Portland, EMM in Seattle, and ICUA in St. Louis — had a wide range of local and metropolitan projects which they sponsored. Thus action-training agencies were not only experimental ministries themselves and involved in training others for specialized ministry in the urban community, but they sponsored other experimental ministries as well.

(1) *Although established as experimental ministries, action-training agencies were not able to communicate their learnings to the denominations that had sponsored them.* In the words of a MUST staff member, that agency turned out to be "simply another of the experiments which the church so ably conducts" — and, it must be added, from which it steadfastly refuses to learn. Heavy research and evaluation were built into each agency's proposals at the request of its sponsors. Yet in most cases the agency did not survive long enough or the agency's program kept changing, so that longitudinal experiments were impossible, and only simpler forms of program evaluation could be conducted. This limitation plagued even the most ambitious research project undertaken by action-training agencies, Research into Training for Metropolitan Ministry (RTMM), which was sponsored by the three pioneer agencies — UTC, CIP and MUST — in 1967-69.

The reports of board and advisory committee meetings, in addition to much of the correspondence from national denominations, are filled with discussions of the need for more reporting by staff concerning the implications of their experience "for the local church," and requests that evaluation be completed to give insights for their own planning and strategy. Staff members from national offices, metropolitan agencies and local projects took up hours of training center staff time discussing the implications of the action-training program for their own work. Yet when decisions were made to cut down financial support or to close any of the centers, those decisions were made almost wholly on budgetary grounds, without reference to what had or had not been learned through the experience.

In point of fact, the action-training agencies were experimental probes into urban mission, especially in the area of civil rights and race relations. Black caucuses and walkouts were happening in action-training programs before they were a phenomenon of denominational life. The stresses and strains of staff relations among an interracial staff were dealt with successfully in these agencies, but that experience was not transferred to the sponsoring church bodies. And from the beginning training sessions were emphasizing the segregated nature of urban life before urban riots and the Kerner Commission Report brought to the attention of the whole society that America already had "two societies — one Black and one White." As a result, the churches and their organizations had to repeat the experience through which the action-training agencies had already gone, and in many cases they did not use the creative solutions and resources that had been developed in the training experience.

Although action-training agencies undoubtedly contributed to the distance that often appeared to stretch between them and the churches, the failure to learn from them as experimental ministries should principally be placed with the churches. In some cases the action-training centers failed to communicate with the churches, but in most instances the church either refused to listen or perpetuated the image that these "experiments" were so different from the existing religious institutions that they had little or nothing to teach them. Having set up experimental ministries, including action training, as a means to learn what to do in an urbanized society, the sponsoring denominations then resolutely refused to learn from them.

(2) *Action-training institutions, like many other experimental ministries, were geared to innovation, rather than being organic developments from existing programs and institutions.* The publicity brochure for the Chicago-based UTC in its earliest years had a cover emblazoned with the title, "The New Thing." This typified the spirit of many of those who served on the statfs of the action-training agencies, as well as many of those who supported their creation. The feeling was that much of what had been tried in urban mission was an extension of earlier approaches in neighborhood church work and the institutional church ministry that had been inaugurated before the turn of the century. If the United States was to have new cities, it would require new churches and new approaches.

As a result, the models that were held up to view and encouraged were those that broke new ground. However, the history of both church missions and church development show that most of the lasting changes have represented an organic metamorphosis from existing institutions and strategies, or have been "exceptions" and "mutations" that have arisen in response to new situations and later have come to be the common practice. When experiments are emphasizing innovation, then those who sponsor them must be prepared for a high number of tests that do not prove out, with resulting negative, as well as positive, learnings. Judicious support of existing programs that show promise and attempts to learn from the exceptions require less effort and resources than trying to break new ground.

Denominationalism and Ecumenism - The ecumenical tides were flowing freely in the post-World War II era. The World Council of Churches was organized in 1948, and the existing national ecumenical agencies were reorganized into the National Council of Churches of Christ in the U.S.A. in 1950. By the beginning of the decade of the 1960's a number of the mainline Protestant denominations were engaged in the Consultation on Church Union, where they were considering the possibility of organic union. In addition, in city after city the same constellations of denominations were engaged in ecumenical coalitions, joint strategies and programs that had common support. Denominationalism seemed to be on the wane.

But American Christianity was still organized on a denominational basis. As greater attention began to be given to declining membership and static revenues by the end of the decade of the 1960's, each denominational body — from its local churches through metropolitan and regional organizations to national structures — was deeply concerned to remain in existence and to give more attention to new church development and strengthening existing congregations. They had been content to leave the breaking of new ground to experimental ministries like the action-training agencies, but they returned their attention in home missions to that part of the task that was responsible for the future health of the denominational structure.

(1) *No mission strategy in American Protestantism can ignore or go very far without the support of denominational structures.* In the case of action training, this study has already told the story of how denominational executives were largely responsible, both at the national and the metropolitan level, for bringing these new agencies and programs into being. The future of action training depended heavily upon: (a) the degree of continued support they could receive from their original sponsors; (b) the ability to attract resources already committed to other forms of church training, such as that conducted by theological seminaries and boards of Christian education (or, contrariwise, the ability of those institutions to move into action training); (c) the degree of satisfaction which clergy, laity and others related to the denominations had in the kinds of training they were receiving from the action-training agencies; and (d) the ability to attract new trainees and funds. Although every one of these factors was in some ways dependent on the leadership of the action-training agencies, they depended even more on the leadership of the denominations and churches, including those who participated in setting up action training in the first place.

(2) *The ecumenical vision was a necessary component of urban strategy.* The natural tendency of denominational leaders, when they look at a metropolitan area, is to see it as a string of pearls defined by the location of the local congregations and community projects related to them. However, a clearer understanding of the nature of the Gospel would show that faithful witness is not restricted to any single denominational organization. And the interrelated nature of urban metropolitan community determines that churches which are part of that community share far more in common with those who work in the same situation than they do with those elsewhere who are not part of that metropolis. The ecumenical vision of action training had both these sources — an ecumenical understanding of the Gospel witness and an ecumenical vision of the nature of urban community.

The nature of this ecumenical perspective varied. For some the meaning of "ecumenical" was a pan-Protestantism which united in a common effort those denominations which were members of the National and World Councils, the so-called "ecumenical" denominations. For others in the period following Vatican II it meant a common effort by all who were Christians, including Roman Catholics, Orthodox, the traditionally conservative denominations who were beginning to claim the title of "evangelicals," and Pentecostals. For still others "ecumenical" activity had to be interreligious and could not exclude the Jews. And for many who were impressed by the growing secularization of North American society, especially in urban areas (as proclaimed by Harvey Cox in his popular work, *The Secular City*) only a "secular ecumenism" that united all persons concerned for the humanization of life in metropolis would be adequate.

(3) *As particularism grew in the wider society, it undercut the understanding of "ecumenicism" as harmony and consensus.* Much of the ecumenical vision as it developed after World War II (similar to the vision of world order through the United Nations and its agencies) assumed that denominations were historical aberrations that would begin to disappear in a renewed and reunited Church. Harmony and consensus would be achieved as denominations worked together and began to care less about their labels and differences.

The Black Power movement of the mid-1960's represented the first public recognition of a resurgence of particularism. It was quickly followed with assertions of Hispanic, Asian-American, Native American, White ethnic, feminist and homosexual identity. In this atmosphere it once again became legitimate to assert denominational identity and roots. However, there is always a tension between the particular and the universal in the life of humanity and in the life of the church as a divine-human institution. A more sober ecumenical point of view needs to understand and acknowledge both the concreteness of incarnation in particular groups of people at particular times in history and the universality and transcendence of the Gospel. The Gospel continues to pull toward the ecumenical, while the humanity of the church will always pull toward the particular, which in American Christianity has expressed itself in denominations.

(4) *Active cooperation with Roman Catholics dramatically increased through action training.* Urban mission in American Protestantism has seen Roman Catholicism as an adversary since the early nineteenth century. As successive waves of immigration brought large numbers of Roman Catholics from Western and Southern Europe, the principal strategies of Protestant churches were directed toward conserving their own membership and proselytizing Roman Catholics. When political control of the cities began to pass into Roman Catholic hands by the end of the century, the stress in church development and mission began to move away from the cities.

Vatican II changed the world-wide stance of the Roman Catholic church, but cooperation had already begun to develop between urban church workers of different faiths as they joined in common support of community organization efforts and tried to focus on racial justice. Several of the action-training centers began with Roman Catholic sponsorship, but most had significant representation of Roman Catholics in trainees and staff by the end of the 1960's. Although there was a parallel development of Peace and Justice Centers by Roman Catholics on the North American continent and several Roman Catholic-based training programs for community organizing, Roman Catholic clergy, religious (members of women's and men's orders) and laity found action-training agencies a viable way to train for Christian mission in the metropolitan areas.

The Black Church - Nothing is more dramatic than to read magazines and reports devoted to urban mission, starting in 1948, and to realize that the photographs change from images of White clergy and church workers surrounded by Black children, youth and adults (mainly women), to images of Black church leaders, male and female, working in their own churches to serve their own communities. The Black churches were already there in the urban ghettos, but the mainline White Protestant denominations shared in the racism of the rest of the United States society. To White churches the Black church was invisible — and often thought to be inferior. Although part of the reason for the presence of White mission workers was a commitment to an integrated church in an integrated society, they also represented the traditional mission emphasis on uplift, bringing the values of the wider culture to what was seen to be inferior and in need of improvement. The Civil Rights Movement and the emphasis on Black Power changed all that, and no future mission strategy in metropolitan areas can afford to overlook the indigenous churches already in existence there.

(1) *The dynamic of race was basic to the existence of action-training agencies, as it was to the life of the metropolitan areas in which they sought to serve.* Although metropolitan areas in the United States had many political

and economic issues that were shared across racial lines, race was (as it continues to be) one of the most accurate indicators, as well as the most highly visible one, of deprivation and oppression in urban areas. Measures of income, employment, housing, health, crime, educational achievement and other basic issues of life all correlated directly with race for both Black and Hispanic residents. For this reason, as well as a basic commitment to racial equality, the action-training agencies gave major attention to the factor of race in urban affairs.

At the National Consultation of Urban Training Centers in 1968, the center staff members who were present were largely White. During the discussions, the small number of Black and Hispanic staff insisted that the agencies could not train in the area of race without having interracial staff teams, and that the time and energy of minority staff members needed to be given more fully to needs of the Black and Hispanic communities than to orientation of suburban Whites about the problems faced by those communities. In his consultant's report Edgar W. Mills said that the racial theme "subtly dominated the entire conference," and that "whenever policy, program and institutional considerations were discussed *apart from* the racial question, they took on a significant measure of unreality." Action-training centers, thus, worked with the dynamic of race in their own organizational life as well as in the wider society. And the decline of support for their programs and agencies coincided with the decline of interest in both the churches and the wider society for the issues of race relations and civil rights.

Action-training leaders probably had some awareness of the ways in which major attention on the factor of race was an invitation to rejection and denial by the majority community. The term "urban" had begun to be understood as a synonym for "minority," Black or Hispanic in common usage by the mid-1960's. Therefore, in taking a title for the organization formed by "urban training centers," the representatives at the second consultation in Kansas City dropped the term "urban" due to "the limiting connotations of the word," and called themselves the "Action Training Coalition." But they also established an Institutional Racism Task Force to prepare a training program in "(a) personal prejudice problems, (b) institutional racism, (c) training center roles, (d) responding to the Black Condition and the Black United Front, (e) relevant curriculum development."

(2) *Action-training agencies worked with the understanding that racism is systemic and institutional.* Although much of White America was busy disclaiming that it had any personal attitude of prejudice, action-training agencies focused on discrimination, which was the social result of a racist society. Using the same analysis of urban society that saw it as "a system of systems" and therefore capable of systemic change and improvement, they located the source of racial issues in that society in "institutional racism" rather than in the actions of its victims.

As much of the orientation to metropolitan life in action-training programs drew attention to the condition of minority residents of the ghettos, so a large share of the analysis of metropolitan society concentrated on the historic institutional patterns that had developed to cause that condition. Both White and minority trainees were coached to develop strategies that would not ignore the factor of racism, but would face it directly and seek to change the deeply ingrained habits and patterns. This concern for systemic evil and institutional patterns led some of the action-training agencies by the end of the 1960's to broaden their attention to the rising expectations of women, homosexuals, the disabled and other groups that were seeking to challenge discrimination. In the process, however, many agencies gave up the primary focus on racism that they had discovered in their first surveys of metropolitan society and to which they had devoted so much of their early programs.

(3) *The Black church, located within the Black community, came to be seen as the primary agent of urban mission.* A great deal of the original concern of predominantly White denominations for urban training was to transmit the knowledge of the Black and Hispanic community that had been gained in cross-cultural urban mission by White pastors and church workers to seminary students and other church workers, both Black and White. At the same time the Black church was forging instruments like the Southern Christian Leadership Conference to take up the civil rights struggle. Increasingly the Black church and the Black community were becoming pro-active in their own behalf. Strategies for urban change were developing out on the field, rather than in denominational and ecumenical headquarters. And the leadership was coming from an extraordinary group of gifted Black male ministers, not from White clergy and mission workers, and their staff supporters.

As a result, much of the agenda of issues to which action-training agencies gave attention was developed by Black-led civil rights groups and community organizations, in which clergy of the Black church played a major role. These were not only the Black clergy who led congregations related to the predominantly White denominations; they included those from the historic Black denominations, principally Baptist and Methodist, and from the more newly organized bodies like the Church of God in Christ, which is today the largest denomination that is almost completely urban in membership. Examples of this shift were the establishment of the Ford Fellows program at UTC in Chicago, the organization of parallel Black action-training agencies or programs by METC in Washington and CIP in Cleveland, and the Brooklyn Mission Ministers program at MUST for pastors of small Black churches. Instead of being seen as irrelevant or an object of mission, Black indigenous churches in the metropolitan areas were now seen to be the primary agents of mission.

(4) *Concern for patterns of racial injustice within the United States opened up action-training for greater attention to international systemic injustice.* The popular way to divide issues in the United States is between those which are "domestic" and those which are "foreign." The issues of race transcended this easy division — even as more careful analysis of the nature of urban community itself showed that it was interrelated with other societies and economies beyond national boundaries. Those of darker skin color were "minorities" in the United States, but they were "the majority" of world population. The oppressed and impoverished condition of so many Blacks and Hispanics in the United States was only a token of the situation of domination and colonialism, hunger and poverty in the so-called "Third World."

The traditional response to situations overseas had been to send North American and European missionaries and to engage in programs of relief, welfare and social service. The post-war Christian community had already learned to place greater emphasis on indigenous church workers than on cross-cultural missionaries, a lesson that was also being learned in urban mission. But it took time for the inadequacy of relief, welfare and social service programs to deal with systemic injustice to become clear to the North American churches. The support of action-training agencies for those who were working to throw off the oppression of urban ghetto communities by the wider society was easily translated into support for liberation movements on other continents. Several agencies produced curriculum on world hunger which emphasized the systemic nature of much of the situation around the world and the need to address causes in North America and Europe, as well as land use and crop production on other continents.

Most action-training agencies enrolled some overseas trainees from time to time. UTC as a national center had a steady stream of visitors and observers from other countries, as well as a number of trainees who worked on "back-home" situations in Europe, Australasia, Latin America, Asia and Africa. Rev. Abel Hendricks and his wife, a Methodist pastor and social worker from Capetown, South Africa, spent several months at MUST taking part in training sessions, and observing urban mission and civil rights activities. Upon their return to South Africa, Pastor Hendricks became a leader in the movement for Colored rights in that country. Relationship and activity with the Third World inside the United States made action-training agencies more sensitive to and more capable of working with international issues involving the Third World.

Social Service and Social Action: The traditional approach of the churches to urban mission, as in most missionary activity, involved evangelization, church development and social service. While action-training assumed that these were necessary components of a mission strategy, the agencies related to the Action Training Coalition laid their principal stress on social action for meaningful change.

(1) *Although social service and social action can be meaningfully distinguished from each other, they are complementary strategies.* Because so much of what churches had been doing in urban areas involved social service (providing help to the victims), the action-training agencies gave principal attention to teaching methods of social action (breaking the cycle of victimization). Even in brief orientation programs, the stress was on forms of political, economic, cultural and community action that would help people to realize their own bondage and find ways to change the systems that were oppressing them.

In practice, the way in which many persons came to trust a church or community organization (and in which those groups themselves found out about the real needs and hurts of people) was through the process of asking for help and finding that the people involved really did care about them. Action-training agencies spent a great deal of time with members of the National Welfare Rights Organization (NWRO) at both the local and national levels. The churches' work with welfare clients went beyond the social service approach that helped them to take advantage of the welfare program's benefits; it also supported the organization of those clients to challenge the system. Thus social service and social action, far from being opposing or contradictory strategies, proved to be complementary.

(2) *The churches found it more difficult to understand or justify involvement in social action.* A mission theology that used the slogans of "the church for others" fitted in well with the benevolent image of churches that saw themselves as helping others. Social service not only had been a customary activity of church people (often symbolized as "baskets for Thanksgiving" by those who wished to highlight social action), but it was supported in many New Testament passages that spoke of service and being a servant. Social action, with its connotations of confrontation and potential for violence, did not seem as compatible with that benevolent image, those customary activities and the customary interpretations of Scripture.

An example would be the resistance of church people to the boycotts organized by the United Farm Workers, first in support of grape pickers and then of lettuce workers. In many metropolitan areas in the United States and Canada local boycott committees, sparked by California farm workers, conducted leafleting, picketing and speaking engagements in support of the union against the growers. Although a great deal of support for the Farm Workers' boycotts came from church organizations, clergy, religious and lay people, there was also a large share of the church population who resisted a boycott as being "coercive" and not in accord with "Christian love." Similar resistance arose to other forms of social action for justice.

(3) *As action-training agencies stressed social action, they moved from seeing the churches principally as a resource to viewing them as targets*

against which action should be directed. Robert H. Bonthius has summarized this development as follows:

> The comprehensive approach to urban mission insists that injustice is a *web of institutionalized policies and practices* (a matrix of all essential systems), and therefore (1) that Christians and their churches are *inextricably complicit* in the inequitable systems, and (2) that Christians and their churches are *either* supporting (by inaction) *or working to change them* (by organized action to which training is dedicated). Therefore, the churches themselves become important targets for intervention. (Black Manifesto, et al.)[4]

In the oft-quoted words of Pogo, the action-training agencies, which were sponsored by the churches and deeply concerned for urban mission, had "met the enemy, and they are us."

Nowhere was this more obvious than in the issues of racism. This study has already described how the shift to Black power from strategies of integration and support for civil rights caused many church leaders and a majority of their supporters to withdraw support from urban mission programs, including action training, and to resist the demands of the Black Manifesto. In its place, they established "urban crisis" funds to raise money outside the regular budgets for grants to church and community agencies engaged in working with urban problems.

At this same time action training began to focus on institutional racism in the society, including the churches. Rather than trying to secure church support to deal with the problems of the rest of society, local congregations and church organizations were being urged to do something about the "log" in their own eye as well as the "speck" they were able to see in the eyes of the racist society of which they were a part. It is to the credit not only of action training but also of many of the denominations that the church as an institution was ready and willing to engage in self-criticism for a while. When that mood began to change in the early 1970's, then support began to dry up for action training, and the churches were being urged to get off what was then being characterized as a "guilt trip."

Churches can engage in social service activities without looking very carefully at themselves, because all the attention is given to the plight of the victims and what is being done to "help" them. When engaged in social action, however, churches cannot avoid looking at the problems as they occur in their own life as well as in the life of society. It is in the nature of social sin (which Walter Rauschenbusch in an earlier era characterized as "the Kingdom of Evil") that it affects all human relationships. Insofar as churches are human institutions, they partake of and are directly intertwined in the life of the whole society in which they exist. Therefore, social action which seeks to oppose and change social evils and injustice must also work for changes of the same kind in the churches. But in the process it will run the risk of losing the support of those church agencies which are not willing to engage in self-criticism. Although this was not the sole reason for the withdrawal of financial support from action training in the period from 1972 on, it was certainly a major factor. While some denominational bodies welcomed the chance to work on rooting out institutional racism in their own life, many others were happier to move to safer targets and forms of action.

Lay Ministry - From the beginning the action-training agencies were interested in lay ministry as an appropriate form of urban mission. They did not always keep this emphasis uppermost, but they were able to make some important breakthroughs in the training of lay persons, especially for social action and roles in community organization.

(1) *Action training designed its programs for both clergy and lay participants.* The statement of purpose and initial program proposals of almost all the action-training agencies involved specialized training for clergy and seminary students, but they also included training for lay leaders and groups of persons from congregations. Some agencies, like the Cleveland Intern Program, began with professional training exclusively and later branched out to training with lay leaders. Some others, like CUE in the Twin Cities and Metropolitan Associates of Philadelphia, were originally interested in lay ministry. Programs which involved long sequences of training or that required trainees to leave their own metropolitan area were principally directed at clergy.

Most of the staff members of action-training agencies were themselves theologically trained and ordained. However, the team style of training and the need to focus on issues in the wider society brought a wider variety of lay staff members than in the mission organizations and local congregations. Increased involvement of lay persons as trainees also produced increased use of lay persons on the training staff.

(2) *Action training moved to understand the importance of the ministry of the laity where the lay members of churches are seen as the principal change-agents in society.* If the ministry of social action and social change is seen principally as an institutional activity of the churches, then theologically trained and ordained clergy will be likely to take the primary role in leading that ministry, as they do in so many other areas of church life. However, theological statements about the church as the people of God and the ministry of the laity, as well as recognition that most action for social change takes place outside or beyond the churches, moved the focus of attention to lay persons as the principal agents of change. MAP in Philadelphia kept this as its main agenda throughout its history. Other action-training agencies moved toward having a greater interest in lay ministry for organizational change by the middle of the decade of the 1970's.

(3) *Action-training agencies shared with the rest of the society in recognizing the need to open up wider opportunities for women in the churches, as well as in the wider society.* The staffs of the action-training agencies at the beginning were heavily dominated by White male clergy, as was true of the urban mission and ministry of the predominantly White mainline Protestant denominations. As time moved along, they began to add more women, ordained and lay, to their staffs, and the agenda of training started to include sexism as well as racism.

Although ordination of women was one of the issues to be faced by the churches in this period, issues of the role of women in the wider society and of lay women in the churches were more far-reaching and involved a larger number of people. Because so large a percentage of the lay members of churches were women, the key to a new understanding of lay ministry was to be found in incorporating women more fully into the leadership of congregations and spelling out more clearly their calling as Christians in the wider society. Action-training agencies began to discover this dynamic in the later stage of their development. Because this was the very time at which denominational support was fading, they were not able to have as significant a role in calling the issue of lay ministry, especially through women, to the attention of the churches as they had earlier with the issues of urbanization and racism.

Fuzzy Goals. - One recurring problem for action-training agencies was the need to clarify the goals for which they were working. The story of every action-training center or program is continually punctuated by the need to work once again on the goals of the agency. In a time of crisis and exciting actions it was easy to add new activities or involvements without asking whether these were in accordance with the original purpose and goals or were calling for a change. Then, when staff became overworked and trainees became confused, the agency would decide it was time to take another look at what they were trying to do.

Although fuzzy goals and unclarified expectations can be endured for a longer period of time by a local congregation or a mission agency that has assured sources of income from general giving and investments, a specialized agency created for a specific purpose or purposes cannot ignore the task of goal clarification.

At times the clear goals which emerged were resisted or opposed by those who had sponsored the action-training agencies. More often, however, their support diminished when they could not be sure what action training was trying to do, or when they felt that the goals were contradictory. Fuzzy goals probably lost far more support and hurt action training more than clear goals which challenged both the church's institutional arrangements and the wider society.

THEOLOGY

Action training began within the theological assumptions of the liberal and neo-orthodox traditions of North American Protestantism. It had some aspirations to assist in making a theological breakthrough, but these were not realized as the task proved more arduous than envisioned.

(1) *While using the action-reflection model, action-training agencies found that theological reflection was a more difficult task than many had assumed.* This approach to training was using a highly inductive model that was concerned to gather the data on a situation of mission or social change before committing itself to the direction of change. Most theological methods are propositional and deductive, not inductive. And even process theology, which was having some vogue when the Action Training Coalition was operating, did not furnish adequate means for understanding the direction that human efforts should take.

As a result, action-training agencies found great difficulty with the theological part of reflection, although most stuck to it as an essential part of their training. Almost no works of new theological or ethical thought came out of the action-training groups. Nor were they able to attract to their efforts any of the theologians or ethicists who were claiming to be "relevant" in the 1960's. The Theological Task Force of MUST, whose roster read like a *Who's Who* of mission theologians and urban pundits, gave notice very early in its deliberations that it would prefer to comment upon what the staff was preparing as a proposal rather than to make suggestions for its direction. In the fall of 1967 UTC called together a consultation to examine more closely the place of theology in the training program of centers already in operation. The general outcome of that session was a renewed commitment to working on the problem, but each agency had to admit that it could not report a great deal of progress in this part of its work. "Doing theology" was a lot more difficult than just talking about it or using the slogan.

(2) *The theological approach adopted by action-training agencies stressed history and human action.* Because they were dealing with contemporary issues and problems in urban life, action-training programs placed their emphasis on history as the arena of God's action, rather than on the transcendent and supernatural. Their eschatology lay less in the future than in the present or what could be fulfilled within human history. Although a great deal was said about "God's action in history" and "the mission of God," the content of these terms was usually some form of human action. The city was seen as a human construction within which could be fulfilled the vision provided by God.

(3) *Justice was the major theme of the set of theological values with which these agencies worked.* Although many persons engaged in urban mission were working with a sense of charity (love), the key issue for society, when

seen from the side of the urban poor and minorities in ghettos, was how to overcome injustice. Most problems were judged to be the result of institutional and organized injustice that victimized many city residents. This meant that major stress was placed on social action to fight against injustice and establish more just systems, rather than on social service to bind up the wounds of the victims of injustice and make their situation bearable.

(4) *The training programs were convinced that lay members of churches and community residents were vital change agents.* A majority of the staff members of the action-training agencies were clergy, but their understanding of the church was based on its nature as the people of God (*laos tou theou*). Both in the church and in the community, they were convinced that lay members/citizens were the source of the power for change. Therefore, they taught various forms of organization and action that would assist the "people" to be change agents. This was seen in opposition to the elitist forms of organization and planning in government, business and industry, as well as in the church, which placed the major sources of action in the top leaders and the efficiency of institutions.

METHODOLOGY

Action training was not simply a methodology, nor did it introduce radically new methods of experiential education. The action-training agencies, however, developed a style of training that brought techniques and approaches from a wide variety of disciplines — applied behavioral science, management theory, community organizing, planning, social, political and economic theory — and combined them into a group of methods and approaches that were unique. At the same time there were a few community training organizations, developed with so-called "anti-poverty" funds from the Office of Economic Opportunity during the administration of Lyndon B. Johnson, which used some of the same techniques and approaches. Yet these did not develop them to the extent that action training did, nor did they last as long as action-training agencies. Therefore, they did not have as much time or as many persons as trainees with whom to improve their methodology.

(1) *The methods used by action-training agencies were principally empirical and inductive.* In preparing for training programs, principal attention was given to developing as wide a range of data as possible about the particular city or metropolitan area involved, about the institutions and issues being considered, and about the trainees themselves. Then, during the training program stress was placed upon having the trainees supply the data. Even though the training staff could recognize patterns and behavior, both institutional and personal, on the basis of their own study, observation and analysis, they chose to have the information come from the trainees and to encourage them to make their own conclusions. In this

sense, the training conducted by action-training agencies was very similar to science labs in secondary or higher education. Some lectures were given and outlines provided, but it was left to each person to verify the truth and usefulness of what had been taught by trying to see it for themselves.

Most action-training programs developed their own form of "situation analysis" or modified the formats developed by UTC in Chicago or CIP in Cleveland. CUE-M in the Twin Cities used for a while a highly ideological approach based on a curriculum developed by the Ecumenical Institute in Chicago. And Black training programs introduced some elements sharing an understanding of "the Black community." However, the principal sources of the kind of analysis used were the structural functionalism of Talcott Parsons and various forms of urban sociology and sociology of institutions that were based on that theoretical approach. Only MAP, with its design for action-research into the urban community, used a full-scale model based on this kind of theory, but other agencies had bits and pieces of it throughout their models of both urban community and religious institutions.

(2) *Action training, as indicated by its very title, was committed to doing its educational work in direct relationship to human action in society.* Training agencies were looking for persons who were already actors in society or who had potential for becoming change agents. They brought in as resource persons those who were already active in areas of social change, and their staffs were usually composed of persons who already had a record for community involvement and social action in urban communities or the civil rights movement. The purpose of most training programs or consultations was to produce action by the trainees or to improve their skills in action. At times the agencies may have overestimated either their own ability to keep in touch with relevant action for social change or the willingness or ability of their trainees to produce such action, but this was a constant theme of training objectives. In addition, the action trainers wanted to be evaluated not by what happened in the training program or session, but by the action which resulted from that training.

Perhaps the best description of action training would be to say that it proceeded from an "action-research" stance. It was continually probing the metropolitan community to find out what could be changed and what kinds of strategies were producing change. It was encouraging and teaching its trainees to do the same, while being willing to change and adapt the very methods of training that were being used. And it was willing to permit others to conduct evaluation of its own activity using an action-research mode.

(3) *Most action-training agencies were committed to community organizing methods as a major tool for social change.* This has already been noted in the summary of the assumptions concerning "power" and "change" that

informed this training. In most cases the approach and methods being taught and used were those developed and espoused by Saul Alinsky and the Industrial Areas Foundation. The three national denominations that formed the Joint Urban Executive Committee were supporting organizational efforts using this model in a number of local situations across the country. However, other persons like Milton Kotler and Richard Hauser were invited to bring their approaches to the development of community leadership and action.

The hallmark of this approach was to assist in the development of group power to produce change. Although cooperation and friendly approaches were not ruled out, it was assumed that conflict would arise whenever people were being challenged to change and existing institutions resisted that change. Conflict was not avoided, and the community organizing approach tried to make positive use of group anger and resistance to authority. In time some of the agencies developed a mixed approach that depended both on external change agents brought together by community organizing methods and on internal change agents who made use of the methods of institutional change. Since so many of the trainees were clergy or persons who were employed by institutions, the latter approach had a particular appeal, since it did not call for them to leave their institutional positions in order to be considered agents of change.

(4) *Most action training was future oriented and also made use of planning approaches.* An important component of most action-training programs was the point where the trainees were asked, "What are you going to do about it?" or "How do you intend to make this happen?" At this point they were usually introduced to some model of planning (often taken from the methodology of "management by objectives" that had been developed for industry and government) and given time to develop their own plans for action. If a training program did not result in such plans, trainees were usually asked to take the model which had been given them and to use it to produce plans as a follow-up to the training.

Most action-training programs were considered to be less than adequate if they did not get to the point of considering strategy and tactics which the trainees and their organizations or institutions were going to use in their own situation in the next period of time. The planning language they used was filled with military terminology — "target," "mission," "strategy," "tactics," "logistics," "intelligence" and the like. In part, this was because much of the theory and approach being used had originally been developed for the military; in part, it stemmed from the essentially adversary position in which the action-training agencies saw themselves, along with others who were dominated by the status quo.

(5) *Instead of limiting training to a narrow range of involvement or to a group of persons who held similar positions in society or its institutions, action-training agencies pressed to include as much diversity as possible in*

leadership and resource persons, as well as in trainees. Urban society was seen as a complex system of interacting systems. Therefore, whatever a person's place of involvement or position in society, they were understood to be interrelated with others.

Training on racism or urban poverty would be conducted by a mixed team of trainers who embodied experience on both sides of the color line or the economic divisions. A wide variety of resource persons would be brought in to speak with trainees. In addition, they were encouraged both in field trips and field engagements to see as wide a range of experience as possible and to listen to a broader span of viewpoints than they were accustomed to hearing. The training groups themselves would often include improbable mixes of suburban pastors, welfare mothers, ghetto community activists, denominational executives and others drawn from different sectors of society. They had a chance not only to learn from one another but to develop action strategies that might involve cooperation with each other.

This sort of approach caused the action-training agencies to move rather quickly away from training directed principally — or exclusively — to clergy and other religious professionals, along with seminary students training for those positions. Instead, the focus became the training of clergy and laity together for action they would be engaging in together. Although UTC in Chicago maintained through most of its career the stance of taking clergy and community leaders out of their local situation and bringing them to the urban laboratory of Chicago for their training, most of the other agencies and programs kept clergy together with interested laity and tried to conduct their training "on-site" where the follow-up action would occur.

CONCLUSION

Action training was a distinctive development in urban mission among the predominantly White, mainline Protestant denominations during the 1960's. For the most part, action-training agencies were developed on an ecumenical basis by national denominational mission agencies or by local denominational bodies. Although their original purpose was to train clergy, religious professionals and seminary students for their role in "urban mission," they moved to training a wider range of persons from both religious and other institutions, as well as residents of urban communities, for "social change," particularly in relation to urban issues and racism. In the course of developing and conducting this training, these agencies adopted approaches and methods that had a wider applicability in education and action.

At an early stage in their organizational history, while most agencies were still in the planning stage or conducting their initial training programs, the action-training agencies organized a national Action Training Coalition, which served as a means of disseminating their innovations and developing common approaches, as well as of exerting influence on the denominations and theological seminaries that had created them. ATC also helped in training staff for the work they had undertaken.

When funding from national denominations began to diminish and it became clear that the support for training was more local, ATC was abandoned. Most agencies either went out of existence or moved to a more mixed approach as United States society became less concerned and less sure about what to do with the issues of race and poverty. Those which survived combined training with consulting, community organizing or education and sought trainees and clients beyond the religious institutions, while continuing to maintain a strong relationship to those institutions which had been responsible for bringing them into being.

Action training is not a distinctive methodology. Rather, it is an approach to training that uses action-reflection and an action-research model to train people to get into action for social change or to improve what they are already doing. It joins both action and learning in an experiential form of education. As a result, the major legacy of action-training is not to be found in the papers and curricula that it developed, nor in the reports and evaluations that it produced, but in the life and experience of those who were trained and those who did the training — and, hopefully, in the life of the urban communities and the churches of which they were members.

Appendices

1. List of Training Centers and Programs

2. Chronological Chart of Members of Action Training Coalition

3. Meetings of Action Training Coalition

4. Case Study: The Institutional Racism Project in the Episcopal Diocese of Southern Ohio (Action Training Network of Ohio)

5. Case Study: Community Organizing through Black Community Developers (Metropolitan Urban Service Training)

6. Theologizing, Sociologizing, Strategizing with Action: The Threefold Curriculum (Urban Training Center for Christian Mission)

7. Chronology of General History and Developments in Urban Mission, Ecumenical Organizations and Action Training in the United States 1962-1975

8. Checklist for Future Research

Selected Bibliography

Appendix 1

List of Training Centers and Programs

ACTION TRAINING COALITION
Canada
Toronto - Canadian Urban Training - CUT
California
Berkeley - Berkeley Center for Human Interaction - BCHI *
Los Angeles - Center of Metropolitan Mission In-Service Training - COMMIT
San Francisco - Glide Urban Center - Glide *
Colorado
Denver - Ministry of Urban Concerns, Colorado Council of Churches
    (began as Ministry of Urban Concerns, Denver Council of Churches) - MUC
District of Columbia
Black Churchmen's Ecumenical Institute - BCEI (joined ATC as Black Churchmen's
    Ecumenical Training Facility - BCETF)
Metropolitan Ecumenical Training Center - METC
Georgia
Atlanta - United Training Organization of Atlanta - UTOA
Idaho
Boise - Ecumenical Training Council of Idaho - ETC *
Illinois
Chicago - Institute on the Church in Urban-Industrial Society - ICUIS (joined ATC as
    Presbyterian Institute on Industrial Relations - PIIR)
        - Urban Training Center for Christian Mission - UTC
Minnesota
Minneapolis - Center for Urban Encounter - CUE-M
St. Paul - Ministry in Social Change, Twin Cities Graduate Program - MISC
Missouri
Kansas City - Midwest Training Network - MTN (joined ATC as Training for Ecumenical
    Action and Mission - TEAM; later became Community 33)
St. Louis - Inter-religious Center for Urban Affairs - ICUA
Webster Groves - Evangelical Academy of Webster Groves - EAWG * ±
New York
New York City - Metropolitan Urban Service Training - MUST
        - Urban Young Adult Action - UYAA
Rochester - Joint Office for Urban Ministry - JOUM (joined ATC as Strategy Training
    in Renewal - STIR; later became Urbex Affiliates)
Ohio
Cincinnati - Center for Human Action, Research and Training - CHART
Cleveland - Commission on Ecumenical Education, Council of Churches of Greater
    Cleveland - CEE
Cleveland/Columbus - Action Training Network of Ohio (joined ATC as Internship
    for Clergymen in Urban Ministry - CIP; then became Community Action Training
    Services - CATS)
Columbus - Columbus Action Training Associates - CATA (now part of ATN)

Pennsylvania
Philadelphia - Metropolitan Associates of Philadelphia - MAP *
    - Training Ecumenically to Advance Mission - TEAM
Puerto Rico
Programa de Renovacion y Investigacion Social para Adiestramiento - PRISA
Tennessee
Memphis/Nashville - Association for Christian Training and Service - ACTS
Virginia
Richmond - Task-Force for Renewal, Urban Strategy and Training - TRUST
Washington
Seattle - Ecumenical Metropolitan Ministry - EMM

OTHERS
California
Mill Valley - Urban Church Institute, Golden Gate Theological Seminary
Oakland - Center for Social Change
Connecticut
Hartford - Center for Urban Ethics
New Haven - Greater New Haven Metropolitan Leadership Training, Church Mission
    Association
District of Columbia
Amilcar Cabral Institute, Interreligious Foundation for Community Organization (IFCO)
Urban Institute for Religious Studies, Howard University
Florida
Miami - Center for Dialogue ±
Florida Training Action Network
Illinois
Chicago - Center for Black Religious Studies
    - Ecumenical Institute
    - Metropolitan Lay Ministry Training Program, Community Renewal Society
    - Urban Ministries Program for Seminarians (UMPS)
Naperville - Center for Parish Development
Indiana
Indianapolis - METRO ±
Merom/Indianapolis - Ecumenical Center of Renewal and Planning
Maryland
Baltimore - Middle Atlantic Training Committee ±
Michigan
Bloomfield Hills - Institute for Advanced Pastoral Studies ±
Detroit - Center for Ecumenical Action Training
    - Inter-Faith Action Centers
East Lansing - East Lansing Ecumenical Associates ±
Mississippi
Jackson - LAOS (also Washington, DC)
New York
New York City - Black Community Developers Program, National Division, Board of
    Global Ministries, United Methodist Church ±
        - Church Management Training Program, National Council of Churches ±
        - United Methodist Volunteer Service ±
Syracuse - Priority One, Metropolitan Action Training Project

North Carolina
Raleigh - Inter-Seminary Church and Society Program for Experimental Study of Church and Society
Winston-Salem - Church and Society Institute
Ohio
Akron - Center for Urban Training, Intergroup Ministry of Greater Akron ±
Cleveland - Black Action Training
Oklahoma
Tulsa - Institute for Urban Ministries
Pennsylvania
Philadelphia - Institute for Black Ministries
- Urban Institute, Lutheran Theological Seminary
Pittsburgh - Urban Policy Studies for Clergy, University of Pittsburgh
Upland - Upland School for Social Change, Crozer Theological Seminary
Texas
Dallas - Dallas Young Adult Institute ±
Houston - Houston Metro Ministry ±
San Antonio/Austin - Lutheran Institute for Religious Studies
Wisconsin
Milwaukee - Center for Civic Initiative
- Milwaukee Institute of Theology

* Associate Member of ATC   ± Nothing in ICUIS files

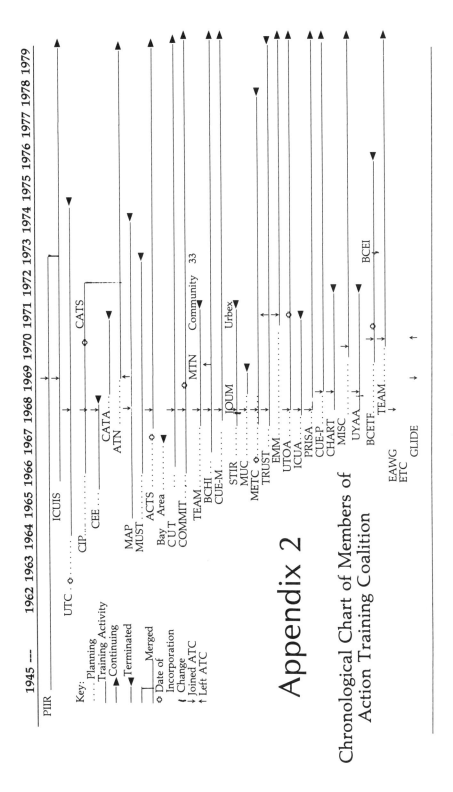

Appendix 2

Chronological Chart of Members of
Action Training Coalition

Appendix 3

Meetings of Action Training Coalition

October 3, 1967 - Washington, D.C.
  Discussion on urban training centers at Episcopal Church House during 50th
  Anniversary meeting of American Institute of Planners
I February 9-11, 1968 - Chevy Chase, Maryland
  National Consultation of Urban Training Centers
II May 24-26, 1968 - Kansas City, Missouri
  National Consultation of Urban Training Centers and Networks
III January 2-5, 1969 - Cleveland, Ohio
  ATC Consultation, "The Black Situation and White Racism"
IV March 30-April 3, 1969 - Cincinnati, Ohio
  ATC Consultation, "Agenda Search: Funding, Functions, Constituencies"
V October 5-8, 1969 - St. Louis, Missouri
  ATC Consultation, "Coalition Social Goals and Constituencies, Proposals for Joint
  Action, Priorities, Plans for Action"
  December 19-20, 1969 - Chicago, Illinois
  Council of the ATC
VI March 20-25, 1970 - Toronto, Ontario, Canada
  ATC Consultation
  ATC Delegate Assembly
  Council of the ATC
  May 28-29, 1970 - St. Louis, Missouri
  Council of the ATC
VII October 26-28, 1970 - Atlanta Georgia
  ATC Consultation, "Sensitization, Analysis, Strategy, Theological Reflection,
  Evaluation" Workshops, and Atlanta exposure
  ATC Delegate Assembly
  Council of the ATC
  February 19, 1971 - St. Louis, Missouri
  Council of the ATC
VIII March 22-24, 1971 - Puerto Rico (followed by visit to Dominican Republic,
  March 25-29)
  ATC Consultation, "Exposure to the Caribbean"
  ATC Delegate Assembly
  Council of the ATC
  June 1-2, 1971 - St. Louis, Missouri
  Council of the ATC
IX October 3-6, 1971 - Los Angeles and Delano, California
  ATC Consultation, "Farm Workers Organizing Committee"
  ATC Delegate Assembly
X March 19-22, 1972 - Chicago, Illinois
  ATC Consultation, "Health Issues"
  Council of the ATC
  ATC Delegate Assembly

XI October 15-18, 1972 - Philadelphia, Pennsylvania
    ATC Consultation, "Lay Ministry for Organizational Change"
    ATC Delegate Assembly
XII April 1-4, 1973 - Chicago, Illinois
    ATC Consultation, "Corporate Responsibility"
    ATC Delegate Assembly

Appendix 4

Case Study:
The Institutional Racism Project
in the Episcopal Diocese of Southern Ohio
(Action Training Network of Ohio)

In May 1970, the Convention of the Diocese of Southern Ohio passed Resolution 55 which asked that "the Diocese of Southern Ohio and its member churches and congregations, in honesty and love, develop plans and programs to deal with the reality of racism in our churches and our Church." After six years of work on this problem by our laity, staff, bishop and clergy, a Special Diocesan Convention in February 1976 adopted as the second paramount program goal of the Diocese the "on-going commitment to search out and eradicate all forms of institutional racism in all programs of the Diocese." Thus, the Diocese of Southern Ohio made a long-range pledge to struggle with the racism inherent in its policies and practices until the time when those problems have been significantly addressed and overcome.

We proclaim in our Handbook that "we believe that the Church had been called by God to exercise a ministry of reconciliation to all people and to witness in its own life that there is neither Jew nor Greek, bond nor free, male nor female, for all are one in Christ Jesus. Institutional racism, largely unconscious and consequently difficult to identify and eliminate, undermines our effective witness to all people. We believe it is essential to the life of the Church that Christians struggle with difficult human problems in order to develop vision and power for a just and humane society."

The problems of racism—both individual and institutional—are difficult and enduring. They gained our attention during the Sixties, a decade of demonstrations, riots, and civil rights legislation. In spite of much effort by concerned Christians, the Kerner Commission reported in 1968 that "our nation is moving toward two societies, one Black, one white—separate and unequal." The Commission said that whites are primarily responsible for this division. "What white Americans have never fully understood, but what the Negro can never forget is that white society is deeply implicated in the ghetto. White institutions created it, white institutions maintain it, and white society condones it."

The Seventies have been more "peaceful" for whites but no less problematic for Blacks. In 1978, a survey of institutional racism (conducted by the New York *Times* and the CBS News Bureau) headlined that "The Black-White Split Persists." Whites believed that progress had been made; Blacks saw it differently. For example,

- In 1968, 49% of Blacks thought there was real hope of ending racial discrimination in this country; in 1978 only 37% expressed that hope.
- In public schools, the actual concentration of Black and Latino children is *greater* than in 1968.
- The unemployment rate for Black people has *doubled* in the past ten years.

The study concludes, "The division between white and Black Americans still exists, and prospects of healing the rift may be more dismal today than they were ten years ago." It is evident that although the problems of racism may be out of the spotlight today, they are not out of existence.

The Diocese of Southern Ohio adopted the Kerner Commission's definition of institutional racism as the basis for its work: institutional racism is *any policy or practice of an organization which benefits one race at the expense of other races.* We focused on institutional behavior because institutions shape the attitudes and behavior of the people within them; therefore, institutions can take significant leadership in bringing about changes in their members. Furthermore, *one* change in institutional policy or practice can affect many more lives than *one* change in any individual's attitudes and actions.

From the beginning, we decided to treat our own membership (Diocesan Council, staff, clergy, vestries, parishioners) as the client, rather than trying to "help" the Black, the poor, the ghetto with their problems; we would work within our own Episcopal institution and membership. As Dr. Archie Hargraves, president of Shaw University, said, "Racism is the white problem, and the Black condition." In its first report, the Institutional Racism Project recommended (and Convention approved) the allocation of $100,000 per year for Minority Empowerment, with the same criteria for control as the General Convention Special Program—regular reporting, but complete autonomy for Blacks. Our primary focus, however, was the white power structure.

We acknowledged that white Christians have inherited, now control, and can change the structures of their church to eliminate (or lessen) racism. This acceptance of responsibility for "the way things are" drastically revised the premise of our church's actions. We stopped studying (and blaming) the victims of racism and began to discover how we shape and participate in systems that create social problems. In the democratic structure of the Episcopal Church, people hold decision-making positions and, therefore, have the power to investigate, to recommend, and to implement. In short, we Episcopalians have the power to act responsibly, as well as the imperative to do so, in the light of the Gospel.

Since the racism of the Church is usually unconscious, we needed ways to identify it. With the help of a Black/white consultant team which had no previous involvement with the Diocese, we began by asking how our Church designed its programs, hired its staff, spent its money, and made its decisions. The answers we received enabled us to see which practices favored whites and worked to the disadvantage of Blacks. We then recommended to Diocesan Convention changes in policy and practice.

The premise of this approach was that attitudes are most effectively revealed when we are asked to do something to change an institution of which we are a part. Therefore, our recommendations for change demanded no special expertise for implementation. They could, however, lead us into new patterns of behavior from which we could learn different attitudes. Since we found these changes both controversial and difficult to make, we were forced to confess the strength of our bondage to racism, and our investigation of the institutional practices of our Church became a journey of self-discovery for each of us.

In our nine years of work, we have learned that the effects of racism are diverse and thorough-going; they afflict both individuals and institutions. We also learned that we must resist the seductive notion that racism is merely a "problem" that can be solved by correct "programs" in a defined span of time. Racism is a complex and deeply rooted manifestation of Sin, and the struggle against racism must be sophisticated, comprehensive, and sustained.

Ultimately, this self-examination of church policy and practice has been for the Diocese of Southern Ohio an initial step in conforming itself to God's will. We discovered and confessed that "we have sinned . . . in thought, word, and deed, by what we have done, and by what we have left undone . . . we have not loved our neighbor as ourselves." In the words of the Exhortation, we are trying to "acknowledge our sins before Almighty God, with full purpose of amendment of life, being ready to make restitution for all injuries and wrongs done by us to others . . . that being reconciled with one another," we may "come to the banquet of that most heavenly Food." We continue to struggle, as individuals and as the Body of Christ in Southern Ohio, to shed the sinful concretions of our history and traditions and thus to recover the image of God in which we were created and to which we are called.

HISTORY

In the United States, racism is a fact of life that none of us can escape. We may fight racism, acquiesce to it, suffer from it, deny it, but we all bear the mark of it in our attitudes and our actions. Through the years, Episcopalians in the Diocese of Southern Ohio have struggled against racism in many ways—each way apparently the best way for its time, all ways working together to do away with the racial schism in the Body of Christ.

Bishop John Krumm, at our Centennial Convention in 1975, cited a text from the Epistle to the Hebrews to help us to put our current actions into a historical context: "One and all gave proof of their faith, yet they never saw the promise fulfilled; for us God had something better in store. We were needed to make the history of their lives complete" (Hebrews 11:39-40, Ronald Knox translation). He commented,

> Originally, that text, of course, referred to the relationship between Israel's past and the new Christian dispensation, but I think it is legitimate to understand it as an insight into God's general use of history. The past is only fully significant as we see its fulfillment in the present. Similarly, the present itself will be revealed in all its implications only in the future. We are, as the Prayer Book says, "Knit together in one communion and fellowship."

We learned several things about racism during the Sixties. The civil rights demonstrations—the marches, the lunch counter sit-ins, the Freedom Rides in the South and the fiery, desperate summers of the North and West—taught us that justice and equality of opportunity are not a reality for Black Americans. We also learned that the conditions of ghetto life could affect lives and liberties in city and suburb as well. Church people responded to these lessons with fear and guilt, good intentions and good deeds.

The churches of the Diocese of Southern Ohio looked outward to the anguished community, seeking ways to serve and to heal. As one of the seven dioceses chosen by the National Church for a Joint Pilot Study on Urban Problems during the mid-Sixties, we learned from local community leaders that the dominant problem was always *racism*. In March 1967, the Bishop and Chapter "reiterated its concern over racial discrimination, and requested that all parishes, trustees, and church bodies within the Diocese examine the policies of contractors and business establishments with which they transact business, to determine if they practice racial discrimination, . . . and if so, to strive to eliminate such discrimination by all legal means."[1] The Diocese also sponsored urban task forces with specialized ministries to ghetto populations. In the major cities of the Diocese, church leaders of many denominations formed ecumenical coalitions so that racial problems, dynamically concentrated in the urban areas, could be addressed with their joint resources of money, wisdom, and planning skills. As chairman of the Office of Community Commitment, Bishop Roger W. Blanchard worked parttime at Cincinnati's City Hall and gave up a sabbatical and attendance at the Lambeth Conference in 1968 in order to work for racial harmony at home.

The Diocese of Southern Ohio supported the National Church's response to the racial crisis, the General Convention Special Program, and in 1969 raised 140% of the pledge it had made at South Bend. Bishop Blanchard and the delegates to that Special Convention spent many hours interpreting to local parishes the decision of the National Church to move beyond parish walls and to touch the lives of non-Episcopalians who were alienated from us by injury and anger. For many in our Diocese, it was their first encounter with institutional remedies for institutional racism.

At the parish level, too, we tried to hear each other in spite of racial differences, to learn of the other's experience, and to help each other over the obstacles of prejudice and injustice. The Diocese helped with its Community Orientation Discussion Series—an educational process designed "to give men, women, and youth an opportunity to get information and facts on crucial social issues; and to develop community leaders within the church membership who can perform effectively with other community leaders." The Diocese also "recruited and helped to place in effective volunteer programs of communities, congregations and the Diocese, the manpower and leadership resources of committed persons who wish to serve and become involved in places of need." [2]

All of these programs were beneficial to us. They helped us to develop skills, knowledge, and sensitivity to some dimensions of the problems faced by Blacks. Frustration swelled, however, as these modes of action brought no change in the situations that caused suffering, even though there was often personal fulfillment for us in our individual tasks.

Resolution 55 (1970), by challenging the Church "to deal with the reality of racism in our churches and our Church," turned our eyes inward to focus on ourselves and our institution as a significant, previously-overlooked part of the problem. It redirected our attention and action from the injustices in the system of the secular community (educational, legal, governmental, medical) and asked us to look for and to accept responsibility for injustice in our own institutions.

WHAT WE DID

We had to decide how to discover and deal with the "reality of racism" within the Church. We saw three levels of racism affecting our life together, and we defined these as

individual racism—personal prejudice and any act which assumes the superiority of one race over another;
cultural racism—any norm or value which exalts one race over another; and
institutional racism—any policy or practice of an organization which benefits one race at the expense of other races.

Because we wanted to effect change in our institution that would endure independent of persons and time, we focused on the racism of the Church-as-institution. . . .

We chose to work primarily at this level because the problem of racism is more than individual attitudes or abstract values. From the Sixties, we learned that real kinds of changes—organizational, institutional, and societal—must take place in order to deal with what racism is. The major institutions of society, including the Church, often operate in ways that reinforce racist beliefs.

We know that institutional racism can be conscious or unconscious. *It is not the motivation of the institution or its members that counts. It is what results from the policy and/or practice that counts and determines whether the institution is racist.* For example, we learned that the Christian education materials we used in our diocesan and parish programs did not include Black Christian experience and contributions to our Church. This was a practice that was not intentional; nevertheless, it prevented Black Episcopalians from seeing their experience and contributions to the life of the Church and the nation affirmed by their church. At the same time, it led the white majority of Episcopalians to assume that there was nothing of special significance to learn from or about Black Christians. Our remedy was to develop eighteen Christian education units for children, youth, and adults to compensate for that lack of inclusiveness. Black contributions to church and nation are now available in our educational curriculum. This has become our new policy and practice.

The group process that we have used in the Institutional Racism Project, "action-training," is designed to enable people to set realistic goals and to achieve them. Everything that participants do is geared to *action*—specific, measurable, attainable, and significant action. The primary reason for people to conduct interviews, to do research, to write reports, to make recommendations, to go to meetings, and to get along with each other is that significant change will occur in the policy and practice of the Church as a result of these actions. *Doing the task*—that is, making changes that last longer than euphoria—is most important. The process itself models what we hope the Church will do: by working in a less racist manner, to become less racist in attitude and action.

There have been two phases of research, followed by recommendations for change that were later validated by vote of the Diocesan Convention—in 1972, seventeen recommendations for the diocesan structure and in 1974, fifteen recommendations for parishes. Since 1972, the research phases have been complemented by the far more difficult work of implementing and maintaining the changes. In both kinds of activity, there are two crucial ways in which the Institutional Racism Project differed from our work on racism in the Sixties: (1) we worked as a group and (2) we worked in a "cool," data-based mode, with specific goals to achieve in a system in which we hold decisive power.

The groups who have worked on the Institutional Racism Project have been a microcosm of the Church itself. We believe it is important for all the people in the Church to see themselves mirrored in the group that want to change the Church. Each group that has worked on the project has been composed of

> —both Blacks and whites, Blacks being at 1/3 of the group to strengthen their cohesiveness and witness as a minority group and to show the Church's seriousness about empowerment of them;
> —laity and clergy;
> —women and men;
> —representatives from various program areas;
> —staff and volunteers, particularly those in decision-making and leadership roles; and
> —a Black/white consultant team from outside the Episcopal Church.

Other criteria for working groups simply try to guarantee the feasibility of a person's participation. For the research phases, for example, we sought people who would spend 5-7 hours every other week for eight meetings, who had the mobility to get to meetings of a diocesan-wide group, who were willing to work on racism with honesty and personal integrity, and who were workers, not just talkers.

As each team began its work, its identity as a task-oriented community helped its members to see personal hang-ups about racism in an institutional perspective. We saw that, as a community, we could take authentic responsibility for the community's rules of life, and that as individuals, we each had to take responsibility for our own attitudes and behavior. In the Institutional Racism Project, we do not try to purge all our personal racism before working to make the Church-as-institution more just, for we recognize that none of us who grew up in a country where skin color still determines response to people is free from prejudice. We acknowledge personal racial prejudice as a persistent impediment to be dealt with by a group only when it threatens the group's task. Prejudice may hamper an individual somewhat but it should not prevent meaningful action by the community. Our working as a group reminds us that liberation comes to the community (Yahweh led the Israelites out of Egypt as a nation, not one-by-one) and is manifested by the creation of a just community.

Setting attainable, yet significant, goals based on data gathered from church members and church records has enabled us to do our task with energy and self-respect. We have a way to learn the intricacies and obduracy of the problem and to measure our progress. We learned by experience what in the Church needed to be changed and how to change it.

We tested our theories about racism in the Church against the facts of Church practice, and we modified our problem statements as we came to know the problems in accurate, verifiable detail. The first research team, for example, began its work with an overnight conference that had three objectives: (1) to meet each other and build the trust necessary for working together on a difficult task; (2) to reach a common understanding of the problems of racism in the Church; and (3) to begin to define some areas of concern that this group would address. In the next three months, the group specified the faults and formulated recommendations for their correction after research.

The primary tool of research was the personal interview; members of the research team talked with four groups within the church—victims, change-agents, powers, and experts. As Dr. Robert Bonthius, one of the consultants for the Project, defines these sources of information,

> Victims are the sufferers in the situation. Change-agents are those who work inside or outside the system to bring about change in policies and practices. Powers are the people who run the organizations of the system. Experts are those who have an accumulated knowledge of the problem through contact with it over a period of time.[3]

Some of the questions to be asked of all four groups, Dr. Bonthius says, are:

1. How many people suffer from the problem?
2. Where are they located?
3. How are they affected?
4. What are the economic, political, and social factors that make this a problem?

Other questions the team must answer are: What are the conflicting values that make this a problem? What are the structures (institutions, agencies, organizations) that contribute to this problem? Who are their key decision-makers? What are the specific policies or practices of these structures which are at fault and need changing? Answers to these questions provide the data from which the team wrote problem statements, goals, and recommendations for action. It also helped them plan the strategy to get the recommended changes approved by the legislative body of the Diocese (Convention) and then implemented.

We have not fooled ourselves that, by implementing some of the approved recommendations, we have eliminated the problem of racism in the Church. However, this way of working has provided a "life-jacket" of self-respect for us when we feel overwhelmed by the enormity of the real oppression that is a traditional and integral part of contemporary social systems. For us, doing a specific, and therefore manageable, task with supportive colleagues is more productive—for individuals and institutions—than solitary, quixotic challenges that never attain palpable reality.

ESSENTIAL RESOURCES

Our effort to change the Church-as-institution has demanded both spiritual and material resources. It began with open and responsible commitment and is sustained by investments of labor and money.

By passing Resolution 55 in 1970, the Diocesan Convention decided to confront the racism that disfigures the Church and hinders both its interior life and its witness in the secular world. Such a commitment means that the struggle against racism takes priority over "business as usual," for the way in which daily business is carried on is the thing to be examined. Such a commitment also demands that we work together in new ways, that we listen to those we have ignored or silenced in the past, that we invent new patterns of actions. It means, fundamentally, that we must give up the old without being certain what the new will be.

In addition to the original commitment to the task, success depends on four other signs of continuing commitment, which must be present at all times—leadership at the diocesan level, adequate funding, serious volunteers (particularly, from the laity), and outside consultants (Black and white).

The Institutional Racism Project has been blessed with strong leadership from the Diocesan staff. Through the Sixties, Bishop Blanchard helped us to face the problems of racism with unflinching honesty and to work on them with energy. Bishop Krumm, who assumed his duties in the Diocese of Southern Ohio in March 1971 when the Project was first proposed to Diocesan Council, has sustained our work in many ways. He has supported strongly the recommendations to Diocesan Convention and the actions necessary for their implementation. He has interpreted the theological aspects of the Project to the Church in sermons and seminars. He has encouraged the diocesan staff to cooperate with us fully and has taken responsibility for change in his own bailiwick.

Adequate funding is another sign of commitment, for achieving change in the policies and practices of the Church costs money. Staff time, consultants' fees, travel expenses, conferences, production of learning materials, coordination of volunteers—all these forms of support can be expressed in terms of dollars and cents, and the budget bears final witness to the seriousness of commitment. "Where your treasure is, there will your heart be also."

Of paramount importance to any attempt to effect change in the Church is the concerned, informed, and active participation of the laity. They are the grassroots of the organized Church, and in the Episcopal Church, the final arbiters of practice. On the diocesan level, their representatives determine the goals and priorities of diocesan policy and elect the Bishop; on the parish level, the laity choose their rector, determine the priorities of the budget, and do the work of the Church. They "work, pray, and give for the spread of God's kingdom," and if they do not support the reforms in the Church, the Church-as-institution will not be reformed. Only a small percentage of the laity need to be change-agents, but the witness of their opinions and their actions is essential.

The fourth essential resource is the presence of outside consultants. It is impossible for those of us inside the Church to monitor our own progress in changing it. Each of us helped to shape the past and the present, and we have a vested interest in the shape of the future. We need the perspective of someone who cannot profit personally by any change we might make in order to do the job of institutional change efficiently and justly. Furthermore, the consultancy in work on racism should be provided by a Black/white team, to insure that both points of view be heard in authentic dialogue. The consultancy for the Institutional Racism Project has been provided by Action Training Network of Ohio. Dr. Robert H. Bonthius, its director (white), has worked with us since the beginning in 1971, and has been accompanied by Oliver O'Conner, James Dunn, and Frank Chiteji, who are Black. Action Training Network was chosen primarily because of its broad experience with institutional change, especially in voluntary groups, and its work on institutional racism in other denominations. The duration of the consultant relationship is testimony to its value to the Diocese of Southern Ohio throughout the years.

HURDLES

Institutional change is hard work. There are impediments everywhere. Some are obvious and some are subtle; all recur. Some of what we face regularly are the reluctance to admit that skin color *does* make a difference, the perception that racism is passe as a critical issue in the life of the Church and the nation, and the desire for the Church, particularly the local parish, to be the final and secure retreat from the ever-changing world.

For many, the highest value that the Church can assert about racial difference is that Christian justice and goodness are "color-blind." After all, God loves us all equally and totally, and so are we tempted to try to treat everyone with divine impartiality, not reckoning with the historic consequences of racial differences in our experience. Color-blindness may be possible in Heaven, but in the last quarter of the twentieth century, it is a denial of reality and turning away from the responsible use of our power. As Bishop Krumm has said, "The Church inevitably as an institution has power. It's not just a heavenly community. It's an institution. It employs people. It pays salaries. It owns buildings. We always have to be embodied in some way, with some structure, and that structure has got to reflect our Christian understanding of these issues of justice, freedom, and dignity."

Using race as a criterion for determining policy also brings the charge of "reverse racism." Bishop Krumm objected to this charge in an address to the clergy in the fall of 1975. He said,

> One refrain I hear, and I think we need to deal with it here, is that by raising this issue and setting targets for progress in overcoming the institutional racism in our church institutions, we become guilty of what is called "reverse racism" . . . I reject that . . . The kind of love which is described in the New Testament is not an impartial attitude toward everybody, treating everybody the same; the

agape love of the New Testament means treating each person or group of persons according to the particular need which is apparent. Our Lord, it seems to me, was very strategic. Consider, for example, the parable of the lost sheep; one sheep is lost and so the ninety-nine are neglected for the sake of the lost one. The ninety-nine might very well have called this "reverse sheepism."

Some church people feel this way. One woman wrote just a short time ago, and said, "I guess you have no room for me in the Episcopal Church—I'm not young, I'm not black, I'm not poor—and I guess you don't want me around since that's what you're spending all your time on."

I wrote her and said in effect, "I think we are justified in spending special time, special effort, special resources on people who have been systematically neglected and lost and alienated over a long period of time.

Now, when affirmative action is being challenged in the courts, we need to remember that the action of Christian love is responsive to need and must be strategically appropriate for historical circumstances, not arithmetically impartial.

Another hurdle to be overcome is the inertia caused by the white majority's opinion that racism is no longer a significant and oppressive reality. Born out of fear and frustration "by the light of burning ghettos," our work slows down when there is little pressure from outside and inside the Church to persevere. Where do we find the vision of a more just society to call forth our energy and dedication, if we believe that all is well in our world just because all is quiet? It is often difficult for white Episcopalians to discover how they would profit from more inclusive ways of worship and church polity; they do not feel impoverished, because the things they have always done have formed the standard by which success was measured. Also, for many Blacks, the Episcopal Church is working well enough—so much better than the secular world that they are not moved to press for more.

Introducing change in the local parishes demands both tact and persistence. Parishioners frequently desire "their" church to be "the one thing in life that doesn't change." Many derive their identity and deep emotional security from its traditions and their participation in them. It is a wrenching lesson to be learned that the Church's structure should manifest the Gospel message, even if habitual ways of action must be changed.

The autonomy of parishes is dear to them and must be respected. When changes in parish practices are suggested support from rectors is crucial, for they are the "gate-keepers" of the parish. The majority of the laity traditionally look to the rector for direction, and the rector often has significant discretionary power in the day-to-day business of maintaining the parish, particularly in the areas of purchasing and hiring. Yet, it is often the laity who find the possibilities of change exciting and can lead their fellow parishioners into new ways of acting. Perhaps the reason for this is that the laity have more autonomy and influence in the small system of their parish life than in the larger systems of their work life.

Work at the parish level brings institutional change back to personal encounter and persuasion. Our goal is to make the Church's policies and practice just, but the power to make the necessary changes belongs to individuals. Some people *must* come to understand the dynamics of institutional racism and want to change the forms of our common life in order for significant change to occur. Thus the research we do on the institutional level brings us to wrestle with the individual manifestations of prejudice and to personal encounters with our brothers and sisters in Christ.

ACCOMPLISHMENTS

The Institutional Racism Project has changed our corporate life in specific and measurable ways. Some of them are described here:

Since 1973, the Diocesan budget has included a $100,000 allocation for minority empowerment. The Minority Empowerment Committee receives and reviews applications for grants-in-aid to minority groups which are ineligible for funding from traditional sources. In addition to providing grants, the Minority Empowerment Committee often offers technical assistance on business methods and advice on alternative funding sources. Under the knowledgeable leadership of Marcus Cummings, the grants are often used as "seed money" to get additional grants from the government or from other agencies. This expertise has enabled the $100,000 to bring up to $3,000,000 to minority enterprise in a single year—to generate *30 times* the original amount. Minority Empowerment grants have helped

  —a Black-owned greeting card company to use modern production and marketing techniques;
  —inmates at London Correctional Institute to develop a program of self-education, personal skills, and family connectedness to break the cycle of recidivism;
  —an Episcopal church in Dayton to work with other churches to prepare for peaceful integration of schools;
  —a highly integrated elementary school to institute a closed circuit television system with programs designed, written, produced, and acted by students;
  —an impoverished neighborhood to gain funds from government and private sources to build its own community health center.

The Minority Empowerment Committee has brought the concern and the economic power of the Episcopal Church in the Diocese of Southern Ohio to many segments of the community—Black and Appalachian, Episcopalian and non-Episcopalian.

Significant changes have also occurred in the areas of staff, worship, education, finance, and leadership.

Staff: In 1975, the Rev. Lorentho Wooden was appointed Community Development Officer of the Diocese, a fulltime staff position at Diocesan House. The number of Black clergy in the Diocese has doubled since the project began. A statement of policy on fair employment practices was written by the Executive Officer of the Diocese and approved by a majority of the parishes.

Worship: A workshop on music by Black composers was sponsored by the Diocesan Music Commission. Absalom Jones Day (February 13) is celebrated in a Diocese-wide service, in addition to local observances.

Education: The Project has produced eighteen Christian Education units for children, youth, and adults, and has developed teams of facilitators in each major city of the Diocese to help local parishes use them effectively. Bishop Krumm has written and delivered a study of the problems of racism from the Biblical and theological perspective; it is now available in print. The Project published the *Racism Handbook*, which provides the history and rationale of the Institutional Racism Project and an introduction to communications skills and group process to help us work together. We have compiled and distributed bibliographies of books on Black history and theology for both children and adults. The *Interchange*, the Diocesan newspaper, regularly carries articles to inform parishes of progress on institutional racism.

A new kind of educational project was conducted by the Church of the Ascension in Middletown, Ohio. Their six-week program of racial awareness helped parishioners focus on the harsh realities of life as a Black in their own city. They asked local Black people with special expertise in housing, education, employment, government services, and health care delivery to meet with them as resources. From this experience, the parish made important linkages with the Black community and learned new dimensions of racial problems by seeing "their" city from a Black perspective. The experience opened doors between the parish and the community. It shows that one way predominantly white parishes can combat their racial isolation is by asking Blacks (not only Episcopalian Blacks) to help them make decisions that will have an impact on the entire community.

Finance: The Diocese of Southern Ohio has conducted its new banking business (loans and mortgages) with minority-owned banks. Trustees of the Diocese have put $40,000 in Unity State Bank in Dayton and $40,000 in Major Federal Savings and Loan Association in Cincinnati, the only minority-owned financial institutions in the Diocese. Also, at least fifteen have put some of their savings into these financial institutions, either in passbook accounts or by purchasing certificates of deposit.

The Diocese has committed itself to purchase 20% of its goods and services from minority suppliers. In 1978, the Ohio Minority Business Development Office compiled a guide to minority suppliers of goods and services throughout the state. This book has been distributed to parishes and church-related institutions, which are encouraged to request bids from minority-owned businesses and to try to conduct a certain percentage of their business with them.

Leadership: Every committee of the Diocese at every level has Black membership. The total percentage of Blacks on the seven most influential diocesan bodies is 22%. The Nominating Committee regularly publishes "job descriptions" and solicits nominations for major program and finance positions in the Diocese.

The latest report shows that in 1978 58 people were actively engaged in decision-making and implementation of the Institutional Racism Project, through the Racism Steering Committee and the three local Clusters (groups of laity and clergy who help local parishes to implement recommendations of Convention). Through the years, people from over half of the parishes in the Diocese (that is, from more than forty parishes) have worked on the Institutional Racism Project.

The plans of the Institutional Racism Project for the future are to work to accomplish the many tasks that remain, particularly to continue developing the local Clusters. We also see the importance of monitoring the progress we have made in the past so that our accomplishments will be maintained.

The "Do-ers" of the Word

The Catechism describes our Christian duties as ministers of the Gospel in this way:

Q. Who are ministers of the Church?
A. The ministers of the Church are lay persons, bishops, priests, and deacons.
Q. What is the ministry of the laity?
A. The ministry of lay persons is to represent Christ and his Church; to bear witness to him wherever they may be; and according to the gifts given them, to carry on Christ's work of reconciliation in the world; and to take their place in the life, worship, and governance of the Church.

Work on the Institutional Racism Project has taught us new ways to fulfill our responsibilities as members of the Church. The participants' new consciousness of the problems of racism in the church (and elsewhere) has been characterized by movements

FROM	TO
reform, civil rights perspective	liberation perspective
individual perspective	systemic perspective
voluntaristic perspective	political action
"your" oppression	"my" oppression
victim as cause	system as cause
powerlessness	empowerment.

Comments by workers in the first phase of our research revealed feelings of frustration and powerlessness. After their first session, they said,

I've come to the stage where I'm aware of much racism but the next step of putting it in its dynamic situation and saying it out loud isn't with me yet.

It's difficult for me to see it when I have been living in it and with it all these years.

I would like to begin to be able to recognize racism without having to have it pointed out to me by a Black.

When asked to state the important learnings when they had completed their task, participants replied,

> The learning for me was to move from a "feeling" that there is racism in the church to discovering actual shocking facts dealing with definite numbers and conditions.
> The most important learning for me is the fact that we did work and we want to eliminate racism. I had always felt that people are quite inadequate to fight socially inherited wrongs and it excites me greatly that we seem to be making some headway.
> . . . how deeply racism is embedded in the policies and practices of the Episcopal church. Also, the disciplined way in which this sin must be approached.

We intend that the Institutional Racism Project be "basic training" for systemic change of unjust structures elsewhere in society, as well as a means of internal reform in our part of the Episcopal Church. Using the power we have within the Church family teaches us how to work effectively for change and gives to us both individual Christians and the Episcopal Church credibility in wider struggles. We hope that participants will use their new skills and insights outside the Church to bring strong Christian witness to their secular lives.

The new power for witnessing is summed up by the comment of a now-anonymous worker in the Institutional Racism Project: "Being a Christian should somehow change a community or a nation in substantial ways."

-Karen E. Steanson
Columbus, Ohio

(This case study has been excerpted from *Journey Toward Justice: A Report on the Institutional Racism Project in the Diocese of Southern Ohio* (September 1979), by Karen E. Steanson.)

Appendix 5

Case Study:
Community Organizing through
Black Community Developers
(Metropolitan Urban Service Training)

In the spring of 1968, at the height of the turbulent struggle of Black people during the sixties for social, political and economic justice in American society, the United Methodist Church launched the Black Community Developers (BCD) program, a bold and innovative church-sponsored and supported, community-based initiative for social change and empowerment in oppressed Black communities. The BCD program was conceived as an instrument to empower the churches serving the Black community, so that they would become a force for liberation and the abolition of the systemic evils of racism and economic exploitation.

In order to advance the church's capacity to be in mission in the ghetto, while at the same time increasing the effectiveness of the role of Black congregations in the United Methodist Church, the Black Community Developers program was funded as part of the Quadrennial Emphasis.[1] It provided for the enlistment, training and ministry of 75 community developers across the United States.

Early in 1969 Metropolitan Urban Service Training, an action-training agency in New York City that had also been initiated with funds from the United Methodist Church, was requested to provide training for the Black Community Developers. The combination of vision, commitment of resources, technical assistance and training furnished by MUST resulted in one of the most effective efforts by Black churches to address the desperate needs and conditions of Black and poor communities in the nation. It has also resulted in a model that has since been expanded to include other ethnic communities and their churches.

The Community Developers were hired by and served on the staff of traditionally Black churches in rural and urban minority ghetto situations. They were recruited locally by the pastors of those churches and a local church Policy Committee, in consultation with national mission staff. The Developers were typically and primarily lay persons (40% were women), and in most instances were young adults who utilized the BCD experience to test the vocational possibilities of careers in professional church leadership.

It was expected that the Community Developer's general responsibilities would include the following:

(1) Developing and supervising a community service program.
(2) Becoming knowledgeable about the total community, its problems and potential.
(3) Relating to existing community organizations and development activities, attempting to strengthen ties between the church and the indigenous community leadership.
(4) Recruiting and mobilizing lay leadership for involvement in community service programs and movements for social change.
(5) Providing linkage between the local church and other religious programs for community development.

MUST was requested to train the Community Developers in such a way as to equip them to be effective community organizers who would deal with both the real and felt needs emerging out of the poor and oppressed communities in which the local Black churches existed. Dr.

Negail R. Riley, founder of the BCD program, has often said, "The program was conceived to empower and enable the Black church to become again, in accordance with the mandate of the Gospel of Christ, an institution in the vanguard of the fight for the liberation of the oppressed."

MUST's responsibility, therefore, was to train the Developers with the intent of making the Black church the center of Black community life, consciously and conspicuously relevant to the struggles of the poor, the dispossessed, the downtrodden and excluded elements of society. MUST was asked not only to train the Community Developers but also the pastors and laypersons who were serving as chairperson of the Policy Committee for each local BCD program.

The training of the Developers was expected to improve their understanding and community organization skills in order to secure the highest demonstration of creative ministry. Moreover, MUST was asked following the training period to provide a continuing consultative relationship with the Community Developers in order to ensure an opportunity for ongoing training experience for Developers, pastors and lay persons.

The syllabus for the MUST basic training sequence, which was given at their headquarters in New York City, included courses in the following areas:

I. The Local Black Church and Community Development
   A. Theological Background
      1. Mission
      2. Prophecy
      3. Cross-bearing
   B. Involvement in large-scale community organization
   C. Denominational relationships
   D. Interfaith cooperation
   E. The cost of church involvement
   F. The benefits of church involvement
   G. The role of the minister
   H. The role of the congregation
   I. Worship as a community factor.
II. Elements of Community Development
   A. Assessment of Pertinent Factors in Community Organization
      1. Authority   6. Reward
      2. Influence   7. Coercion
      3. Decision-making   8. Expertise
      4. Force   9. Reference
      5. Political power   10. Economic
   B. Elements of Community Organization
      1. Issues
      2. Change
      3. Conflict
         a. Utilization
         b. Management
      4. Organization
         a. How to organize
      5. Techniques of Community Organization
      6. Strategies
      7. Skills
      8. Situation Analysis
         a. Problems   d. Actors and agents
         b. Conditions   e. Goals
         c. Structures

III. Issue Areas
  A. Black Economic Development
  B. Health and Welfare
  C. Housing
  D. Police-Community Relations
  E. Education
  F. Drugs
  G. Black Theology
IV. Leadership Development and Black Empowerment
  A. Sensitivity Training
  B. Leadership Development
    1. Leadership—a definition
    2. A look at several models of Black leadership
    3. Self-examination, definition, direction
    4. Leadership—responsibility of
    5. Myths and symbols
      a. Attitudes
      b. Values
      c. Behavior
  V. Practical Community Organization and Leadership Administration

As a consequence of the MUST training, evaluations of the 75 BCD projects reflected a qualitative development in community leadership and organization, characterized by an increasing ability of community people to engage in the determination of their economic and political destiny. An examination of the efforts and programmatic activities of local BCD projects clearly illustrates the effectiveness of the MUST training in helping communities to address social, political and economic injustices through Black empowerment and development.

Some local programs wrestled with the dehumanizing evils of deplorable housing conditions manifested in the blight of crumbling Black ghettos throughout the nation. Some programs were projected toward economic development in an effort to lift communities from the grave of economic deprivation. Some were concentrated on the crippling, killing, insufficient—and in some cases total lack of—medical and health services in the communities where Black churches and Black people were located.

All of the Community Developers were involved in the mobilization of church and community folk to wage non-violent war upon the many forms of systemic violence that were heaped upon them, and consistently were blocking their efforts to emerge from the prisons of their poverty and legalized oppression. As a result, Black United Methodist churches in several communities were engaged in supporting and participating with those communities in their battle against such deeply entrenched problems as widespread, debilitating drug abuse, unemployment, inadequate and inefficient school systems, corrupt and discriminatory political policies and practices in government, inequitable and failure-oriented welfare programs; and the polluting effects of deplorable prison systems and unfair court systems, where equitable justice was a promise reserved for the prestigious, the influential, and the politically and financially powerful.

Fifteen years after MUST provided the initial training, its significant and continuing impact upon the Black Community Developers, as well as upon poor and oppressed Black communities, is evidenced in people like Bob Ford, who was trained as Community Developer with special emphasis upon political action, and is now a city councilman in Charleston, South Carolina. Ford organized other Blacks to run for political office, and several of them were elected. He himself was elected to the City Council in 1975, and became the first such Black city official in Charleston since Reconstruction. Bob Ford is featured as one of the most prominent Black political figures in America in an article in *Ebony* magazine (August 1984).

Several Community Developers in the original group of 75 have chosen community development as a full-time career. Most striking of all, 50% of those who participated in the program have chosen a life of Christian ministry and are presently ordained clergy, serving as effective pastors who still maintain a commitment to effect social change through the church's involvement in the community as a liberating vehicle for empowerment, self-determination and development.

The Community Developers program, under the National Division of the Board of Global Ministries, has now been expanded to include Asians, Hispanics, Native Americans and poor Whites. With the direction and impetus provided by the initial training design at MUST, Community Developers continues to be a major vehicle to extend the ministry of the United Methodist Church to hundreds of poor and oppressed communities throughout the nation.

Negail R. Riley
National Division
Board of Global Ministries
United Methodist Church
New York, New York

Appendix 6

Theologizing, Sociologizing, Strategizing with Action:
The Three-Fold Curriculum
(Urban Training Center for Christian Mission)

For people of Judeao-Christian faith, as indeed for all citizens, the metropolis requires intensified actions in many situations. Such engagement, moreover, must be kept reflective, that is, rooted in the understandings and imperatives of one's faith. This is needed if people are to be fully critical and constructive participants in unprecedented situations, within established institutions, in supplemental demonstration or pilot projects, and among the consumers or clientele of any institution.

The Urban Training Center seeks to discover the nature of *faithful participation* in a wide variety of public, urban situations. It is devoted to developing *ministries* which facilitate such reflective-inductive action at many new points of decision and movement in metropolis. It is in this way that faith will find its appropriate expression in our time, and participate in decisions by which changes in the city of man will be for the better rather than the worse.

Training at the Urban Training Center accordingly focuses on specific points of public decision and development in the society, both at more "established" points and more "insurgent" points, in places of accumulated power and present powerlessness. Faithful participation at such points includes attention both to the historic sources of faith, Judeao-Christian faith, and to current forms of understanding and organization. It must do so in a fresh and radical way at a time when both Judeao-Christian doctrine and practice have been subjected to rigorous historical inquiry, and when specialized concepts and skills characterize activity in a pluralistic society. Conception and development of appropriate ministries require, therefore, actual engagement with urban actors and specially guided reflection on their actions. "Christian thinking, speaking, and organization must be reborn out of this praying and this action." (Bonhoeffer)

AN OVERVIEW

. . . Each participant is involved in individualized field work, study, and reflection; supervisory and consultative conferences; small group participation for exploration, review of reflective work, and of proposals for ministry; seminars in specialized practices within which ministry is to be fashioned and plenary sessions of the school as a whole for major lectures, forums, and corporate worship. The life of each participant alternates between *work at the Center* and *work in the field*.

There are two major options for training at the Center: *shorter term training*, ranging from four weeks to ten weeks, and *longer term training*, extending for a period from three months to two years in three month units. In the shorter period, the primary focus remains on problems brought by the participants from their home situations. Field study is, therefore, necessarily limited to survey, analysis, evaluation, and consultation in the Chicago area and occasionally by visits to significant projects elsewhere. In the longer term of training, trainees actually go to work on the Chicago scene, often helping to develop policy and strategy in selected agencies or organizations. In both programs, each participant develops capabilities for effective gathering and sorting of data from the situation which he addresses, doing theological and sociological analysis of such data, focusing on a limited problem or problems, considering strategic options and program models, the selection of a program for his situation, and the anticipation of immediate steps to be taken in action.

The intention of the UTC is that each participant, at the conclusion of his stay at the Center, will have clearly located that social and political program in operation, or proposed, which most responds to the problems he has defined. In relationship to that social program, the participant is also to identify the relative role and functions of the institutional church or churches in relationship to that program, and the particular role of a corporate ministry growing out of the life of the church in that setting. Finally and most pointedly, he is to define his special role(s) in relationship to that problem, the program directed toward it, and the task of the Church in regard to both.

To achieve such results, it is our understanding that a threefold practice may be identified: *theologizing, sociologizing, and strategizing with action.* They are respectively weighted to past, present, and immediate future considerations. However, each is here assumed to incorporate past, present, and future considerations and necessarily to be wedded in the process of developing both social programs and forms of ministry in, with, and under them. In addition to *seminars* in each of these practices, *workshops* are also regularly offered in such *skills* as work with task groups, management, planning, and organizing communities. Other workshops are organized around *program patterns* such as cooperative economic enterprises, the use of housing legislation and other governmental programs, and the programs of the War Against Poverty.

The entire community is invited to share a weekly lecture in Biblical, historical interpretation and to share in preaching at the weekly celebration of the Eucharist. These contribute to theological reflection both in the midst of the community gathered at the Center and also in regard to the home situation and the Chicago scene. . . .

SHORT TERM TRAINING METHODS

The basic short term course consists of a ten-week session (4-3-3) with the first four weeks spent in orientation at the UTC, the middle three weeks devoted to research by the participant in his home situation, and the final three weeks back at the Training Center focused upon specific mission project development. Each participant is expected to develop a strategy for his home setting through the use of a UTC-developed discipline known as "Situation Analysis—Back Home."

PREPARATION

The form, "Situation Analysis," has been developed in two parts. The first is a manual to be utilized by prospective UTC participants for the purpose of introducing them to selected procedures for development of relevant forms of ministry. Part II is a questionnaire for participants preparing to attend in-service training programs at the Urban Training Center and is usually filled out immediately prior to coming to the Center. The manual acknowledges the threefold practice to be developed at the Training Center: appreciation of historical and social settings and targets of Biblical and *theological* texts; *sociological* analysis of current situations under consideration in terms of their material conditions, structures which obtain in them, the agents which function or fail to function in them, and the various sorts of goals appropriate in the situation; and *strategy development* with faithful Christian interpretation and action, relevant ministries, and mobilizations. A preliminary step is described and suggested as the participant delimits the situation which he accepts as his responsibility for study and work. Identification and definition of problems to be found in the situation; identification and evaluation of solutions or answers that have been or are being applied to these problems; and critical comparison of the problem definitions developed by the participant with those of the solution- or answer-givers in that setting are scrutinized. Help is given in developing interview techniques, the use of other research and documentary resources, recording procedures of the student's own work and interventions in the situation, and his record of helping processes, not his own, being directed to the problem.

. . . [T]he model of the Situation Analysis is founded on the notion that in any situation four basic elements can be distinguished. These basic elements are *material or economic conditions, structures, agents,* and *goals.* In reality all four elements are intricately intertwined.

Simply for analytical purposes, the participant is required to single out the four elements as though they could be isolated one by one. Yet, he can only realistically study them by continuously reminding himself that each single element has to be understood and interpreted in the light of the others. The manual then develops definitions for the elements with sources for additional understanding of them and for data regarding them as related to particular situations. In summary, pre-entry tasks for the participants include: delimitation of the to-be-analyzed situation, a general situation analysis, identification of selected and accepted issues found in the situation, and a definition and analysis of priority issues. Three such issues are to be described in terms of their nature, their characteristics, and the essential terms of debate. Finally, certain problems are singled out by the participant for special attention during his stay at the UTC.

THE "ROCK-BOTTOM PLUNGE"

Upon arrival at the Training Center, each participant introduces himself by giving a brief report on his pre-entry research and an interpretation of his roles in the home situation. He then enters into an orientation process designed to free him and open him up for participation in the city and for increased understanding of the nature and methods possible for societal or issue-directed ministries. The initial event for this sensitizing and exposure is known as the *"rock-bottom plunge,"* sometimes called "the poor plunge," or "the powerless plunge," In four or five continuous 24-hour periods, the trainee is immersed in a port of entry and/or skid row section of the city with only the clothing on his back and coins in his pocket. It is: (1) an effort to act on the commitment to be with people in other than our own stream of life in a metropolis; (2) to undertake to communicate in languages new to us, within para-communities with which we are inadequately familiar; (3) to be open to sense the chaotic and redemptive, the horrifying and vivifying forces in our metropolitan society; (4) to begin to isolate social "problems for solving" in the midst of a more general problematic situation; (5) to increase our sensitivity to the Word as it may be coming to expression in particular situations; and (6) an indication of our willingness with the Church to be changed and/or to participate in directing change as the city of man requires. The participant is cautioned not to plan his strategy in advance but to play it by ear, to rely on oral communication in discovering from local people available options for meals, housing, day labor, other income, etc., "where the action is." Varieties of recording experiences such as anecdotal or TV-logging, or analytical reference to the four elements of conditions, structures, agents, and goals are offered. Participants are urged to sample a variety of experiences typical of everyday life for the down-and-out: sleeping in transient hotels, staying up all night in coffee houses or movies, seeking at least one day's casual labor, participating in actions on the street or demonstrations within the area. It is recommended that they venture into areas in which ethnic makeup of the people is different from their own. The trainee is also given a series of questions which he is encouraged to ask himself about the people he meets, the institutions in that area, evidences of the work of the Church, about his own reactions and reactions to him, and indications of significant breaking through of humane forces within the situations.

Such a rock-bottom plunge has been supplemented with *other similar existential events*: a suburban plunge, in which issues involving power groups vying with one another have been analyzed; a public education plunge, with visits in the homes of families with school-age children and in the schools attended by the youngsters; live-ins with persons ranging from public aid recipients to top management in steel companies; and so forth. In the case of all such experiences, significant amounts of time are allowed for feedback and critical review in small groups. In each case, theological, sociological, and strategic questions are raised and used for learning both the essential practices of the Center and an increased awareness of the realities of metropolitan life.

WORKSHOPS AND SEMINARS

A workshop for participants' developing of their own *skill in making good use of the three major types of group meetings* occurs next in the program sequence and is provided in cooperation with the Industrial Relations Center of the University of Chicago. The three types of gatherings are identified as (1) "information presentation meetings," (2) meetings in which "advice" is sought by the participant from those in the gathering; and (3) meetings in which "problem-solving" is done jointly by those present, with the participant helping to moderate the session and provide direction in defining and working on the problem. This training experience assists participants in developing useful patterns of participation in the small and middle-size groups of the Training Center, and also in developing skills in enabling others to participate in such small group experiences in which theological and sociological reflection may contribute to sound strategizing for mission.

During this early orientation the very basic and central *theological orientation seminar* is directed toward developing a faithful or theological mode of interpretation and action in social contexts. Historical studies of prophetic roles and servant deeds in Biblical settings, as well as in subsequent social contexts, help to form expectations and intentions concerning faithful participation in new contexts today. These studies also provide formative conceptions for development of ministries of word and sacrament in new unprecedented settings.

A sequence of subjects used at the UTC for developing a theological practice in urban situations has included one called, "Polis, Politics and Pastorate," which deals with the changing scope and shape of human community and the promises, perils, and political responses to such change. Urban political activity is described as ancient vision and neglected American project, with emphasis upon the responsibilities of churches and other institutions to understand institutional revolution and the responsibility of faithful revolutionaries. A study unit on "Prophetic Roles of Faith from Biblical Scenes to Modern Pavements" analyzes the relationship between Biblical prophets and kings, and between prophets and the temple, with some attention to persisting themes concerning religion and power, and with reference to prophetic "success" and "failure." Students investigate the basis and authority of prophetic utterances, the prophetic office, and the Gospels, and sample translations of prophetic speech to the new city. Another study unit on "Servant Roles of Faith as Seen in Biblical Songs and Modern Settings" reexamines the servant in Deutero-Isaiah, Jesus Christ as servant, his followers as servants, and ministry aimed at more than simple equity in society. "Organization for Prophetic Words and Servant Deeds" picks up the problems and proclamations at Corinth, words to the Church and the authority of the apostolate, ministries of word and sacrament amidst social change, and theological reflection on keeping peace and being responsible for consequences within the society. Using considerations suggested by Gibson Winter, trainees consider such questions as "Does metropolis viewed as New Creation imply any particular program for the city?" The question is raised as to how the New Creation functions with respect to faithful participation in social programs. In the light of New Metropolis the memory of the Judaeo-Christian community is used to illuminate the question of the participation of the faithful in the reorganization of the society.

Closely intertwined with the theological seminar is the concurrent seminar series which deals in a radical way with the *development of liturgies and discipline* within forming and reforming Christian groups. In the secular context of our mission today, many questions are posed: Is there any necessary relation between public ministries on the one hand and worship, prayer, corporate discipline, ordination, and the gathering of the faithful on the other? Is one for the sake of the other? Can one be dropped today? The purpose of this seminar is to question this relation between public ministries and liturgies, between relevance in the world and peculiar actions of the church as gathered. The modern intellectual crisis matched by the emotional, cultural, and institutional crises are summarily analyzed, and the current Christian church crisis is then looked at in cross-cultural perspective. The question is raised as to "What is new?" with due reference to an appropriate return to the roots of our being. An invitation emerges for the Church to exercise the sacred word and action in profane places, new words and actions in old places, rather than keeping holy actions only in holy places. Further, parochial preoccupation is examined in contrast to community celebration, solidarity, needs, and understandings which do minimize religious ghettos and Christian imperialism and contribute to more open Christian presence and ecumenical participation. Finally, in this series power and the churches' institutionalization or institutional use of it is treated in connection with developing "the church for others." Suggestions regarding missionary structures of the congregation and implementation of planning processes within denominational judicatories are made.

Further orientation to analysis of field situations includes a series of *current issue seminars* on a major subject such as public education, housing and renewal, political processes and the governing of metropolis, communications and the arts, and so forth. In each case, such a series includes approximately eight seminars during three weeks, five guided field surveys, selected assigned readings, and feedback analysis of these in both small and large group discussion. Participants encounter together the ways in which interests and systems intersect and conflict in specific urban problems, the relationship between technology or planning and political decision, and the complications perpetuated by hardened attitudes concerning race and class. A beginning is made in the practice of relating material and economic conditions to appropriately chosen goals through organizational or structural efforts. Field study examines both established systems and demonstration or pilot projects, and the actions of organizations of consumers or clients as they press their positions in regard to the issues in question. . . .

WORK IN A TASK GROUP

Beginning with the second week of orientation and running simultaneously with the other general experiences described above, each participant becomes a member of a *small group* organized around comparable problems which the members have identified. The third phase of the threefold practice, strategizing, is done in individualized fashion. Informed by planning seminars held weekly and one major strategy workshop held during the first month, the small groups range widely in field exploration and analysis of going models; in addition, the groups hear and criticize the strategizing and the proposals presented by each member. This combined effort comes to fruition in a proposal presentation by each participant both to the small group and to a larger "hearing." His proposal treats (a) the social and political project indicated by the problem(s) he has defined, (b) the relative role and tasks of the institutional church, (c) corporate ministries of task forces initiated by the church, and (d) the particular role of the participant himself in enabling problem-solving.

THE THREE PANELS CHART

A graphic presentation of the steps through which the trainees begin to move toward such proposal presentation is indicated in the accompanying "Three Panels Chart" (Figure 1). Panel I, entitled "Analytics," begins with the *broad situational analysis,* and in this stage, as in the Back Home Questionnaire, the participant identifies his situation in terms of material conditions, the structures mediating between those conditions and the actors or agents actively or potentially active within the situation with specific regard to the goals operating within that situation. A second step involves an *analysis of a major process-system* within that gross situation. The identity of the culture of that process-system, its history, traditions, and structures are to be identified along with the tactics and methods that prevail within that system and help to characterize its style of organization and action. Additional study is made of the subjective commitments and disciplines required in that system, and the skills and resources needed for functioning within it. A third phase within analytics is *analysis of selected organizations* with an eye to assessing the impact of the current strategies vis-a-vis their understanding of the problems within the system and the gross situation. Such organization analyses would include basic acquaintance with the purposes, history, current program, and personnel of each project, its principles and methods, some acquaintance with a variety of perspectives of both operators and consumers, as well as of other publics related to the project. Most useful, then, is the critical evaluation of its social impact. It is as a result of this combined analytical work that the participant selects from the priority issues and finally decides and defines the problem to which he will devote his efforts. To this point, the project design may be described as focusing on a public or societal problem, theologically and sociologically understood. The participant next, using the best of his logical capabilities, defines theoretical, strategic options both for solving the focal problem and for peculiar strategic roles for corporate ministry in the form of both the institutional church and task forces from within it. Particular deliberation occurs with reference to his own specific role options, such as initiator, or enabler, or expert (or a combination of these). Some theoretical strategic options are then expressed through the design of tested models or models proposed by other persons, or models invented by the participant and his colleagues.

Table 1

Panel I ANALYTICS	Panel II STRATEGY-DEVELOPMENT	Panel III CRITICAL PATH (Action)

Theo- and Socio-logical

1	2	3	4	5	6	7	8	9
Situation Analysis	Systems Analysis	Organizations' Analysis (assessment of current strategies)	Problems and possibilities	Basic Strategies	Models of Action	Operational Requirements	Next steps in preparation of 9 →	Implementation of strategy accompanied by reflective and evaluative procedures, aimed at testing, readjusting of strategy in view of critical conditions that affect or are called forth by it

for purpose of:
Priority Issues
Selection and
Problem Definition

Evaluation   Selection

a-Societal Program
b-Institution's Function
c-Corporate Ministry
d-My Role(s)

Pre-Entry Task	Introduced at UTC and practiced illustration-wise, if not in reference to own problem selection (for back home or Chicago field placements)	To be practiced back home (and by long-termers in Chicago field placements

During this period of strategy development and model reviewing, field trips on both a general and elective basis are arranged in collaboration with the staff of the UTC. Directories of some among the many promising ministries in the Chicago metropolitan area are identified and briefly interpreted in group sessions with particular reference both to churchly efforts and the efforts in which churches have substantially collaborated with others, such as community organizations, community economic enterprises, civil rights movements, and so forth.

Each of these models for action is subject to evaluation for its strength and weaknesses vis-a-vis the particularities of the participant's situation. Once an action model or complex of models is finally selected as a result of evaluation, operational requirements are now clarified and additionally influence final design of the mode of action. With such general strategy and model for action in hand, the participant next plots a time sequence of specific steps, simultaneous or in succession, which will lead to the various stages of fulfillment of the proposal. Formal moves to marshaling what resources are needed for implementation of the strategy may now occur. During the period of implementation, all of which occurs after his final stay at the Training Center, the participant is encouraged and helped to anticipate evaluative and reflective procedures aimed at testing and retesting, adjusting and readjusting the strategy in view of critical conditions and responses that occur as a result of the action.

Such are the program and the methods developed during the shorter term training for participants at the UTC, a rather cursory introduction to a threefold practice: theologizing, sociologizing, strategizing—for ministries which facilitate faithful participation in metropolitan society.

LONGER TERM TRAINING

During the four-week orientation period, the program for longer term trainees is basically like that for the shorter term; however, longer term trainees during the latter stages of that period select a specialized program of study, field work, and skill development for ministry. Such specialized work at the Center and in the field continues in three-month units for periods varying from the remainder of the three-month period up to two years. The UTC expects the longer term trainee to become increasingly aware of both the actual and potential conditions, the agents and actors, structures, institutions and organizations, and operating goals of the various parties to metropolitan life. The trainee becomes specifically acquainted with a limited number of programmatic theories and practices which effect social maintenance or social change. He is expected to develop a method of Judaeo-Christian theological reflection which includes historical analysis, inductive analysis of current social situations and applied societal strategies, and strategy development for Christian ministry now. He is to learn to enable others of the *laos* to do such reflective-inductive action, insofar as is possible during his stay here. He is given the opportunity to develop a competence in selecting programmatic skills, such as organizing for political action, economic enterprises, educational programs, and so forth. Such organizational skill includes analysis, strategy development, enabling group action, evaluation of effectiveness and the posing of emerging new problems. Learning such languages and behaviors of the systems in which the participant finds himself increases the probability of effective ministry.

The *field experiences* for the longer-term participant vary according to the relative opportunity available and the intention of the trainee. The UTC has identified five degrees of field engagement: (1) to be *exposed* and receptive to circumstances especially where groups are "hurting" or are in conflict, such as among the poor and among racial and ethnic minorities; (2) to *explore and analyze social situations and programs* presented to those situations in agency and organizational terms, (3) to *learn the specific rationale* and procedures of operative agency patterns and programs; (4) to *develop specific skills* comparable to those used in the field of specialization such as working with groups, organizing communities, doing planning and administration, providing for communication and education; and (5) to *practice faithful, reflective-inductive ministry* in the formulation stage of agency and community policy-making.

Fields of specialization for field work and study are currently designated by the professional practice most required in that specialization:

(1) *Ministries in the field of planning and administration.*
(2) *Ministries in face-to-face groups.*

(3) *Ministries in federated community organizations.*
(4) *Ministries in communication systems.*

Field placements are approved for the participant by the UTC in the light of the trainee's sense of vocation and readiness, current estimates of societal urgency regarding the problem, priorities for mission established by church bodies, the potential in the setting for the participant's involvement in metropolitan dimensions of the problem and its solution, the opportunity for the trainee to be close to decisive action, and the relative capacity of the agency or organization for communicating and teaching its own philosophy, knowledge, and skill. Attention to the task of the definition of a "community," its organization and/or reorganization is sought in all field placements. Agencies and organizations providing placements accept participation in their life and work by UTC participants and recognize that such participants, in light of their faith and citizenship, will be both respectful seekers and workers in that setting, and have an additional commitment to seek out faithful roles as servants and prophets. No social arena, no set of problems, no form of response to problems is prejudged by UTC as out-of-bounds for exploration and field learning. Individual and group consultation regarding the trainee's selection is accompanied by specific exploratory, analytical attention during the trainee's initial weeks at the Center. The trainee himself makes the final determination of the site of his field engagement and bears responsibility for activating its full potential and/or alerting the agency and the UTC of placement problems needing attention. . . .

The receiving agency commits itself to a variable and negotiable degree of educational responsibility for the UTC participant. Primary tasks assigned the UTC participants are appropriately focused and limited but with an agreed upon job description, usually in writing, to which trainee, agency, and UTC bring concurrence. Secondary opportunities provide the trainee with broader views of agency operation and its community context through participation in wider staff, board, committee,. and community meetings. Time for recording, reflection, research, and attendant work are allowed as necessary during the period in the field. Weekly or biweekly conferences are scheduled between the field supervisor and the student.

The *UTC participant* commits himself to responsible and regular participation in the efforts of the agency or organization with which he accepts placement. He participates in establishing a work schedule for himself with his supervisor and assumes responsibility for its fulfillment. He, himself, determines the variety and use of analytical records for his own reflection, planning, and action in that setting. Similarly, he formulates his own questions and bears responsibility for the basic academic considerations within the supervisory relationship. He bears the initiative in continuing efforts regarding his own self-awareness and self-use, as well as social awareness and effective collaboration in action. He bears the primary responsibility for identifying with or assembling a "congregation" of the faithful for theological reflection in the field, with due recognition of agency intentions and policies.

Each trainee is provided a *field supervisor* identified with the field agency who assumes administrative responsibility for the work in the field and a variable proportion of the academic responsibility for the trainee's growth in his field practice. *Field consultants*, specialists in the skills needed for the particular situation chosen by the trainee, hold regular conferences with him. *Pastor-tutors*, usually of the same denomination as the trainee, are available by special arrangement. The *UTC staff* is committed to fulfilling the continuing functions of liaison and consultation among the trainee, the field agency, and the UTC program, as well as with the sponsoring denomination, as needed. UTC staff, as situations demand and time permits, will fill out deficits in trainee and UTC expectations for field analysis, theological reflection, development of knowledge and skill, and the content of the field work itself. . . . In addition to this basic support of the trainee and his development, UTC staff members endeavor to involve themselves, to the maximum extent practicable, in the life of the Chicago community and its organizations. They strive for increasingly close working relationships with a selected number of field operations, including as much collaboration with trainees as feasible.

Longer-term trainees do have the responsibility for developing several forms of *recording for analysis and strategizing*. Among those suggested are the following:

(1)   General suggestions for *analyzing the field placement agency*. The trainee is expected to acquaint himself with the purpose, history, current program, and personnel of the project, and he analyzes its operating principles and methods. He makes an effort to meet with and describe all persons involved in the project: staff, board, consultants, supporters, and—most important of all—the consumers or clientele of the program. He studies who plays what roles, both in setting goals and policies and in carrying out the programs of the agency. Other publics related to the operation are observed and interviewed for the purpose of recording their reactions and evaluations. The trainee records in summary fashion all important meetings, the substance discussed in them, and the efforts of the meetings and actions on the program of the organization and its clientele. Each trainee aims toward eventual assembly of an objective, concise, and readable account, chronologically annotated, of the project or agency, from its inception to the current impact of its operation. Each trainee also interviews and reads accounts of other specialists in the same field of action to enhance his general comprehension of the issues, philosophies and approaches currently being debated. Each trainee is encouraged to submit monthly records of this material for review to his field supervisor or reflection group staff member.

(2)   Each trainee is urged to complement such a close look at the agency or organization for which he works with a *community situational analysis*, comparable to that described for the shorter term trainees, giving attention to the material conditions, social structures, agents, and goals. In addition, he develops an open-ended analysis of the system within which his organization is operational, such as that system which includes schools, centers, families, and other agencies participating in the socialization process; or the economic-productive process-system with its occupational groups, industry, business, finance, and other components.

(3)   The trainee is expected to *record the process* occurring in the specific social action group or groups with which he is working and for which he assumes responsibility in the field. He prepares a fact sheet with the general description of the group, its name, its purposes, methods, past accomplishments, present agenda, participants, and something of its immediate social context, and allies or opposition. The record of the group process itself indicates the objectives stated or assumed for each gathering of the group and also picks up with as much fullness as feasible the record of meetings between the UTC participant and his co-workers, the members of his social action group, and also the group-as-a-whole in meeting. He adds the more factual observations of non-verbal communications and actions as well as factual descriptions of his own participation. He records behavioral indications of the relationship among the participants and the roles and functions of the participants in assessing such factors as dependence and independence, cohesion and disunity, cooperation and conflict, and the effects of each in guiding the group to appropriate focus and action.

He pays particular attention to the decision-making processes, both those that occur in more formal occasions and those done informally or on the run. He is careful to identify those who contribute to the formulation of policy, and who make the final decisions; furthermore, he pays careful attention to the assignment of responsibility and accountability in the execution of policy. The trainee assesses the external factors which give rise to issues emerging within and around the group he serves which affect the nature and range of their reactions and the interaction between the group and external forces or groups. To each factual record he adds his own interpretation of his understanding of causal connections and what he surmises to be movement in the process going on within the group and its implications for his objectives and those of the group. After early verbatim recording on such items, the trainee moves (with the approval of his supervisor) to a combination of summary, anecdotal, and intepretative records. Meantime, he tries to maintain copies of any formal or informal minutes developed by the group and keeps a secondary file of correspondence, results of pertinent studies, newspaper clippings, organizational releases, annual reports, and interpretative brochures which indicate both what is happening in and by the group and give clues to the nature and quality of his own work in relationship to that group.

(4)   The longer-term program includes a continuous seminar giving attention to the first of the threefold practice: *theologizing*. With particular stimulation from that ongoing seminar and increasing capability in terms of his own skill, the trainee logs *his theological thinking and acting*. This log and reflective use for it is used by the trainee in his own more disciplined practice, for weekly reference in the small reflection-review group, and for use with any supervisor-reflector within the agency organization or from the UTC. It should be useful in discerning the emerging Word as it comes to expression in specific field work situations, in both servant and prophetic terms. Field work presents an opportunity to deal with the specific social situation with its material conditions, its agents active and inactive, its structures through which social processes function, and the implicit and explicit social goals operating as the result of varied interpretations of the situation and its problems. Less apparent in field work are the historical word-events which cause us and others to be who we are and who they are in the situation, and which are determinative for Judaeo-Christian interpretation in the current social situation. Theological reflection provokes a faithful interpretation and expectation of the present situation, and we are freed by faith to cope with it. This interaction of "past" and "present" may, by the Spirit, lead to a more accurate interpretation of the meaning of current affairs, and therefore a more clear call to obedience and service in the "future," through proclaimed words and action, or through deliberate inaction. The logging is to focus on the UTC participant's individual or collaborative work in the social project which he enters. The social data, the Biblical or other historical stimulant, the participant's interpretation of the situation he faces, his action in words and deeds, and the reactions of others to his word and deeds. These are reexamined in the reflection-review group.

For discussion purposes it is recommended that there be a limited focus on one definable problem or set of problems in the current field situation as selected by the trainee. "Prophetic" interpretation may arise through such questioning as the following: What are the folk religions or the delimiting ideologies that are operative here? What effect do they have? What organizational goals must be challenged by a faithful interpretation? What is the influence of modern formal religion in the situation? How is it contributing to interpretations and/or to freeing or ensnarling folks and their organizations? What is the nature of the power complex, the power order, and what effects does this order have on doing justice and equity in the portion of society under consideration? What is needed to extend the reforming processes in that setting? What is needed in the event that social structures are judged either irredeemable or quite adequate and good? Indications for "servant" deeds may be suggested by asking what is needed within the organization by reference to free manhood and full community as indicated in the Biblical servant and his song? What is indicated as action alongside present organizational actions? What is demanded as action in tension with the focal organization? What is the movement out of the movement in which the trainee is participating? Concurrent Biblical study at the UTC or other materials suggested by those closer to the focal situation may be useful stimuli. Logging units may well be divided thus: (a) the situation empirically described; (b) a theological interpretation or understanding of what's happening in it; (c) words and deeds in response to the situation, including interpretations actually offered in concert with and in response to others; (d) reactions to our words and action; (e) implications for next steps in the process at hand.

The UTC has developed some minimal guidelines for practices to be used within the reflection-review groups of the longer-termers. Such practices include, among others, the following:

(1)   primary attention to the role and roles of the trainee in relationship to others in that setting;

(2)   analysis of the forms of sanction and auspice with their implications;

(3)   identification and analysis of the consumer or client groups served, and their needs and interests in the light of the larger situation analysis done by each UTC participant including theological considerations;

(4)   system analysis of the process-system context of the agency or organization;

(5)   problem selection and definition with both socio- and theological reasoning;

(6)   analysis of the strategizing occurring in that situation and potential strategic options with reference both to the social process and corporate personal ministry;

(7)   periodic review, for each participant in the reflection-review group, of the development of his understandings and definitions of problems, the findings regarding effective practice by the trainee, and the evaluation of the impacts of the organization in that setting;

(8)   periodic attention to the psycho-social dynamics, with particular attention devoted to specific analysis of the trainee's action and reactions to it. As a result, either at the terminus of each three-month period and/or as a *final major written project*, each participant combines a proposal regarding a societal form of action, or the description of one currently in process, with his proposal for corporate ministry, both formal and informal, including his personal role in that ministry. UTC participants thus make their own efforts more understandable to themselves, more available to one another, and contribute to the ongoing research and development efforts of UTC.

RESEARCH, DEVELOPMENT, AND CONSULTATION

Persistent research is devoted to the Center's own program in the settings in which it is developed. Five questions are under constant exploration in a research program which is carried on in close collaboration with other training programs of a similar nature: (1) Which urban issues are most relevant for urban training and how are these issues to be conceptualized? (2) Which curriculum components are most needed and what does each accomplish? (3) What is the impact of training and how do our participants change? (4) How do their back-home situations show the effect of training? (5) What new models of ministry arise our of field placements and experiments? The UTC recognizes that unless the institution sending and receiving trainees is prepared to develop new roles and practices, the whole training process becomes a kind of "urban peep show." The transformation of theoretical options into practical possibilities, however, is an operation not entirely within the power of either the Center or each trainee. Therefore, the UTC is now deliberately arranging development and research projects in collaboration with church institutions in the Chicago area to define specifically replicable and supportable ministries within the public sphere. This promises to be a significant step toward solution of the problem of cooperation between the UTC and the institutional matrix from which it comes, the judicatories and agencies of the churches. The Director of Research also receives and processes requests from former trainees and other inquiries, and communicates useful findings to appropriate agencies inside and outside the church. Summaries of such findings are available upon request from the Center.

The national "Urban Training Center for Christian Mission" is attempting to develop increased competence for ministry to facilitate faithful participation in the precedented and unprecedented situations of metropolitan society. It is developing a threefold practice: theologizing, sociologizing, and strategizing for action. It is a development and research effort barely on its way, but there is good reason to believe that significant findings and capabilities are already emerging. The opportunities and dangers of our changing time and our complex situation demand no less.

(This account has been excerpted from the chapter, "Urban Training Center for Christian Mission: Its Primary Intention and Its Principal Methods," by Carl Siegenthaler in Henry Clark, ed., *Manpower for Mission: New Forms of the Church in Chicago* (New York, NY: Division of Christian Life and Mission, National Council of Churches of Christ in the U.S.A., 1966). Reprinted by permission.)

Appendix 7

Chronology of General History and Developments in Urban Mission, Ecumenical Organizations and Action Training in the United States

Year	US and World History	Ecumenical and Urban Mission	Action Training Coalition
1945	First atomic bombs exploded. End of World War II		PIIR founded
1948	Berlin blockade Executive orders ending segregation in armed forces and federal employment	East Harlem Protestant Parish (EHPP) organized	
1949	North Atlantic Treaty Housing Act of 1949		
1950	Korean War Internal Security Act	National Council of the Churches of Christ in the USA (NCCC) organized Department of City Church, NCCC 1/23-24—Convention on the City Church, Columbus, OH	
1951	Universal Military Training Act Executive order on non-discrimination in government contracts		
1952	Immigration and Naturalization Act National Negro Labor Committee		
1953	McCarthy hearings Refugee Relief Act		
1954	Housing Act of 1954 Brown vs. Board of Education decision (5/17/54)	12/1—Division of Home Missions, NCCC Assembly, "The Church Confronts the City"	
1955	Southeast Asia Treaty Organization (SEATO) formed AFL-CIO merger	4/24-26—Conference on "The Effective City Church" 11/1-4—Conference on the Churches and Social Welfare, Cleveland, OH	

Year	US and World History	Ecumenical and Urban Mission	Action Training Coalition
1956	Federal Aid to Highways Act Montgomery bus boycott ICC order on segregation in interstate bus travel	Detroit Industrial Mission (DIM) organized	
1957	Confrontation over de-segregated schools in Little Rock	Support for Industrial Areas Foundation (IAF) organizing in Chicago Home Mission study, "Christ, the Church and Race" 5—"The Impact of Urbaniza-tion on the Churches," report to NCCC General Board 10/8-11—Evangelical United Brethren Church Urban Convocation 10/29-31—American Baptist Convention Urban Convocation Reuel Howe organizes Institute for Advanced Pastoral Studies (IAPS)	
1958	Soviet Union launches Sputnik NASA formed Supreme Court school decisions uphold Brown vs. Board of Education	1/7-9—United Church of Christ Urban Convocation 2/18-20—Methodist Church Urban Convocation	
1959	Inter-American Develop-ment Bank organized "Co-existence" replaces "Cold War"	11/18-20—Consultation on Personnel Needs in Planning and Research	
1960	Greensboro sit-in	11/17-19—Report on Effective City Church Study	
1961	Peace Corps Berlin blockade Bay of Pigs invasion of Cuba Freedom rides Fair housing laws	University programs and seminars for urban clergy organized by Department of City Church, NCCC	
1962	Cuba missile crisis James Meredith admitted to University of Mississippi Albany, GA protest Manpower and Develop-ment Training Act	10/11-12/8—Vatican II, Session I (John XXIII)	

Year	US and World History	Ecumenical and Urban Mission	Action Training Coalition
1963	Birmingham AL protest Nuclear test ban treaty Assassination of President John F. Kennedy	NCCC organizes Commission on Religion and Race Urban America organized to consult on non-profit housing 9/24-12/4—Vatican II, Session 2 (Paul VI) 11—Conference on Training for Urban Ministry, Detroit Episcopal Church Pilot Diocese Program	UTC founded
1964	Gulf of Tonkin resolution Civil Rights Act of 1964 (voting, education, employment, public accommodation) Poll Tax Amendment Urban Mass Transportation Act Economic Opportunity Act ("War on Poverty") COFO and Mississippi Freedom Summer Riots in 7 cities (New York Bedford-Stuyvesant, Harlem; Elizabeth, Jersey City, Paterson, NJ; Dixmoor suburb of Chicago; Philadelphia, Rochester)	Division of Home Missions NCCC becomes Division of Christian Life and Mission Coalition on Religion in Appalachia (CORA) organized Project Equality Ecumenical Institute formed in Evanston IL CORAR participates in Freedom Summer Urban seminars held at metropolitan universities by NCCC	CIP founded
1965	Dominican Republic intervention US military build-up in Vietnam Elementary and Secondary Education Act Medicare Selma AL demonstrations Voting Rights Act Riot in Watts, Los Angeles (also Chicago, San Diego, Hartford, Springfield) McCone Commission report on urban violence	Joint Urban Advisory Group ("Troika") formed by United Church of Christ, Episcopal Church, United Presbyterian Church in USA CORAR conducts city projects in Cleveland (voter registration), Detroit (housing) 9/24-26—Consultation on Christian Education for Inner-City Children, Atlantic City, NJ	ACTS founded CEE founded MAP founded MUST founded
1966	SNCC raises slogan of "Black Power" SCLC "open city" campaign in Chicago Riots on West Side of Chicago	Industrial mission programs establish National Industrial Mission (NIM) 4/19-20—Joint Urban Advisory Group conference, Chicago	Bay Area proposal BCHI founded COMMIT founded CUE-M founded CUT founded ICUIS founded

Year	US and World History	Ecumenical and Urban Mission	Action Training Coalition
	Miranda ruling on self-incrimination Department of Transportation established Demonstration Cities and Metropolitan Development Act (model cities) Consumer laws (National Traffic and Motor Vehicle Safety Act, Fair Packaging and Labeling Act) Adam Clayton Powell stripped of House Committee posts	7/12-26—World Council of Churches Conference on Church and Society, Geneva 10—"Generating Manpower for Mission" conference, Chicago	TEAM, Kansas City, founded
1967	Riots in Detroit and Newark (also Pontiac, Grand Rapids, Albion, Saginaw, MI; Toledo, Hough area of Cleveland OH; Waukegan Il, South Bend IN, East Harlem, Rochester NY; Englewood NJ; Cincinnati OH; Mount Vernon, Albany, Poughkeepsie NY) Stokes elected mayor in Cleveland, Hatcher in Gary IN Air Quality Act Wholesome Meat Act Newark Black Power Conference Increased anti-Vietnam War activity Milwaukee housing marches	Interreligious Foundation for Community Organization (IFCO) Joint Educational Development (JED) Joint Strategy and Action Committee (JSAC) 10/22-26—US Conference on Church and Society, Detroit 9/14-15—NCCC Resolution on Urban Concerns 10/1-6—American Institute of Planners 50th Anniversary Conference, Washington DC 11—National Committee of Negro Churchmen organized, Dallas TX	EMM founded ICUA founded METC founded MUC founded STIR founded TRUST founded UTOA founded Bay Area Proposal dropped 10/3—Representatives of 7 urban training programs and denominational executives meet in Washington DC during AIP 50th Anniversary Conference
1968	Soviet Union invades Czechoslovakia Civil Rights Act (open housing) Omnibus Crime Control and Safe Streets Act Black Panthers gain national visibility King and Robert Kennedy assassinated Chicago Democratic Convention	Church and business leaders establish Operation Connection 2/28—NCCC begins "Crisis in the Nation" emphasis 3/28-29—JSAC Mission Strategy Development Conference, Washington DC Episcopal Church begins General Convention Special Program	BCETF founded CHART founded CUE-P founded CATA founded MISC founded PRISA founded UYAA founded ATN founded STIR becomes JOUM CEE closed ATC Consultation I 2/9-11, Chevy Chase MD

Year	US and World History	Ecumenical and Urban Mission	Action Training Coalition
	Poor People's Campaign Campus demonstrations (Columbia, Howard Universities) New York City teachers strike (Ocean Hill-Brownsville)		ATC Consultation II 5/24-26 Kansas City, MO
1969	Anti-Vietnam War demonstrations Tax Reform and Relief Bill Astronauts land on moon Riots in smaller cities Trial of Chicago 8 Philadelphia plan for employment in construction Shoot-outs in cities and college incidents (San Francisco State, Cornell) Rising protest by Native Americans	United Ministries in Public Education (UMPE) organized 4/25-27—National Black Economic Development Conference, Detroit MI 5/4—Black Manifesto read at the Riverside Church	TEAM Philadelphia founded TEAM Kansas City becomes MTN MUC closed ATC Consultation III 1/2-5, Cleveland OH ATC Consultation IV 3/30-4/3, Cincinnati OH ATC Consultation V 10/5-8, St. Louis MO
1970	Cambodian invasion Omnibus Crime Control Act National Environmental Policy Act Occupational Health and and Safety Act Postal Reorganization Act Welfare reform (Family Aid Program) rejected SDS Weatherman bombings May Day at Yale HEW eases on school desegregation Gibson elected mayor in Newark NJ Young Lords active in New York City Cesar Chavez and Farm Workers Nixon announces new policy for Indian lands	4—JSAC hired full-time staff 11/30-12/1—Florida Mission Strategy Development Conference Interfaith Center for Corporate Responsibility (ICCR) organized	CIP becomes CATS MTN becomes Community 33 ATC Consultation VI 3/20-25 Toronto, Canada ATC Consultation VII 10/26-28 Atlanta GA
1971	China seated in UN Voting age lowered to 18 Wage-price controls and public service employment		JOUM becomes Urbex Affiliates CATA closed ICUA closed

Year	US and World History	Ecumenical and Urban Mission	Action Training Coalition
	Attica Prison riot Formation of Congres- sional Black Caucus Riots in Wilmington NC, Jacksonville FL, Columbus GA, Chattanooga TN, Newburgh NY; and among Puerto Ricans in Camden and Hoboken NJ		MTN closed JOUM closed ATC Consultation VIII 3/22-24, Puerto Rico ATC Consultation IX 10/3- 6, Los Angeles and Delano CA
1972	Revenue Sharing Act National Black Political Convention Nixon visit to China US-USSR agreement on anti-ballistic missiles (ABM) Paris peace talks End of Apollo space program Urban Development Cor- poration formed in New York State Bombing of Hanoi		CATS becomes ATN CHART closed UYAA closed ATC Consultation X 3/19- 22, Chicago IL ATC Consultation XI 10/15-18, Philadelphia PA
1973	Vietnam cease-fire Rise in food prices Native American confronta- tation at Wounded Knee Watergate investigations Allende overthrown in Chile Nixon impounds Federal funds, vetoes appropriation laws Agnew resigns as Vice- President Fuel shortage	Division of Christian Life and Mission NCCC becomes Division of Church and Society	BCETF becomes BCEI PIIR merged into ICUIS MUST closed ATC Consultation XII 4/1-4, Chicago IL ATC Consultation XIII planned for 10/14-16 in Seattle WA, then cancelled
1974	Political change in Portugal World-wide inflation House impeachment hearings Nixon resigns and is succeeded by Ford Fear of "petrodollars"		MAP closed UTC closed
1975	Vietnam War ends Portugal leaves Angola and Mozambique		

Year	US and World History	Ecumenical and Urban Mission	Action Training Coalition
	Israel condemned as "racist" in United Nations Congress investigates CIA and FBI New York City fiscal crisis		
1976			BCEI closed
1978			METC closed
1979			TRUST closed

Appendix 8

Checklist for Future Research

— The Idea of "Urban/City Church" - content analysis of *The City Church, Church in Metropolis* and *JSAC Grapevine*

— Interdenominational Agencies for Urban Mission - history of Department of Urban Church, National Council of the Churches of Christ in the USA, and Joint Strategy and Action Committee (JSAC), possibly compared with some of metropolitan agencies established during the same period

— Race and the Policies of Major Denominations in Urban Mission, 1948-1972 - consideration of the importance of the factor of race, even when it is not explicitly mentioned

— White and Black Urban Church Activists: A Comparison- study of background, ideas and activities of a selected group of urban activists to show their differing perceptions of both society and church

— The Inner-City Parish Movement and Its Effect on Protestant Mission Policy in the United States Cities - effect of the East Harlem Protestant Parish as a model for other parishes and mission programs in cities

— Mission Policies and Major Denominations in Relation to Cities, 1948-1972 -longitudinal studies of the development of denominational mission policy for city work

— The Struggle over Community Organization in National Denominations - the development of policy and program for community organizing in the major Protestant denominations and Roman Catholicism

— The Struggle over Community Organization: Chicago as the Battleground - study of the role of Chicago in precipitating conflict over Alinsky-style organizing

— Urban Church Research: The Heirs of H. Paul Douglass - study of the development of church planning and research as a profession, and reasons for its decline

— Uses of the Social Sciences by American Religious Groups after World War II - study of the ways in which certain social science disciplines were more likely to be used than others, and in which areas of church program

— The Retreat from Organized Labor by Protestantism in the United States - decline of interest in labor ministry and industrial chaplaincy after World War II, and the role of urban mission and industrial mission in encouraging that development

— The Effects of Anti-Communism on Religious Activism in the United States 1948-1972 - study of the way in which the Cold War atmosphere and anti-subversion campaigns limited the areas in which religious activists moved

— "Doing Theology" as a Theme in American Religious Thought - sources of both the title and the various meanings of "doing theology," with an analysis of principal exponents and schools

— Religious Activism in the United States after World War II - comparison of Protestant, Roman Catholic, evangelical and Jewish statements and activities

— The Adoption of Planning by Protestant Denominations in the United States - study of the key people and institutions, and the kinds of planning that were taken up by church bodies

— "The City" as a Metaphor - study of theological statements made by urban theorists, theologians and missioners, 1940-1975

— "Mission Theology" - A Movement or a School of Theological Thought? - study of principal thinkers and whether they were developing an apologia for particular mission strategies or represented a separate form of post-Barthian theology

— The Role of Social Theory in the Development of Urban Mission Strategy - study of ways in which the Park-Burgess school of urban sociology and the structural functionalism of Talcott Parsons influenced the social analysis underlying urban mission strategy in the period from 1940 to 1970
— Black Caucuses and the National Committee of Black Churchmen - study of the interweaving between the traditional Black denominations and the Black caucuses of predominantly White mainline denominations in the development of NCBC
— History of the Urban Training Center for Christian Mission - deserves a full-scale historical study
— Biographical Studies of Key Leaders in Urban Mission and Urban Training (or Oral History interviews):

  Vann Anderson (Kansas City, MTN)
  David Barry (New York City, UTC, MUST)
 *Donald Benedict (East Harlem, Cleveland, Chicago, UTC)
  Robert H. Bonthius (Cleveland, ATN of Ohio)
  Jon Brown (Columbus, ATN of Ohio)
  Paul Buckwalter (Cincinnati, ATN of Ohio)
 *Tilden Edwards (Washington DC, METC)
  Bryant George (United Presbyterian)
  Edgar M. Grider (Atlanta, UTOA)
  J. Archie Hargraves (East Harlem, Chicago, UTC)
  Mance Jackson (Atlanta, ACTS)
  Paul Jones (Kansas City, MTN)
  William Jones (Memphis, ACTS)
  Paul Kittlaus (Los Angeles, COMMIT)
  Walter Kloetzli (Lutheran Church in America, UTC)
  Norman Klump (Evangelical United Brethren, United Methodist, UTC)
  Speed Leas (Los Angeles, COMMIT)
  Ted McEachern (Nashville, ACTS)
  Joseph Merchant (United Church of Christ, UTC)
 *Paul Moore (Jersey City, Washington DC)
  James P. Morton (Jersey City, Episcopal Church, UTC)
  C. Kilmer Myers (Jersey City, New York City, UTC)
  Randolph Nugent (MUST)
  David Ramage (United Presbyterian)
  Negail Riley (United Methodist Church)
  J. Metz Rollins (United Presbyterian, NCBC)
  Meryl Ruoss (National Council of Churches, United Presbyterian)
  Carl Siegenthaler (St. Louis, Los Angeles, UTC)
  Arthur Stevenson (United Presbyterian)
  George Todd (East Harlem, United Presbyterian, UTC)
 *C T Vivian (SCLC, UTC)
  John Wagner (National Council of Churches, Los Angeles, UTC)
  Leon Watts (New York City, NCBC)
  George W. Webber (East Harlem, New York City, MUST)
  George W. Woodard (Episcopal Church)
  George D. Younger (New York City, MUST, UTC)

---

* Autobiography or memoir has been published.

Selected Bibliography

Urban Mission:
Armstrong, J.A., "Mission to the City," *Encounter,* 25 (Autumn, 1964), 507f.

Benedict, Don, *Born Again Radical.* New York: The Pilgrim Press, 1982.

Callahan, Daniel, ed., *The Secular City Debate.* New York: Macmillan, 1966.

Clark, Henry, ed., *Manpower for Mission: New Forms of the Church.* New York: Division of Christian Life and Mission, National Council of the Churches of Christ in the U.S.A., 1967.

Cox, Harvey, *The Secular City.* New York: Macmillan, 1965.

Cully, Kendig B. and Harper, F. Nile, *Will the Church Lose the City?* Cleveland, OH: World, 1969.

Edwards, Tilden, *All God's Children.* Nashville, TN: Abingdon, 1982.

Ellul, Jacques, *The Meaning of the City.* Grand Rapids, MI: Eerdmans, 1974.

Freire, Paulo, *Pedagogy of the Oppressed.* New York: Herder and Herder, 1970.

Fry, John R., ed., *The Church and Community Organization.* New York: National Council of the Churches of Christ in the U.S.A., 1965.

Grace, William R., "The Church and an Urban Way of Life," *McCormick Quarterly,* March, 1966.

Kloetzli, Walter, ed., *Challenge and Response in the City: A Theological Consultation on the Urban Church.* Rock Island, IL: Augustana, 1962.

Kloetzli, Walter, *The Church and the Urban Challenge.* Philadelphia: Muhlenberg, 1961.

Kloetzli, Walter and Hillman, Arthur, *Urban Church Planning.* Philadelphia: Muhlenberg, 1958.

"Learnings from GCSP, A Report on Five Years' Experience with the Episcopal Church's Most Controversial Mission Program," *The Episcopalian,* 137:11 (1972), 47-51.

Lee, Robert, ed., *Cities and Churches: Readings on the Urban Church.* Philadelphia: Westminster, 1962.

Lee, Robert, ed., *The Church and the Exploding Metropolis.* Richmond, VA: John Knox, 1965.

Loeffler, Paul, "Theology as Process: Theological Reflection in Urban-Industrial Mission," *Study Encounter,* 7:2 (September 7, 1971), 1-6.

Michonneau, G. Abbe, *Revolution in the City Parish*. Westminster, MD: New-Man, 1963.

Modeste, Leon, "The End of a Beginning," *Black World*, January, 1974, 86f.

Moore, Paul, Jr., *Take a Bishop Like Me*. New York: Harper and Row, 1979.

Moore, Paul, Jr., *The Church Reclaims the City*. New York: Seabury, 1974.

Moore, Paul, Jr. and Day, Duane E., *Urban Church Breakthrough*. New York: Harper and Row, 1966.

Norton, Perry L., *Church and Metropolis*. New York: Seabury, 1964.

Poethig, Richard P., "Urban/Metropolitan Mission Policies: An Historical Overview," *Journal of Presbyterian History*, 57 (Fall, 1979), 315-52.

Rose, Stephen C., *Who's Killing the Church?* Chicago: Renewal Magazine, n.d.

Sanderson, Ross W., *The Church Serves the Changing City*. New York: Harper, 1955.

Schaller, Lyle E., *Community Organization: Conflict and Reconciliation*. New York: Abingdon, 1967.

Schaller, Lyle E., *Planning for Protestantism in Urban America*. New York: Abingdon, 1965.

Schaller, Lyle E., *The Church's War on Poverty*. New York: Abingdon, 1967.

Shippey, Frederick A., *Church Work in the City*. New York: Abingdon, 1952.

Takayama, K. Peter and Darrell, Suzanne B., "The Aggressive Organization and the Reluctant Environment: The Vulnerability of an Inter-Faith Coordinating Agency," *Review of Religious Research*, 20 (Summer, 1979), 315-34.

Todd, George E., "New Strategy for the Church in Metropolis," *McCormick Quarterly*, March, 1966.

Turner, Warren H., Jr., "Draft Staff Paper on Councils, Consortia and COCU." Unpublished paper, Joint Commission on Ecumenical Relations, Episcopal Church, February 1, 1969.

Vivian, C T, *Black Power and the American Myth*. Philadelphia: Fortress Press, 1970.

Watts, Leon, Jr., "The National Committee of Black Churchmen," *Christianity and Crisis*, xxx:18 (November 2 and 16, 1970), 237-43.

Webber, George W., *God's Colony in Man's World*. New York: Abingdon, 1960.

Webber, George W., *The Congregation in Mission*. New York: Abingdon, 1964.

Webber, George W., "The Struggle for Integrity: American Church Experience
over the Last 30 Years," *Review of Religious Research,* 23 (September, 1981),
3-21.

Wickham, E.R., *Church and People in an Industrial City.* London: Lutterworth, 1957.

Winter, Gibson, *The New Creation as Metropolis.* New York: Macmillan, 1963.

Winter, Gibson, *The Suburban Captivity of the Churches.* New York: Macmillan, 1962.

World Council of Churches, "Becoming Operational in a World of Cities,"
International Review of Missions, 58 (January, 1969), 90-100.

Wright, Kenyon E., "Urban Industrial Mission: Humanization or Evangelism?"
International Review of Missions, 60 (January, 1971), 81-88.

Younger, George D., "Mission of Christ and the Work of the Church in Chicago,"
International Review of Missions, 63 (April, 1974), 256-63.

Younger, George D., *The Church and Urban Power Structure.* Philadelphia:
Westminster, 1963.

Younger, George D., *The Church and Urban Renewal.* Philadelphia: Lippincott,
1965.

Action Training:
Bonthius, Robert H., "Resources Planning in Theological Education: A Response
and an Offer," *Theological Education,* v:2 (Winter, 1969), 67-72.

Bonthius, Robert H., ed., "Action Training Centers' Challenge to Theological Education,"
Theological Education, vi:2 (Winter, 1970).

Bonthius, Robert H., "Twenty Elements in Action Training, 1965-1975."
Unpublished manuscript, March, 1980.

Carr, Helen C., "Report to Floyd B. Shannon: Preliminary Study of Feasibility of
Establishing a National Program for the Training of Civil Rights Community
Development Executives, Management and Staff Personnel, and Elected and/or
Appointed Public Officials." Metropolitan Applied Research Center, New York, NY,
March 20, 1968.

"Educating Churches for Urban Environment," *Home Missions,* x1i:6 (June, 1970).

Fisher, Neal, "Memorandum to Persons Interested in Action Training Coalition."
Unpublished paper, October 28, 1969.

Hermanson, Robert F., "Abandoned Offsprings." Unpublished report to Department of
Strategic Studies, United Presbyterian Church in the U.S.A., and Department of
Planning, National Council of the Churches of Christ in the U.S.A., March, 1971.

Koller, H., "Action Training: A Methodology and Theology," *Theological Education,* vi:1
(Autumn, 1970), 57-65.

Kraemer, Paul E., "Urban Training — Formation and Re-Formation." Unpublished paper, February 25, 1969.

Little, Bryce, Jr., "Report of Visit to 5 Action Training Centers and ATC Consultation." Unpublished report, December 21, 1970.

"Local Church Social Action: Why and How," *engage/social action*, January, 1975.

Luecke, Richard H., "Protestant Clergy: New Forms of Ministry, New Forms of Training," *The Annals of the American Academy of Political and Social Science*, 387 (January, 1970), 86-95.

Morton, James P., "Who Should Be Trained and What Does Training Mean in Our Churches' Structures?" addresses at Conference on Training for the Urban Ministry, Episcopal Church, November 10-11, 1963.

Poethig, Richard P., "Developing a Theology for Metropolitan Ministry," ICUIS Paper No. 7. ICUIS, Chicago, IL, 1977.

Riley, Negail R., "Reflections on Action Training." Unpublished manuscript, May 28, 1971.

Roessingh, Karel H., "Adult Education and Community Organization in the U.S.A. and Canada," report prepared for Technical Assistance Operations of United Nations, 1970.

Ruoss, Meryl, "Working Papers for Southern Regional Training for Christian Mission." Unpublished manuscript, April 15, 1967.

"Training for Ministry: Views and Projects," *Probe: The American Sister Today* (National Assembly of Women Religious), 11:1 (October, 1972).

"What is Action Training?" *JSAC Grapevine*, 2:4 (October, 1970).

Winter, Gibson, "Reflections on the Development of Urban Training Centers." Unpublished manuscript, May 17, 1966.

Winter, J. Alan; Mills; Edgar W.; Hedrick, Polly S.; with Younger, George D., *Clergy in Action Training: A Research Report*. New York: IDOC, 1971.

Younger, George D., "Action Training in Ohio," in Biersdorf, John E., ed., *Ministry in the Seventies*. New York: IDOC, 1971.

Younger, George D., "Do Training Centers Know What They Mean by Training?" Unpublished manuscript delivered to Action Training Coalition Consultation II, May 24-26, 1968.

Action Training Coalition Members:
ACTS, Nashville, TN:
Fisher, Neal; May, Forrest; and Riley, Negail, "Assessment of Learnings, 1967-71." Unpublished manuscript.

ATN, Ohio:
Action for Earthcare. New York: Friendship Press, 1973.

Bonthius, Robert H., "So — You Want to Change the System?" *Trends, A Journal of Resources,* 4:2 (October, 1971), 28-33.

Bonthius, Robert H., "Theological Education for Revolutionary Response," *The Drew Gateway,* xxxix (1968), 50-69.

Bonthius, Robert H., "The Impact of the Urban Crisis on Pastoral Theology," in *The New Shape of Pastoral Theology.* 1969.

Bonthius, Robert H., "Action Training Network," *engage/social action,* May, 1975, 27-37.

Bonthius, Robert H., and Brown, Jon K., "The Metropolis as the Context for Theological Education," in *Explorations in Ministry.* 1971.

Steanson, Karen E., "Journey Toward Justice, A Report on the Institutional Racism Project in the Diocese of Southern Ohio." Manuscript report, September, 1979.

CHART, Cincinnati, OH:
"A Selected Bibliography for the Training of Citizen-Agents of Planned Community Change," Council of Planning Librarians, April, 1970.

"Conflict: The Conditions and Processes in Community Organizations and Interpersonal Relationships," Council of Planning Librarians, May, 1971.

JOUM, Rochester, NY:
Finks, P. David, *The Radical Vision of Saul Alinsky.* New York: Paulist Press, 1984.

METC, Washington, DC:
Palmer, Parker J., "Action Research: Perspectives, Program and Some Techniques," Washington Center for Metropolitan Studies, n.d.

MUST, New York, NY:
Younger, George D., "Who Goes There—Friend or Foe? Action Training and the Churches." Unpublished manuscript, 1971.

"Worksheets on Researching Power," in *The Whole Church Catalog.* Washington, DC: Alban Institute, 1984.

PRISA, Puerto Rico:
Torres, Irvin, "Puerto Rico: A Moral Dilemma and Responsibility." Unpublished manuscript, 1971.

UTC, Chicago, IL:
Hargraves, J. Archie, "Seminary Must Go to the Streets: The Conditions and the Systems," *The Drew Gateway,* 39 (Autumn, 1969), 32-49.

Hauser, Richard and Hepzibah, *The New Society.* Draft copy of manuscript for private circulation, London: The Centre for Group Studies, 1969.

Illich, Ivan, *The Church, Change and Development*. Chicago: Urban Training Center Press, 1970.

Luecke, Richard Henry, *Perchings*. Chicago: Urban Training Center Press, 1972.

Younger, George D., "Mission of Christ and the Work of the Church in Chicago," *International Review of Missions*, 63 (April, 1974), 256-63.

(Note: Urban Training Center for Christian Mission published and distributed over 600 mimeographed documents on the subjects of urbanization, theology, proposals for ministry, church institutional renewal, model and experimental ministries, community organization and community development, racism, health, curriculum and research, and other reference materials, as well as many internal UTC documents. These are cataloged in "List of UTC Mimeographed Documents," published in November, 1971. Most of the documents are on file in the UTC collection at ICUIS.)

UTOA, Atlanta, GA:
Grider, Edgar M., "New Patterns for Urban Ministry," *Review and Expositor*, 66 (Spring, 1969), 197-203.

NOTES

Chapter II

1. Much of this background is documented in Loren Bavitz, *The Servants of Power: A History of the Use of Social Science in American Industry* (New York: John Wiley and Sons, 1960).
2. A history of the development of NTL methodology is found in Leland P. Bradford, Jack R. Gibb and Kenneth D. Benne (eds.), *T-Group Theory and Laboratory Method* (New York: John Wiley and Sons, 1964).

Chapter III

1. Robert H. Bonthius, "Resources Planning in Theological Education: A Response and an Offer," *Theological Education*, V:2 (Winter 1969), 67-72.
2. Robert H. Bonthius, "Action Training: What Is It?" *Theological Education*, VI:2 (Winter 1970), 94.
3. George D. Younger, "Do Training Centers Know What They Mean by 'Training'?," pp. 2 and 5. This and all subsequent unpublished documents cited are in the files of the Institute on the Church in Urban-Industrial Society (ICUIS), Chicago, Illinois.
4. James P. Morton, "Who Should Be Trained, and What Does Training Mean in Our Church Structures," Addresses at Conference on Training for the Urban Ministry, Nov. 10-11, 1963, p. 11.
5. "A Tentative Proposal for an Urban Training Center." Presented to the Division of Home Missions of the National Council of Churches by Rev. Donald L. Benedict, General Director, Chicago City Missionary Society, May 23, 1969, p. 3.
6. For full identification, see Appendix 1, "List of Training Centers and Agencies." All will be described more fully in Chapter IV, "The Development of Action-Training Programs."
7. Minutes, Consultation V, Action Training Coalition, October 8, 1969.
8. These statements are included in the Methodology Packet produced by ICUIS. Centers included are ACTS, CATS, CUE-M, CUT, METC, MUST, TRUST and UTC.
9. George D. Younger, "Who Goes There—Friend or Foe?" pp. 39ff.
10. Most of the elements of UTC curriculum are described and discussed in Carl Siegenthaler, "Urban Training Center for Christian Mission: Its Primary Intention and Its Principal Methods," in *Manpower for Mission: New Forms of the Church in Chicago* (New York: National Council of Churches, 1967). This has been reprinted here as Appendix 6. A later description is found in Paul E. Kraemer, "Urban Training—Formation and Re-Formation." Many of the definitions of specific terms used in UTC training are in "Situation Analysis—'Back Home,' Pt. I," the manual used by prospective students to fill out a questionnaire before attending training programs at UTC. "Problems" were to be "specific elements for solution within the 'issues' . . . .: a clear question proposed for solution" (*Loc. cit.*). This very specialized terminology used at UTC distinguished between what was wrong and needed to be changed, as defined by those who were affected ("issue"), and what, upon further analysis, proved capable of being changed ("problem").

11   *Ibid.*, p. 11.
12.   Described in Siegenthaler, pp. 44-46; see Appendix 6.
13.   "The Plunge," UTC pamphlet.
14.   "Basic Commitments of Community Action Training Services," pp. 1f.
15.   "Action-Research: Perspectives, A Program and Some Techniques," p. 7.

Chapter IV

1.   Reports on the rise of the consortium style of regional and local ecumenism, as well as the origins of JSAC, were prepared by Grace Ann Goodman of the Department of Strategic Studies, Board of National Missions, UPCUSA, between 1966 and 1972 and constitute the only adequate secondary source on this form of ecumenical organization.

2.   Leon Modeste, "The End of a Beginning," *Black World*, January 1974, pp. 86f.

3.   Many of these documents were published in *Renewal*, X:7 (October-November 1970). A brief history of NCBC may be found in Leon W. Watts, Jr., "The National Committee of Black Churchmen," *Christianity and Crisis*, XXX:18 (November 2 and 16, 1970), pp. 237-43.

4.   This summary is based on an outline history and a manuscript that carries the story through 1969, which were prepared by the author from source materials in the files of UTC and personal experience.

5.   *A Prospectus for a Proposed Urban Training Center for Christian Mission in Chicago, Illinois*, p. 2. This and all subsequent unpublished documents cited are in the files of the Institute on the Church in Urban-Industrial Society (ICUIS), Chicago, Illinois.

6.   Minutes, Continuing Education Committee on an Urban Training Center, January 4, 1962.

7.   A staff member of the Episcopal Church later identified the UTC as the first such interdenominational consortium which that national body took formal action to join. Warren H. Turner, Jr., "Draft Staff Paper on Councils, Consortia, and COCU," February 1, 1969, table on pp. 7f.

8.   *A Prospectus for a Proposed Urban Training Center for Christian Mission in Chicago, Illinois*, p. 9.

9.   This summary is based on materials in the files of ICUIS and interviews with those who conducted the program.

10.   This summary is based on annual evaluations prepared by the author in the first program years; a manuscript five-year evaluation, "Who Goes There—Friend or Foe?" written in 1973; and a manuscript prepared by the author from source materials in the files of MUST and personal experience.

11.   "Metropolitan-Urban Service Training (MUST)," June 1965, p. 6.

12.   "Working Document Re: Racial Justice," October 24, 1967.

13.   1975 is chosen as the year to make this distinction both because it marks the end of the period (1972-1975) when the greatest number of action-training programs and agencies were closed, and because it is the period in which the active research for this study was undertaken.

14.   No information is available on three programs that had peripheral relationship to ATC.

15.   All summaries are based on materials in the files of ICUIS, questionnaires that were completed in 1975 and personal experience. In some cases there have also been interviews with those who conducted the programs.

16.   *Purpose*, January 1974. Since 1975 ATN has continued to work with church and community groups with an emphasis on the issues of poverty and hunger. In 1980 ATN offices were moved to Hancock, Maine, where its work has been with church bodies at the national level and with labor and community organizing at the local and state levels.

17.   *Southern Regional Training Center Project*, Spring 1966.

18.   ACTS continues to be active throughout the Southeast with an increase in research services and consultations for church leaders. In addition to the core staff, consultants are available, particularly for churches in racially transitional communities. The self-perpetuating board remains broadly ecumenical.

19.   "Guest Editorial," *Urban Institute Newsletter*, Council of Churches of Greater Washington, IV:6 (June 1967), 2.

20.   "Guest Editorial," *loc. cit.*

21.   "Summer Report 1973," p. 22.

22.   METC Quarterly Report, June 1970, pp. 1f.

23.   TEAM is now organized with a board of directors that has individual membership, as well as representatives of congregations and Philadelphia area judicatories. A core staff plus other consultants work with congregations, denominations and church-related agencies and publish a newsletter for religious leaders.

24.   Charles Lutz, Memo, "To: Members of the GUP Board of Directors," June 19, 1969.

25.   At the time of writing CUE-M was continuing its basic activities of training and consulting with community organizers and community organizations. It has since been disbanded.

26.   "Proposal for a Community Development Project," January, 1973, p. 1.

27.   *Ibid.*, p. 2.

28.   UTOA has continued with an interracial staff engaged principally in community development activity in the Atlanta area, along with consultation for congregations and denominational bodies.

29.   *A Short History of COMMIT*, pp. 1f.

30.   *The Purpose of COMMIT.*

31.   "Proposal for an Ecumenical Training Facility for the Black Churches of the Washington Metropolitan Area," pp. 1f.

32.   Brochure, "Portland's Center for Urban Encounter," 1969.

33.   Stephen Schneider, "Imagination and Change: Notes on the Center for Urban Education," p. 1.

34.   CUE-P has continued with its educational and media activities in the greater Portland Area.

35.   The program is now called Ministry in Pastoral Care and Social Change and enrolls new graduates as well as returning pastors and missionaries. Close cooperation is maintained with the D.Min. program of the Twin Cities Consortium of Seminaries.

36.   ICUIS was reorganized in 1982, when the concerned denominations and McCormick Theological Seminary sought direction for a new form of national resource center. Its files continue to be maintained by the Library of McCormick Theological Seminary.

37.   Since changing its name to The Strong Center, BCHI has emphasized environmental values and ethics.

38.   EMM is now called EMM/Northwest Second Harvest and concentrates on hunger programs that sponsor food banks and on-site feeding programs, with support from churches, businesses and the general public.

39.   This summary is based on materials in the files of ICUIS, interviews with those who conducted the programs and personal experience.

40.   "Interim Constitution of Canadian Urban Training Project for Christian Service," May 18, 1966.

41. "Information Re: Clergy Training Opportunities, September, 1966, to September, 1967."
42. CONNEXIONS, V:1.
43. See Irvin Torres, "Puerto Rico: A Moral Dilemma and Responsibility," PRISA, 1970, for a clear description of the parallel development of relations between United States Protestant denominations and their structures in Puerto Rico.
44. See "Puerto Rico: Its Right to Self-Determination and Independence," Presentation Addressed to NCCC, by Rev. Mrs. Eunice Santana de Velez, Prisa International Bulletin, No. 1, December 1976.
45. TRUST Staff Report No. 2, January 1968.
46. "Position and Planning Paper on the Urban Mission Strategy Component of TRUST, Inc.," October 1, 1968.
47. "The 1971 Program of the Inter Church Association."

Chapter V

1. Minutes, ATC Organizing Committee, November 10, 1967. This and all subsequent unpublished documents cited are in the files of the Institute on the Church in Urban-Industrial Society (ICUIS), Chicago, Illinois.
2. Robert H. Bonthius, "Report of Ideational Development, Consultation II on Action Training."
3. Paul Kittlaus, Action Training Consultation III, The Black Situation and White Racism, p. 24.
4. Minutes, Consultation III, January 5, 1969.
5. Minutes, Consultation IV, March 31, 1969.
6. Minutes, Consultation V, October 8, 1969.
7. Neal Fisher, "Memorandum to Persons Interested in Action Training Coalition," October 28, 1969.
8. Minutes, ATC Council, February 19, 1971.
9. William E. Ramsden, Letter, January 30, 1974.
10. Robert H. Bonthius, Letter to Carl Siegenthaler, March 31, 1972.

Chapter VI

1. Minutes, Organizing Committee, November 10, 1967. This and all subsequent unpublished documents cited are in the files of the Institute on the Church in Urban-Industrial Society (ICUIS), Chicago, Illinois.
2. See Chapter III, Table 2, "Analysis of ATN Projects from Inception to December 31, 1974."
3. Yoshio Fukuyama, "Reflections on New Forms of Ministry" (New York: United Church Board for Homeland Ministries, unpublished research manuscript, 1964).
4. Robert H. Bonthius, "Twenty Elements in Action Training 1965-1975," ms. March 1980.

Appendix 4

1. Abstract of Minutes of Bishop and Chapter, Convention Notebook, 1968.
2. "Programs of the Diocese," Diocesan Journal, 1970.
3. For a more comprehensive description of the methods of Action Training, see Dr. Bonthius's article, "So—You Want to Change the System?" which originally appeared in *Trends*, October 1971.

Appendix 5

1. Every four years the United Methodist Church holds a General Conference. In 1968 it adopted a Quadrennial Emphasis Program on Reconciliation. The Black Community Developers program was one of the major programs supported by the Quadrennial Emphasis funds.

Index

STUDIES IN RELIGION AND SOCIETY

edited by

Robert L. Moore, W. Alvin Pitcher,
W. Widick Schroeder and Gibson Winter

Other CSSR Publications in the Series:

Charles Amjad-Ali and W. Alvin Pitcher, eds.,
Liberation and Ethics: Essays in Religious Social Ethics in Honor of Gibson Winter (1985)

John B. Cobb, Jr. and W. Widick Schroeder, eds., *Process
Philosophy and Social Thought* (1981)

Bruce Grelle and David A. Krueger, eds., *Christianity and Capitalism:
Perspectives on Religion, Liberalism and the Economy* (1986)

Philip Hefner and W. Widick Schroeder, eds., *Belonging and Alienation:
Religious Foundations for the Human Future* (1976)

Paul E. Kraemer, *Awakening from the American Dream: The Human Rights
Movement in the United States Assessed during a
Crucial Decade, 1960-1970* (1973)

William C. Martin, *Christians in Conflict* (1972)

Robert L. Moore and Frank E. Reynolds, eds., *Anthropology
and the Study of Religion* (1984)

Victor Obenhaus, *And See the People* (1968)

W. Widick Schroeder, Victor Obenhaus, Larry A. Jones, and
Thomas Sweetser, SJ, *Suburban Religion: Churches and
Synagogues in the American Experience* (1974)

W. Widick Schroeder and Gibson Winter, eds., *Belief and Ethics:
Essays in Ethics, the Human Sciences and Ministry in Honor
of W. Alvin Pitcher* (1978)

Walter M. Stuhr, Jr., *The Public Style: A Study
of the Community Participation of Protestant Ministers* (1972)

Thomas P. Sweetser, SJ, *The Catholic Parish: Shifting
Membership in a Changing Church* (1974)

Lawrence Witmer, ed., *Issues in Community Organization* (1972)

Other Books in the Series:

Thomas C. Campbell and Yoshio Fukuyama, *The Fragmented Layman* (1970)

John Fish, *Black Power/White Control: The Struggle of the
Woodlawn Organization in Chicago* (1973)

John Fish, Gordon Nelson, Walter M. Stuhr, Jr., and Lawrence Witmer,
The Edge of the Ghetto (1968)

W. Widick Schroeder and Victor Obenhaus,
Religion in American Culture (1964)

Gibson Winter, *Religious Identity* (1968)